ABOUT THE AUTHOR

During November of 1989 I took up a post as a power station superintendent, working for the Saudi Arabian Air Force at a remote site one hundred kilometers from the holy city of Medina Wa Munawarra. The desert village of Hanakia in which our accommodation compound had been established was typical of the mixture of old Arab settlements, and the new structures established by entrepreneurial newcomers taking advantage of the road that had been built from the south of the country to the north, and on to Jordan.

Summer temperatures in this desolate area approached fifty degrees centigrade, so the surrounding desert was completely devoid of flourishing vegetation. The only creatures braving the midday sun were the myriads of crawling insects, and most ominous of all, snakes, scorpions, and camel spiders as big as the opened hand of a man.

There was one other creature; not indigenous to this remote area, that was alert at all times to whatever moved in its vicinity. This creature was the domestic cat turned completely feral. Their intelligence was so greatly superior to any other creature that could be classified as probable prey for a cat that they survived, and multiplied extremely successfully. They were seen to attack, kill, and devour the three dangerous creatures already mentioned, and they certainly kept human habitation free of small rodents and lizards.

For me, watching these intelligent animals in my rest periods turned from casual interest into a determined research project, although I didn't use the research material until 1999, when I had acquired a quiet area in Cyprus to begin my fight to become an author.

DEDICATIONS

This book is dedicated to my wife Marian, affectionately known as Maz. She was responsible for saving the lives of many beautiful kittens, all of them nursed back to health by just giving a little of her time to their immediate needs.

ACKNOWLEDGEMENTS

Microsoft Office.com/en-us/images. Thank you for the replica of the main protagonist in the three editions of Nine Lives of a Feral Cat, Amazon Kindle Direct Publishing and now in this combined book.

McDonald's Fast Food Restaurant Limassol, Cyprus.
A big thank you to your representative in the above restaurant for his kind words when my agent visited him with the relevant pages of the finished novel, and allowing me to retain all references to McDonald's.

Rupert and Mary Elliott.

Thank you for your efforts acting as my agent in Cyprus during my absence, and presenting the above references to McDonald's on my behalf during the final preparation of this novel before presentation for publication.

FOREWORD.   By the author.

Although I did not immediately realize it at the time, the area of Cyprus I had chosen was also a haven for feral cats, so this time I could write my first draft of the manuscript watching truly feral cats, whom we shared an area of Governors Beach with.

Our first contact with a feral cat occurred when a mother was dispersing a weaned brood. For some reason best known to her alone she forcibly abandoned a female kitten in a hedge bordering our plot of land.

Three times the kitten tried to follow her, and three times she snarled at it and drove it back. We watched this scene, and my wife was heard to say sympathetically, 'Oh! Look at that lovely little bundle of fluff.' Hence the name of Fluffy stuck with her, lacking in originality or not.

The story will show how this kitten reacted to natural kindness, and stayed with us until she reached maturity, and of course motherhood. During this few months she did reach a level of domesticity which was very beneficial to her, particularly when hunting and scavenging were a little sparse.

It was at these times-usually during the winter months- that she opted to stay with the humans she had adopted. It is a fact that this delightful example of grey; black, tan, striped, and spotted tabby was far too intelligent to be ignored.

Fluffy's earlier life, occasionally spent with her adopted humans on a caravan site overlooking the sea about eleven kilometers east of Limassol, gave her a trust in humans that was to serve her well. Other feral cats could be seen scurrying around in typical feral feline style with their bellies close to the ground for reasons of low profile. These cats knew they had to fight for every morsel of food that became available. The law of the wild dictated nature's most basic tenet: survival of the fittest.

Fluffy, however, had learnt that humans on the whole, are very kind to cats, therefore, during the necessary absences of her chosen humans, found sustenance by being very nice to other humans. One Cypriot family had actually taken her home with them to Nicosia, but very quickly brought her back, because living in a house was totally alien to her nature.

At an early age, her superior feline instincts led to her becoming the alpha female in the area, and her absences became longer. Some inner memory, or need, always brought her back, even after weeks. These absences, with a little imagination, come to life in this book.

William Thomas

CONTENTS

NINE LIVES OF A FERAL CAT

. HUMAN CONTACT

A dark shadow in the form of a bird of prey swept quickly along the rocky ground, then stopped suddenly as the huge bird spotted a target below. This moment could have been the last for any unaware victim, but today the Eagles intended meal was not lacking in the knowledge of survival.

My mother reacted in the instant it took for the shadow to register in her brain. Scowling loudly she hurried us under a thick hedge. The shadow disappeared immediately, and we followed the huge birds path with our eyes pointed skywards as we took in the ominous shape of this deadly predator, and consigned it to memory.

I am a feral tabby cat born close to the sea in Cyprus. My mother is a beautiful panther like black cat with yellow eyes, and a wisdom that can only be learnt when every fibre of ones being is highly tuned to the art of survival. She also understands the sounds a human makes when it opens its mouth.

By the time we were three months old, my brother and sisters and I had learnt to catch anything that we could successfully hang on to and kill, and eat. Our mother's milk had almost run dry, so she had to wean us swiftly, and set about regaining her bodyweight ready for her next tour of duty, after a short rest period.

My brother and sisters and I did not know it, but today was the day when all the cuffs around the ears, and the impatient hisses as she moved away to prevent us suckling, would become more brutal, as her instincts told her that this brood must now fend for themselves; nature must now take its course, and the devil take the hindmost.

Our first instinct was to suckle, as the fear of the huge bird waned. This time our mother's refusal took the form of a fang showing snarl and cuffing round the ears with claws retracted. She sprang to her feet suddenly and pushed me away from the others.

I tried to get back to my brother and sisters; they in turn tried to follow her. She scowled nastily at them, and they shrank back from her. She again forced me away, and did not stop until I was under the fronds of the opposite hedge. I stared back at her as she withdrew, and jumped up to follow her. She drove me back, savagely this time, holding me down with her teeth around my neck, growling horribly into my fur. She let me go, and withdrew again.

So recently chastised, and remembering the strength of her mouth around my neck, I made no move to follow her. She edged back to the other hedge, not taking her blazing eyes of me.

From my vantage point, I became aware of two humans talking to each other. My first thought being this close to a human for the first time was, 'How big they are.' One had thick legs and big feet covered in leather strips, and the other had thinner legs that were very brown. Her feet were a lot daintier also.

I did not understand the noises that they made, but the first reaction of the one with brown legs upon seeing me in the bottom of the hedge was instantly interpreted as friendly. She said something to the one with big feet, and he went into a big white box and came out with milk. Brown Legs poured the milk into a dish and gently edged it towards me. The noise she made interpreted as, 'Come on you lovely bundle of fluff, don't be frightened.'

She backed away as I cowered lower to the ground, ready to run. Feeling less afraid as the distance between us increased slightly, I eyed up the dish, knowing full well the desirable taste of its contents. They watched me silently, and remained still as I summoned up courage, and edged towards the dish. A quick taste reassured me of its contents, and, still keeping my eyes on the humans I lapped up the lot. It tasted very nice, different than my mother's milk, but that did not bother me because I was very hungry.

I finished the milk, and crept back into the hedge, glancing to where I had last seen my mother. She was not there. For a moment I panicked, and mewed loudly with fear. I turned to run after her, but then some inner sense stopped me. Whatever it was, the kind voice of Brown Legs quietly calling, 'Here, here kitty kitty, 'drew my attention back to the humans again. She was pushing a dish of fish towards me; that quickly took away my apprehension, and soon, my belly was full for the first time in my memory. Thoroughly content, I fell asleep in the bottom of the hedge.

I cat napped for some time, one eye fluttering open occasionally, and my ears swiveling in all directions ready for any sign of danger. Brown Legs and Big Feet did not bother me, although I could not help but notice that every time I opened an eye, Brown Legs was looking my way. I met her glance now and again between dozes: she always seemed to be smiling at me.

I woke up feeling reassured, and then, after stretching and yawning widely, settled down to watch her pottering around. I met her gaze every time she looked my way. I was beginning to feel very much at home in her presence.

My mother had taught us to watch humans carefully from a safe distance. The good ones threw food to us, but the bad ones shouted and sometimes chased us away. We soon learnt to tell the difference between an arm raised to toss food, and an arm drawn back to throw a stone. For this reason I did not shrink back when the two humans tossed me titbits whilst they were eating.

The dangers our mother had protected us against during our learning process seemed far away at this moment. Bad humans seemed not to exist as I stared into the friendly eyes that seemed never to stray far from me. Even all the tensions that occurred between others of my kind, like mothers chasing us away from their area if we strayed, and bad old Toms who would have snatched us if mother had dropped her guard. Stray hunting dogs that would have gobbled us up in a moment if they had caught us. They had been left in the wild because their humans no longer found them useful. Fortunately they could not climb trees, whereas we could, and with great speed when our lives depended on it; the trick was learning to get down again. All these things were forgotten at this moment, and I was beginning to feel very much at home.

When my mother forced me to stay at Brown Legs caravan plot, I was left with no idea of where she had taken my brother and sisters. I spotted my mother many times scurrying through the bushes, belly close to the ground. She never came near me; she would simply glance my way, and then disappear. It was as if she had planned my meeting with Brown Legs, and just turned up now and then to check on the success of her plan.

I soon learnt that I was not the only kitten that ate at this plot, but I was the only one who was fed in the plot. In the evenings other youngsters had learnt that food had been left for them on the other side of the hedge, so they never had to fear about contact with a human. It did however have the effect of encouraging them to turn up at the same time every day, and very soon other plot owners began to throw their leftovers out for the poor bedraggled specimens that jostled and sometimes fought savagely for every morsel. Soon it became noticeable that these same cats began to walk around with their tails in the air, showing just how useful a little human help could be.

The big white box became a source of great interest in my life. Whenever she opened it I would stop at her feet and watch her rummage around in its cold interior until she found what she wanted. She always gave me something, and then stood there laughing while I licked it around the floor until the chill wore off and I could eat it. It did not take long for it to become a daily joke. Brown Legs would wait until she thought I was nowhere in sight, then she would open the door.

She did not fool me very often; my mind was seriously tuned in to that wonderful white box.

As time went on my training as a tree climber became very useful. Sometimes during the night, the upper branches of a tree were the only escape route from stray hunting dogs that entered the site under the cover of darkness. I was almost caught napping one night not long after I had been put outside for the night. I was sitting on my haunches grooming myself in the moonlight, when all of a sudden a huge hunting dog burst through the hedge scattering Brown Legs flower pots all over the place. In an instant I was on my feet and running for my life, the hot breath of the desperately hungry hound rasping hard on my heels. I leapt at the trunk of the Mimosa tree in the middle of the plot, and the dog's front paws scraped my hindquarters, before the weight of his own body reacted to gravity and he descended to the bowl of the tree barking with frustration.

The noise brought Big Feet running out, and seeing the dog's purpose, he chased it away waving a big stick determinedly. He returned to the base of the tree just in time to see Brown Legs grabbing hold of me as I climbed down. They both soothed me, before putting me down, but they did not take me in with them, Big Feet did say however, 'Come on dear, this is her world out here, and she must learn to contend with it.' I had ran up trees quite often in my young life so I soon recovered from that short sharp shock, but like any life threatening event it made my awareness just that little bit sharper.

I think the small amount of domestic training that they felt they had to give, was harder to learn than a feral cat's continuous fight for survival, not all domestic issues are natural to a cat, particularly when it comes to the place where certain functions of the body have to be attended to.

The first thing they taught me was not to scratch a hole in the plot we lived in. Big Feet dug up a patch of earth outside the plot to make it soft and easy for me to scoop out a hole. I made a few mistakes, and if they caught me at it, they would pick me up, and rush me to the soft patch laughing, and saying, 'Naughty Fluffy! Poo poos are done out here.' It did not take me long to get the message.

The play fighting we learn as kittens, strengthens our small bodies, and establishes a pecking order, but once we are weaned the constant search for food leaves little time for playfulness, that is, until you adopt a human. A cat soon learns that animal loving humans will share whatever they have with any animal that is in dire need. I found myself in that situation, but whether by accident or design, my mother made the separation between us not three yards away from two humans, and now they have befriended me I wonder if this had been a purposeful action by her, or otherwise.

The truth is, we are hereditary egotists, only our own desires at a given moment matter. We show our feelings, but they cannot be regarded as emotions. Even Brown Legs must have known that, because she always encouraged me to hunt, and to pounce on a rag mouse she had made. A strong pole was made into a scratching post with an old beach mat wrapped around it; very soon I was joined by other kittens wanting to share my new toy with me. The play descended into fighting at times, because we all wanted to be best, even so, if any kitten played a submissive role as a fight progressed, tooth and claw were never used. We played to our rules, so even if any fight did appear to be an expression of feline savagery, we became fitter and stronger for it.

****

By the time I was eight months old, I was an extremely proficient hunter, and had become less reliant on Brown Legs. My scavenging tactics were honed to perfection, and my range had extended to include all the Taverna`s down by the beach.

Quite a few cats` had established themselves with families who had a caravan on the site, and who visited every weekend regardless of the weather. This meant that I could spend the night hours strolling around being sociable and meeting the Toms. Everything I do is dictated by the natural order for felines, and it is this inner urge that guides me to do things as the time arrives.

When it is time for me to become a mother, my kittens will have different fathers; this ensures our survival as a species, as well as ensuring a wider selection of the gene pool. Sadly, as happens all around me continuously, the weaker kitten in a brood does not survive, and that will happen to me in times of hardship, no matter how good a mother I am. The fittest and the fastest, and sometimes the most aggressive, will go on to provide the next generation.

One morning I strolled into the plot; not having had a very good night. It had been raining for three days and nights with little let up, and I was very hungry. My first thoughts were of food and shelter from the consistent rain. A lot of activity was taking place, but that did not stop Brown Legs from feeding me the moment her eyes fell on me.

'I think something told her we were going,' she said, staring down at me wolfing down a lump of liver. Big Feet did not reply, but he glanced my way smiling, and then continued packing things. After a final look around the plot they stopped and looked down at me, 'We're going to miss you Fluffy, I hope your still here when we come back,'

Brown Legs said, her voice tinged with sadness. I had got used to the expressions on her face, but I had never seen this one before. She was not jolly or playful, or gently scolding. She was sad, and I knew it was because she was leaving me.

They put on big round hats, climbed on their beast with two round legs, and roared away out of my life. I stared after them as they disappeared out of sight not knowing if I would ever see them again. The roar of the beast gradually faded into the distance, and I was left alone with the whole plot to myself.

They did not know I was expecting my first litter of kittens, but their final thoughts must have been about me. I nosed around the awning, and found a little gap that Brown Legs had left open for me. Just inside the opening

I found a strategically placed polystyrene fish box which had been lined with a blanket. She had also left a large lump of liver in my dish, so big that I could not eat it all at once, so while I didn't have to hunt and scavenge, I pulled and tugged at the blanket until it was an untidy mess, but it was a comfortable untidy mess, the wrinkles and folds I had created made it much more individual, as a matter of taste.

All the other feral cats in the vicinity obeyed the law of the wild. After I had screamed and scowled at a few of them, they did not bother me in my home again. This protected area under the awning, and my comfortable little nest, soon became the home of my family, so I could not allow old Toms and wandering stray dogs to be too nosy. None of them sniffed around the area again after I surprised one or two of them with a vicious attack to their rear ends with weapons unsheathed. I was an adult cat now, and more than able to defend my territory.

My first family was born some weeks after the disappearance of my humans. For two days I was tied by motherly concern for the first most important few hours of the lives of my kittens. They fed and slept in short intermittent periods, after which I groomed them thoroughly. I had to choose my moments to tend to my own needs with great caution, only being able to leave long enough to carry out my own toilets for two days. After two days they had received enough nourishment to ensure that no weaknesses due to lack of sustenance would harm them.

They were all soundly sleeping rolled up in one big ball of fur, so I took the opportunity to consider my own needs. Stepping out of the box, I stretched luxuriously, and gave a wide satisfied yawn.

Hunting around the bushes and hedgerows of my territory, I managed to catch a few lizards. These sated my hunger a little, but it would take a much larger meal to really satisfy my needs. The urge to return to my kittens quickly overcame the urge to find more food, so I hurried back to them and woke them to feed. They nuzzled and fed instinctively, then passed water and milky excrement as I cleaned them with my rough tongue, this kept our nest clean and free from harmful bugs that caused cat dysentery and other sometimes fatal diseases to immature cats. Some days later their eyes began to open, and by ten days old they could see, and were beginning to crawl around the nest inquisitively.

My motherly fussiness continued in this strict manner for two weeks, by which time I was really desperate for a satisfying meal. It was also becoming harder to keep the box clean, so I dug another nest in the soft soil underneath the caravan close to a round leg. I then moved my family into their new nest.

It was their first experience of being carried by the scruff of the neck in my gentle jaws, but they instinctively knew that this was the carrying position for felines, so made no fuss.

By this time my serious need for a good meal had reached the point where chances have to be taken. It was in fact a fifty-fifty situation; we all died of starvation, or I eat my own kittens to survive to breed another day; or I leave them for as long as it takes to feed myself thoroughly, and chance that another creature does not find and eat them during my absence. My body fat had reduced to the point where my skin hung loosely on my flanks, and there was little flesh left to cover my bones.

As of this moment, the hazards of being born completely feral were a stark reality. It was the rainy season, and there was little to scavenge on the caravan site, so therefore I had to range further afield to satisfy my needs.

I scanned the area around my plot, and then crept through the hedges to sniff out any fresh scent that a predator may have recently left. This helped to tell me if I was being watched or not. Satisfied with my findings I sneaked away carefully, slinking from bush to bush, and through the hedgerows on low belly. I had purposefully chosen the time of day to hunt when other cats would be napping, but I still had to move with watchful caution so as not to alert anyone to my absence. Whilst they thought I was still at home, they would not dare incur my wrath so keeping out of sight was of prime importance; I was desperate not to have to abhort the hunt.

The perimeter fence was a strong well posted construction, with barbed wire angled outwards at the top; very effective as a barrier against dogs and other large animals, but certainly not effective as a cat deterrent.

We had made places to crawl through underneath, this was our quick route to the shore side Tavernas.

Unseen by prying eyes, I reached the Tavernas. I had caught one or two lizards as I crossed the scrubland, and these morsels served to encourage me to fully satisfy the aching need in my stomach.

I scavenged around one Taverna after another, spitting savagely at the odd resident cat who resented my presence. Slowly but surely I filled myself up with all the scraps that the resident cats had turned their noses up at. A very varied diet, but it filled me for the first time since I had given birth.

I returned stealthily to my kittens, and mewed with relief as they fed, then succumbed to a thorough washing. Some complained plaintively as my rough tongue pushed them around.

When satisfied that I had finished my chores, I lay back, and let them nuzzle at me until they dropped off to sleep. Full for the first time in weeks, I soon joined them and enjoyed a very good cat nap.

That large meal sustained me for three days, with a few things caught locally in my territory.

The kittens were now crawling around on splayed unsteady legs but had not ventured out from underneath the protective umbrella of the caravan yet, natural caution made them respect the boundaries to the outside world.

Fate had been kind to my kittens and I thus far, but it in no way reduced my continual alertness to possible danger.

It was this inherent caution that saved my kittens from a bad old Tom who by some misfortune had come to notice my family. He had probably been skulking around and heard my kittens mewing. Unbeknown to me this ragged eared old Tom, veteran of many a territorial skirmish had been watching me from the cover of some bushes on the opposite side of the garden that formed the centre of the site, and was biding his time to close in to see if any of my kittens were weak enough to be snatched and eaten.

My kittens were now of an age where they could lay back on their haunches and present a spitting four pawed defence that could blind an attacker, but there was always that small one in a litter that was a bit behind its siblings, and that would be the one that the old cannibal would go for. Any one of them could be vulnerable though if caught unawares from behind.

Oblivious to his watchful glare, that evening I kept the kitten's awake making them feed and continually cleaning them, until I was sure they would sleep for hours. I sneaked away, but remained watchful from a favourite vantage point until I felt that it was safe to continue on my hunting expedition.

A movement caught my eye. I froze, hugging the ground beneath me, every sinew tensed. A dark shape, belly close to the ground, was edging its way through the fronds of the garden bushes heading towards my patch. My heart raced, blood surged into my muscles ready for the attack.

The old torn eared Tom did not know what hit him, I was on him in a flash, claws and teeth tearing at his tatty multi coloured hide. One of my slashes seared an eyeball making him turn away from my savage attack. Now I took full advantage of his move to retreat. I clung to his backside, clawing and tearing at him as he tried to escape my onslaught.

My hideous screams added great fear to his discomfort, as he scrambled to make good his retreat from my territory. Completely demoralized, he scurried away to lick his wounds. I simmered down slowly and returned to my kittens, I would have to stay hungry until a feeling of security returned.

The old Tom would not forget his confrontation with me in a hurry, and could probably add a blind eye to his list of battle scars. He would not venture near to my kittens again, that's for sure.

Next morning, I was staring out towards the road, when I became aware of familiar noises beginning to echo around the site. The sun was shining in a cloudless sky, and I knew instantly that the humans were returning for their weekend barbecues. A time of plenty was about to begin, the hardships of the rainy season were coming to an end. I knew that today I would eat well; these people were the sort of people who always threw food to us watching cats.

I steered clear of the places where I knew I was not welcome, these were doggy people, and of course their animals loved nothing better than chasing us cats. I was in no danger from these dogs, because they generally chased us full of boisterous playfulness. None of these dogs would ever consider killing and eating a cat.

Sometimes I would sit cheekily at the entrance to a doggy owner's site just to tease the dog; I could play games just as annoying as his. Usually the dogs owner would get fed up with his dogs antics, and put him on a lead, this way I extracted my revenge. Invariably the owner would toss me a morsel, rubbing salt into the dogs wounded pride. It was we cats who kept this site free of vermin and snakes, and these owners knew it.

I fared much better at the begging game than many of my feral equals. Because of my association with Brown Legs, I had become trusting towards other humans, and they in turn rewarded me by feeding me any time I passed by their plot This site was full of people like that, so at times like this I fed very well.

Cats that scurried around furtively were at a definite disadvantage, they could only feed by stealing, whereas I just had to sit quietly and attentively knowing full well I would be fed.

There are many advantages to being human friendly; being nice to them is a dead sure way of being able to exploit their superior intellect, and need to show kindness.

Of course the small male humans can be very annoying. They chase us with absolutely no hope of catching us; they are so easy to dodge. After a few yards they give up the chase, and then throw a badly aimed missile as if annoyed at their inability to catch us. How the human race has survived I will never know they never chase anything until it is caught, yet their cold white boxes are always full of good things to eat.

I did not have to travel far to eat well, and very soon was full to bursting. Suddenly I realized that I had been away from my kittens for a long while, and the urge to return to them came on strongly.

I ran the few metres back to my plot and dived underneath the caravan. I froze on stiff legs, back arched, hissing, and spitting aggressively. Staring back at me impassively was the form of my mother. She gave a soft mew, and looked from me to my kittens, and then back to me.

Her stance was not threatening; she looked at me quietly for a moment, and then was gone. Humans might say she had come to see her grandchildren, but that is not so in the feline world, once the bond is broken, relatives can be as dangerous as any other cat in times of hardship; it's all a matter of survival, regardless of the cost to another of our species. As mothers we defend our kittens with great ferocity, but once we have weaned them and taught them to hunt, our job is finished, there are no extended families in our world. If any of our last brood is still present when we are preparing for another litter, we will drive them away in a most assertive and ultimately cruel manner. In the wild they can be a danger to their new brothers and sisters, so a mother must protect her new young from this possibility.

Many of the cats that share this area with me would not have survived without human intervention. We are not house pets like the conventional domestic cat, but we do enjoy human companionship. To have the scope to live a satisfying life free from the restrictions of total tameness, yet retain the ability to be attractive to humans is truly a wonderful life while you are young, fit, and healthy. The downside of this lifestyle does not appear until frailty sets in with old age, it is at this time we need our human friends. For sure, they make the twilight years of a feral cat much easier to contend with than a life spent totally in the wild, like my stealthy peers.

The time soon came when my kittens were two months old, and due to their size my milk was insufficient to satisfy all four of them. For a short time I had been bringing them solid food, but the time had become right for me to take them out and start to teach them how to kill, and fend for themselves.

The hunting trips had the effect of sorting out the quick from the slow, and the greedy from the desperately hungry. Nature, as always, found a way of creating order from chaos, soon all four were on a par with each other, and some real cat fights occurred.

Fortunately my kittens were growing up in a time of plenty, so hunting failures could be subsidized by showing off my kittens to humans who knew me and always tossed something my way. Fish, and pork barbecues were popular at weekends, and all of my kittens were gradually learning that humans were very handy to have around if hunting was not as successful as it needed to be. The battle for personal survival however, was fraught with the dangers of competition amongst a species so well equipped for survival. As usually happens in the feral world, the females had the edge on their brothers at this early stage in their lives. We seem better equipped to put up with the trials and tribulations of our harshly competitive world, and were much faster on the kill, and much faster to escape once we had grabbed our prey.

My one male kitten was beginning to show the effects of not being quite as spry as his sisters; he was in fact becoming very thin. His condition was not helped by the fact that he had caught a bug, and suffered terribly from cat dysentery. The continuous and involuntary nature of this severe case of diarrhoea weakened him dreadfully, and malnutrition became evident by the thinness of his flanks, and the wobbly nature of his hind legs. His head also began to droop, as total lethargy crept up on him.

One of the females had lost an eye completely, another had been clawed badly, and lost the use of one eye, and was only partly sighted in the other one. The third female who would become to be known as Tiger had to wobble around on three legs due to a thumb claw hanging off. With all these injuries and disease, it was beginning to look unlikely that any of this litter would survive.

Just as I was beginning to lose all hope, something happened that jogged my memory. I stopped and listened intently. A sound was in the air that seemed familiar. Something drew me to the sound of voices coming from my plot. By habit, I came through the hedge and broke cover at speed; this was a defensive tactic in case a larger enemy was on the other side. This time however, there was no enemy. Memory flooded back. I mewed and purred plaintively as I stared up at a very welcome figure, perhaps all was not lost.

"Fluffy!" Brown Legs squealed with delight, then sobered as she took the sight of me in. 'Oh but you are so thin, you poor darling!'

Big feet passed a carton of milk to her, interrupting her verbally expressed sadness at the sight of me. For a moment she searched around for my dish, then rinsed it out before Big Feet poured milk in whilst she held it. With no thought for my kittens skulking under a bush, I lapped the milk up greedily.

Meanwhile Big Feet opened a tin of fish, and handed it to Brown Legs. She tipped it into my food dish, and I immediately left my milk dish to gobble down the fish. She was murmuring gently to me all of the time, saying nice things as she stared at me.

All of a sudden my world seemed free of cares, my favourite human had reappeared, and all the hard times were forgotten. I purred contentedly, and rubbed myself against her legs, she reacted by bending over and stroking my flanks. I stiffened for a moment at the touch of a human hand, but then relaxed. I felt secure; after all, this was my human.

'Look, she hasn't forgotten a thing,' Brown Legs said.

Big Feet, ever practical, smiled, 'She knows which side her breads buttered on,' he said, looking down at me before continuing making our plot fit for human habitation again.

It filled me with great confidence to see him coiling up the lines that he had removed from the awning. Brown Legs joined him, and got on with the job of cleaning our seaside home. I licked my dish clean, and while they were busy, went back to my kittens. Even though they were in such a bad state, I was still preparing them for a life independent of me. Without a doubt they would need human help to survive, regular human help, not just a hearty meal at weekends when the locals arrived for their barbecues.

Determinedly I led my kittens back to the plot. The four of them followed me, one after the other, and sat around me staring at the awning.

Brown Legs noticed me, and her mouth fell open, 'Good Lord! look what Fluffy has brought home,' she gasped, total amazement alight in her features.

My kittens shied away as she approached them, this sort of closeness represented a threat. She saw their apprehension, and came no closer, instead she went to the big white box, took out the milk, and poured a liberal amount into a square plastic container. The instant she stepped back, the kittens dived at it.

Another tin of fish came out of the big white box. The kittens devoured it, growling at each other as they gobbled it down. They did not fight this time; they knew there was enough for them all to be satisfied.

Big Feet grinned at the sight, 'Looks as if your milk bill's just trebled,' he chortled.

'Don't laugh too loud,' Brown Legs replied smiling. 'If they get rid of fish this quickly, your fishing stories had better not be about the one that got away.'

They both laughed heartily, but their light hearted banter soon took on a different tone as they began to notice the poor state my kittens were in.

'I don't think that little fellows going to make it,' Big Feet voiced his concern as he tried to get a closer look at my black kitten. Almost as he spoke my poor black one crawled towards the hedge.

'It's got dysentery,' Big Feet murmured. 'The poor thing looks beyond help.'

'It did eat some fish,' Brown Legs said, and then added hopefully, 'Perhaps a few days of regular feeding may improve his condition.'

They stared after me as I led my kittens from the plot. I knew they would talk about me and my first family, and try and find a way to help the black male. I however, had decided that it was time for them to fend for themselves, so now, with food in their bellies was the ideal time to start the process of separation.

The feline schedule, dominated by my chemistry, would not be delayed by personal events, life must go on. If any of this litter is still hanging on when the seeds for my next litter are sown, I shall have to disperse any hanger on brutally.

Next morning, fate played a part in my duties, and had taken the only male from us during the night. We left him where he had died underneath some bushes, where, after a few curious sniffs his siblings ran after me, and left him as if he had never been a part of the litter. His ravaged body would become flyblown, and riddled with maggots, in a few months only his black hide would remain.

For most of the day of Blacky's death, I led my kittens around parts of the site that they were not familiar with, showing them the places under the fence, and certain caravans that no one ever seemed to visit. The underneath of these caravans were a very useful protection from the winter rains.

During the afternoon we dropped in to visit Brown Legs. Her instant action on seeing us was to provide a large dish of liver which she had got free of charge from a butcher that day. Cypriot butchers gave this offal to their customers if they had animals to look after.

This time the kittens did not growl at each other, there was plenty on the dish for all. When they had filled their bellies I polished off the remainder.

'No Blacky I see,' Big Feet said, looking meaningfully at Brown Legs. She nodded, but made no comment.

Big Feet tried to get a closer look at my kitten with the broken thumb claw, but she was not ready for any human attention and shrank away, her eyes looking straight into his with feral caution. Her eyes gave the message, 'You can look, but don't touch.'

'Have you noticed her colouring,' Big Feet said, more as an idle comment than a question. 'Mainly grey and black tabby at the flanks, with a bushy tail, but look at the yellowish tint, almost tawny, leading to a glowing brunette at the base of her tail around her haunches. Almost Tiger like across the back, wouldn't you say?'

'Mmmm, it is a bit unusual,' she leant across and answered. Tiger cringed back, now deeply suspicious of all the attention. This did not deter Brown Legs. 'The claw doesn't look that bad when you get a closer look,' she changed the subject. 'Perhaps it will heal better if we entice her to stay here with us for a day or so.'

'Leave the food out,' Big Feet suggested. 'There's nothing like a regular food source as an enticement to an animal that is used to constant hunger.'

Their attitude showed kindness and concern, but I had a different agenda. This was my patch, and my next brood would be born here. Tiger will have to be taken to another area, just like the others, regardless of any infirmities.

The kittens did not want to leave the plot because it had registered in their little minds that this was definitely better than having to scramble for every morsel of food that past their lips.

I mewed at them, and then used my 'follow me or else tone.'   They obeyed that instantly, so I led them out with the intention of taking them further afield.

For two days we stayed at a Taverna out of sight of the caravan site. Tiger, and the one Big Feet had named "Blind Pugh" soon began to get the idea of survival in this tourist friendly setting, so at the end of the second day, while they were being spoiled by friendly tourists, I sneaked away with the one named "One eyed Jack". She was very alert; the female in her knew very well what I was doing. She never the less followed me obediently, and made a futile attempt to snuggle up to me under a remote caravan placed in the scrubland by some freedom loving Cypriot family.

I scolded her spitefully; ears laid back, and mouth displaying fangs. I cuffed her viciously around the ears, and as she shrank to the ground submissively, I sank my teeth into her neck, just above the shoulder blades strongly enough to convince her that I meant it.

She squealed, horrified, and now dreadfully afraid, she ran from beneath the caravan genuinely in fear for her life.

The following morning I returned to the plot on my own. 'Hello Fluffy,' Brown Legs greeted me, 'Where's the babies then?'

I mewed at her, looking up with a feed me expression that she could not resist. I was very soon tucking into a bowl of liver with a side dish of milk to wash it down with.

'We thought you had gone away and left us,' she chided me gently as I gobbled down the food.

When I had finished eating, I jumped up on one of the chairs that had my cushion on it. I noticed by the smell that it had been in water, but it still had my scent mingled in with the freshness. I wriggled contentedly until totally comfortable. Feeling absolutely secure, and free from responsibility for the first time in months, I was soon absorbed in a cat's favourite pastime, "Snoozing".

'Wonder what she's been up to for this last three days?' Big Feet said, nodding my way.

'Whatever it was, it obviously involved her kittens, and I wonder where she left them?' she replied, and then added, her face showing concern, 'They did not look well enough to survive to me.'

'Aw, don't worry dear,' Big Feet soothed. 'At least you had filled their little bellies before she took them away. Summers coming, there will soon be plenty of visitors around to throw scraps to them.'

Life became idyllic again. I followed Brown Legs as she pottered around enlarging her pile of rocks, and adding plants between them. The rocks were great to perch on and survey my domain; but I soon learnt not to take advantage of the soft soil between the rocks at toilet time. I was put through a refresher course of essential training to become house trained again, when sharing their territory.

She chatted to me continuously as she placed little brown pots everywhere with flowers in them. She took every opportunity to stroke me now that I had succumbed to the touch of a human, and really, I began to enjoy the sensation very much.

Like all cats that have become comfortable with their situation in life, I was very nosey. I just had to sniff around all the bits and pieces, nooks and crannies to see if I could find anything that interested me.

My nosiness backfired one day. Big Feet left the door of his work shed open, so I sneaked in while he was not looking. Suddenly the door closed behind me, and I heard it being locked. My heart stopped as I heard the beast with round legs burst into life with a loud growl.

It ran out of the plot, and I heard it roaring up the road. Were they leaving me again? Apparently not. Sometime later, my ears caught the sound of the beast returning. I started doing a wall of death around the walls of the shed, making a terrible din. The door burst open, and I hurtled out between Big Feet's legs and found solace rubbing my head around Brown Legs ankles.

The shed was never left open again, but it did remain in my mind as a suitable place in which to have my next litter of kittens.

Big Feet knew what was on my mind, and every time I appeared when he opened the door, he would scold, 'I've got my eye on you madam,' as he stepped over me and closed the door.

A week soon passed by since I had dispersed my kittens, and settled into a life of ease between feline duties. I had apparently underestimated the intelligence of one of my offspring. One colourful youngster, who had been blessed with a better memory, or a more acute sense of direction than her siblings, had found her way back. Brown Legs was first to see her, as she limped through the hedge. 'Oh!' She shouted, somewhat surprised, and then called to Big Feet, 'Tigger's found her way back!'

This popular variation of Tiger was to stay, Tiger had now become Tigger, and nobody would dare change Brown Legs mind. Without any hesitation, a bowl of fish appeared, and Tigger demolished it greedily.

'Poor soul hasn't eaten for days by the looks of her,' murmured Brown Legs, looking down concernedly at the new member of her cat family.

If I had been human at that moment, I would have been terribly ashamed. Fortunately self-blame is not within the limits of a cat's conscience. We show a few reactions, but shame and self-blame are not amongst them; love, and anger are, when the occasion arises. However, I don't think Brown Legs would have ever forgiven me had I chased Tigger away at that moment. I just sat there and watched her gobble up the fish, and resigned myself to the fact that I would have to share Brown Legs affections with one of my daughters.

As the days passed, Tigger sniveled her way into my affections again and very soon snuggled up to me in my basket. I could just not be bothered to stop her, this was my relaxation period, and I was not going to exert myself one little bit, I just laid back and went along with it.

Her walking began to improve as the care she was getting kept her less mobile, allowing her claw to heal naturally. Very soon she was fit and agile again, and very playful.

By the time Brown Legs had persistently toilet trained her, and rubbed the rough edges off with a bit of affection, she had become a member of their family.

'Don't forget she's feral,' Big Feet warned her. 'Don't get too attached, Fluffy may still chase her away.'

'I know! I know!' She replied rattily, not liking what she took to be a criticism. 'At least she will be fit and well if that time comes.'

'Well don't feed her too well,' Big Feet went on insistently. 'She must practice her hunting skills, don't make her too reliant upon you.'

As it turned out, my daughter joined me on my nightly hunting forays. Her natural instincts and new fitness soon made her an excellent hunter. She became what all cats are in their natural habitat; matchless hunting machines, with the speed and agility to leap and catch small birds hastily departing a low bush.

She learnt not to panic when a snake she had grabbed behind the head threw its coils around her body. It was the first snake she had snatched, not a large one, and not poisonous; it is called the "Small Whip Snake", and is less than a metre long and about three centimeters in diameter. We could not eat it all, so Tigger buried what was left for later. She did not have to be taught this, it was a natural instinct, but only truly comes to light when a cat is feral.

The "Small Whip Snake" has a larger cousin, the "Large Whip Snake". It can be two metres long, and six centimeters in diameter when fully grown. It is also nonpoisonous, but far too strong for a solitary feline to do battle with.

Although Tigger became a deadly hunter, and a good companion, I frequently had to cuff her, and scold her nastily for persisting to try to suckle sneakily. In this sense she seemed determined to keep her kittenish ways, and took every opportunity to remind me that I was still her mother, and she was my daughter. She did not want me to forget that fact.

Later that afternoon, we were strolling side by side across an open area beyond the caravan site, when a large shadow flashed along the ground. For an instant I froze, and then memory surged back to a time long ago when such a sight had sent my mother and us kittens rushing for cover.

Instinctively I rushed for cover, and Tigger alerted to danger by my swift movement followed suit. We disappeared under the fronds of a large bush just as a swishing sound filled the air behind us, and then over us.

One of us had escaped death by a whisker thanks to a panther like feral cat with yellow eyes, who had passed on the fear of a shadow from the sky. We watched it soar upwards again, and then take a dive from the sky. Seconds later a horrific screech filled the air shattering the quiet of the afternoon.

The Eagle soared upwards, a kitten of about two month's old hanging lifeless beneath it. Instant death: and a harsh warning to all who witnessed its triumphant escape with a limp victim clenched in one talon. A mother had relaxed for a moment, and one of her kittens had paid the price of her negligence.

We found the hole in the fence, and crawling underneath dashed for cover. All was safe, so keeping close to the hedgerows and bushes; we made our way back to the plot.

Brown Legs always seemed a bit surprised when I showed no eagerness to feed. How could we tell her that the hunt had been good, and that we were full of snake and lizard?

'Oh suit yourself then madam!' She said feigning a huff, putting the liver back in the big white box.

'She's not limping now,' Big Feet nodded towards Tigger as he spoke. He knelt down to take a closer look at Tigger's leg. She however, was having none of that and shrank back apprehensively.

Big Feet did not let her reaction discourage him; he became more persistent with his overtures of friendship. Tigger just moved further away every time without making a great effort to distance herself; just sufficient to stay out of arms reach. She showed no fear of him; her actions were just simply inbred caution. It was Brown Legs who finally cracked Tigger's reserve. The old pretend mouse was rooted out, and that did the trick. Within a few days Tigger was eating out of her hand, and was accepting the touch of that human hand. Kindness and familiarity had won the day, from that moment on Brown Legs and Tigger became firm friends.

Their mutual understanding became so close that Brown Legs only had to raise her voice and say: 'Ah-Ah! That's naughty,' and Tigger would immediately behave herself and sit upright with head cocked to one side with a look that said, 'What's wrong now?'

She learnt to play football with a bottle cap, just like me. She even went to the lengths of hiding the bottle cap in the hedge, and then retrieve her toy when the mood was upon her. Big Feet watched her actions laughing like a drain, and shouting encouragement.

'If anyone saw you, they would swear you are ready for the funny farm,' laughed Brown Legs. Big Feet just made funny faces at her, and laughed even more.

Tigger, as if enjoying the attention, showed off by throwing the bottle cap in the air, and then jump and catch it, rolling and twisting in midair, shooting the cap along the ground as she landed.

'Goal!' Screamed Big Feet, roaring with laughter as the bottle cap shot between two plant pots.

'That's enough for you my lad,' Brown Legs chortled, making a playful grab for his beer bottle.

'Gerroff!' He roared tears of mirth appearing as he theatrically cuddled his beer bottle to his chest.

The scenes of play continued for ages in this safe and happy atmosphere. Cats just love to play, and always welcome this sort of attention to their playful habits.

With no kittens to care for, my life of ease soon came to an end. Nature took charge, and very soon I was expecting another litter of kittens. This meant absolutely nothing to me in human terms; I was just living out the cycles of a cat's life. We bring up a litter, wean them, and have a little rest, and then the cycle starts all over again.

A month later during one of my visits to the plot, I was enjoying a good meal of chopped liver and chicken necks watched casually by Big Feet.

'Are you enjoying that fatty?' He asked. His statement attracted Brown Legs attention, 'The way she's tucking into that, I would say she hasn't eaten for a while.'

Big Feet nodded acknowledging her observation, 'The size of her can only mean one thing then, can't it?'

'Not already surely, poor things only just got rid of the last lot.' Female concern showed on her face as she kept looking at me.

'This is not a front room and cosy fire cat, you know. The only rules she abides by are survival at any cost, no niceties in her feral life out there, crack on regardless, and live by the rules for feral cats.'

Brown Legs face had not lost its look of concern as she replied, 'But she seems so tame and homely when she's with us.'

'Ah! That's when she's with us,' Big Feet replied strongly, emphasizing the point that I spent more time on my feral life than I did with them. 'You've seen how she goes for anything that comes near this plot, this is her territory, and everything that's in it belongs to her, including us,' he added, bending over to stroke me.

I shrank back, and gave him a cold stare, and then carried on eating. They always talked about me when I spent time with them. Very soon they will have to put up with my new babies; that will give them something else to talk about.

My birthing spot was already selected, under their caravan, unless something better turned up in the meantime. Humans always seem to create nice little nooks, many of them suitable for the first two weeks of my kitten's lives. I still had my eye on Big Feet's shed, bet he wouldn't throw me out if I had kittens in there; or would he?

I was still a bit unsure about him, even though he is kind to us cats. I remember how he scolded that naughty dog who wrecked Brown Legs garden. I am sure that if he could have found the owner of that dog, he would have scolded them also.

Whenever he opened the shed door, I tried to be near.

'I know what you're up to madam!' He would say laughing, and then immediately shut the door. Never the less there was always the chance of a moment of carelessness. Like my entire breed, I was a great opportunist; you never know your luck.

'That inquisitive madam never misses a chance,' he said. 'She appears from nowhere whenever I put the key in the lock.'

Brown Legs thought for a moment, and then made a suggestion, 'I'll put that polystyrene box in that space between the back of the caravan and the hedge, if she's determined to have them here; I will feel better knowing exactly where they are.

She spends a lot of time underneath the caravan lately; in fact I think she is there when we think she is off on one of her adventures. I'm not sure I like the idea of a family of cats living underneath my bedroom; tell you what! Let's get that sheet of galvanise that was left over from the alcove, and make a lean to.'

'Great idea,' Big Feet said enthusiastically, I'll get to work on it immediately.

Sometime later, they had built a cosy little shelter at the back of their caravan, with the sheet of tin making a nice little cubby hole. When it was complete, I gave it a thorough inspection, and decided this would be the birth place of my second family.

Because of my condition, my territorial senses became very acute, cats whom I would normally ignore, and others who I had spent a playful moment with, suddenly became a threat. Tigger kept well clear of me now, not just because her instincts told her to, but because my body language was such that every movement I made while she was around could be interpreted as determinedly aggressive. She knew that the smallest offensive act could produce an attack if I was so minded.

As time passed I needed more to eat. My night forays did not always satisfy me. I began to wait for Brown Legs early in the morning. The first time, she chortled, 'Oh, you're joining us for breakfast now, are you?'

My answer was to gobble up everything she put in front of me greedily, and then relax with a saucer of milk.

She said to Big Feet, 'Do you think I should feed her twice a day now she's like this.'

'No I do not!' He replied gruffly. 'I know you have grown very fond of her, but I really do think that it is not wise to overdo the kindness bit. We humans have the habit of making our pets a bit too dependent upon us, sometimes even attributing them with human emotions. It is essential; to be kind to animals, but we should resist the urge to overdo it, or worse still, become domineering with our possessive feelings.'

By way of answer to his lecturing, I finished the milk and then rubbed myself affectionately against her.

"Oh look!' She exclaimed she's saying thank you.'

Big Feet flicked his eyes upwards in mock exasperation; his little lecture had not affected my association with Brown Legs in the least.

As if I had understood him, I raised my tail, and my head haughtily in the air, and sauntered off to my recently established position behind the caravan, there to sleep off my hearty breakfast.

'Hey look!' Big Feet shouted, pointing to the caravan across the road. Two tabby ears tipped with a ginger tuft showed Tigger peering furtively from behind a piece of board under the van. Brown Legs eyes followed the direction of his finger.

'It's Tigger!' she cried, 'I wondered where she had disappeared to.'

I heard her cry of delight, and leaping from my box, peered around the side of the awning. The fact that my daughter was ravenously hungry meant nothing to me. I watched her gorge a meal down, and then gaze apprehensively at me. I returned the frightened gaze with an air of aloof authority. My look had the desired affect; she finished her meal, darted into the hedge, and disappeared. I relaxed and returned to my box.

Some weeks later, I reacted to a sudden pain, and crawled into my box. 'Here we go again!' I sighed, and waited to give birth with an air of resignation.

A MOTLEY LOT.

'Is it that time again?' Brown Legs stared down at me, her gentle voice tinged with concern. She then stayed with me for the next two hours; by which time five new lives were on the earth. 'There's a clever girl,' she cooed as each new life appeared. Not once did she touch me or interfere, and somehow her presence was reassuring.

As with my first litter, this could be a dangerous time for my kittens, at a time when my retaliation to an intruder was hindered by the act of giving birth, even though I would not hesitate to retaliate, even with a kitten hanging from me, half born. So having Brown Legs watching over me was particularly comforting. My kittens were absolutely safe.

'Five seems to be it,' she called to Big Feet. 'One of them is very small compared to the biggest of the brood, but it seems to have the same urge to suckle as the rest.' There was a slight pause, and then she continued, 'It's not defective, it's just small.'

Big Feet came round the back of the caravan to look at me stretched out in the polystyrene fish box. By this time, my young were nuzzling at my belly, and two of them had been successful in finding a nipple, and were feeding. 'My word, they are a motley lot!' he said, grinning widely, then went on wryly, 'How many husbands have you got then, at least five looking at that lot.'

I gave him a look that said, 'Okay, I don't mind you looking, but you touch one, and I'll have your fingers off!'

'That smallest one is a pretty little thing now it's dry,' said Brown Legs. 'But look at the size of that tabby kitten, she struggled a bit with that one, it was first born, and first to reach her teats, so it looks as if that one is the pride of the brood.'

'Don't you think it's time you had a cup of tea now, you've been standing there for over two hours. Have a break and let her get on with it now.'

'I think I will call that little one Cleopatra, and the big one will be Tabitha.' She retaliated, ignoring his plea to have a rest.

'Oh! You're expecting to keep all of them, are you?' he retorted, and once more issued that short lecture about not getting too attached. 'She may have other ideas,' he added, and then emphasized his point further, 'She took all the last lot away, and only Tigger came back to you.'

'Yes but we were not here when she was born,' she replied, obviously searching for excuses.

The little one she had named Cleopatra, had made a lasting impression on her, and even at this stage she was bonding with the little mite. 'I think Tigger is the only survivor of the first lot,' she added, trying to lend strength to her overt desire to keep at least one of this brood. 'The black one must certainly have died, and the two with eye defects must find life very difficult, even if they have survived.'

'Not necessarily,' argued Big Feet. 'The very fact that they have a defect means that they will have to try harder. You look at some of the opportunists around here, not one of them is free of a battle scar or two. They survive by feline instinct and wiliness, they learn as they go along.'

'Fluffy has not got a mark on her, so she does not fall into that category,' she replied defensively.'

'I know she doesn't!' big feet answered a hint of exasperation in his tone. 'She has been more or less brought up by you which puts her on both sides of the fence so to speak, that is why she is the alpha female around these parts: she certainly wields authority on this patch.'

Brown Legs looked up at him, and said defiantly, 'Well I am not letting her take Cleopatra away; I'll put her in a carry cage when the time comes if I have to.' Big Feet gave her a quirky grin and threw his arms in the air theatrically, realizing that this was one difference of opinion he would not win.

He was right about my authority around these parts, but perhaps, on second thoughts, not totally right. That trespassing elder daughter of mine: the one they had named Tigger, had inveigled her way into their affections and was now treated with equal status to me. I shall have to review her situation again when it's time for her to become a mother, we cannot have two bosses strutting around this plot.

Before a week had passed, Brown Legs had her hand in the nest stroking the kittens with her finger. 'Hey look at this!' she called to Big Feet, not removing her hand, and then, as he poked his head around the corner she explained, 'Every time I go to stroke them, she tries to cover them up, and cuddle them between her front legs.'

'She's just telling you that they are hers, go and get your own babies.'

Brown Legs laughed saying 'Oh she'll share them with me, she's my pal.'

'She's a clever pussy cat,' he replied emphatically, then added in a different tone of voice, 'When I get a chance, I'll see what genders they are.'

I knew already that all of my kittens were girls, but Big Feet had to wait until I had gone for a walk to stretch my legs and do my toilets, before he found out, and then he got it wrong.

'Four little girls, and this young fellah,' he said, holding the black and white kitten out to Brown Legs.

'Oh good, that means that little Cleopatra is a girl after all,' she replied happily.

'And that big lump,' he laughed, pointing to Tabitha.

I knew someone had picked up my kittens as soon as I returned to them, I could smell Big Feet all over them. I quickly washed the scent of all of them. Nice as these humans are, I could not have their scent all over my kittens.

'We are the fussy one, aren't we?' Big Feet said, highly amused by my fastidious actions. I glowered at him as if saying, 'Don't you dare touch them again.' But of course the big oaf found it all terribly amusing.

'She doesn't look very pleased, does she,' Brown legs said. 'I really think that scowl means: keep your smelly hands off!'

Two weeks later, I had moved the kittens out of the box, and placed them in a comfortable spot surrounded by the gas bottles and crates, and other bits and pieces that always clutter at least one hidden part of a caravan plot. They were crawling now and needed wrestling space.

By the time two months had passed, I began the gradual weaning process. The kittens were still losing most of the lizards I brought for them, but Brown Legs, as always, helped out with a bowl of liver, or fish.

My gradually decreasing milk supply was sustained a bit longer due to the regular meals I received; it seems that comfortable living delays the usual rush to get my offspring fending for themselves. This was very evident due to the fact that this litter had no defects at all; hence they were stronger and fitter than their peers when out in the night time world of the feral cat.

Individual traits began to appear as they grew older. Two of the females who were identical stood out from the rest. They were quicker to grab food, and always seemed very alert, and certainly one jump ahead of their siblings. Their colouring was grey tabby saddleback, head, and feet, the remainder pure white. Brown Legs named them, 'Poser and Sneaky'. Although twins they were most definitely rivals,

Poser would strut around impressively preening herself at every opportunity, while Sneaky preferred to watch everything from the cover of the hedge very much on her own, but poised to dart out and grab anything that she could reach first. It was always a race between these two whenever I brought a catch to the litter.

They did not always succeed in being first, and very often would harass the winner until she dropped the morsel to defend herself, then one of them would pounce and be off growling with the ill-gotten gains. Sometimes it was the other way around. If one of them had been first to snatch the morsel, the other would fight for it, the net result of this was that Tabitha would seize the opportunity and grab the prize while they were momentarily diverted by each other's animosity. I did not pick and choose who won the product of the hunt, the fittest would survive, and that was the balance of things in the feral world.

When there was a surfeit of scaly or furry little things to eat, the cat population would increase, because there was plenty to eat. But when an area had been cleared, and our victims became hard to find, only the fittest and fastest survived, the others moved on or died of starvation, unless they had a human to rely on in hard times.

Little Cleopatra had her own way of ensuring her survival. She had quickly learnt that if one is petite and cuddly, and definitely attractive to humans, all one had to do was purr, and rub oneself around a human's ankles; look up at them appealingly, and they could just not resist you.

Her bonding with Brown Legs had reached the stage of possession: She now wore a pretty red collar around her neck. The result of this was that other long stay caravan owners took a liking to her. This was

Brown Legs way of ensured that Cleopatra would go to a good home and be cherished forever.

She was being reared as a house cat, and when weaned would be off to a new home.

TC had been wrongly gendered by Big Feet, possibly because she was a furry lump and not easy to categorize at that early age. But who am I to burst his bubble, there was no way I could convey the truth to him; but nature will as time goes on. I hope I am here to see his face when he discovers the truth. TC is a naturally quiet cat. She keeps her eye on everything, but gives the impression of complete disinterest. Her sisters bully her unmercifully, but when she mews in distress, they ease off. This is a clever ploy; as soon as they let her go, she will get her own back by jumping on the nearest one, rough her up a little, then dart away before she can retaliate. TC likes the simple things of life; good food, somewhere comfortable to lay her furry head, and the attention of a chosen friend.

It became noticeable as TC matured, that she divided her attention between my two humans according to her needs at that moment. Quite naturally she soon found out that Brown Legs was an easy touch, no matter what she was doing. Big Feet however was her main interest, she followed him everywhere which further assured him that he had got her gender right. He would lead her around the gardens and the bushes, and then he would encourage her to follow him along the hedgerows encouraging her interests and feline curiosity.

It was a while before she caught her first lizard, and then lost it immediately as she was distracted by another one. Later on he introduced her to the scrubland outside the site by lifting her over the fence, and dropping her on the other side. She panicked at first, but her interest was quickly restored by the scents and sounds of this strange environment. She sniffed through the grasses beneath the carob trees, and the very gnarled old olive trees while Big Feet watched her through the fence. Suddenly she froze, her back arched on stiff legs, her eyes gazing down at something in the grass.

Whatever it was, it was obvious that the object of her intense stare was backing away from her, the tufts of grass were moving very slightly in reaction to some slow moving body. Slowly her stance returned to normal, she backed away a few paces, then turned and ran for the fence.

Whilst in flight she selected her escape route over the fence and with one determined leap she reached the lower branches of the carob tree. From there all she had to do was drop down at the feet of her friend.

Strangely, it was the two who by choice had become closer to my humans in a domesticated sense, who began fending for themselves first. Both of them spent a lot of time familiarizing themselves with the Tavernas. They also visited other humans, and did not run away if not immediately welcomed.

Their persistence paid off, and they became very popular amongst plot owners, and hence well fed. Cleopatra had found her own human, and coincidently it was the same lady who was waiting to become her companion.

It pleased Brown Legs greatly whenever she passed Cleopatra's new home, and she ran to her to rub her head around her ankles. She never ever followed Brown Legs when she left after a chat with the Cypriot lady, because of course this very nice cat lover had also introduced Cleopatra to her home in the city, so she now had two homes to call her territory.

The dozy TC became her new companion's lap cat, which was a good thing, because she really enjoyed a quiet life. The twins found a slot for themselves at the beachside Tavernas, and Tabitha disappeared with a nice human who had been visiting a friend on the site, and fell in love with the big lump, who incidentally had turned into a slightly bigger version of me.

So here I am again all on my own. Oh, except for that overly affectionate elder daughter of mine. I have noticed the local gentry cautiously sniffing at her and then moving on as she snarled at them. What they can see in her I shall never know. Her coat does not have the sheen that mine has, she is far too straggly haired, and very pushy in company: The brazen hussy was brought up better than that. Mind you, I blame Brown Legs, and Big Feet for spoiling her, she would not have come back, had they have been easily forgettable. Ah well! I suppose I shall just have to put up with it, and carry on as if she wasn't here.

A short time after Tabitha and the twins had disappeared; my humans were visiting friends who lived on the other side of the site, close to the main entrance. I knew it was the friends turn to have a barbecue, so I pottered along behind them to share in the goodies.

During the latter part of the afternoon, an earth shattering scream came across the site from the direction of our plot. Big Feet jumped up, 'What on earth was that?' he said, rising to his feet his face creased with concern.

'It sounded like a cat's reaction to fear and pain,' his friend said.

The humans all stood up and looked across the intervening space. Several more cries came from the same direction, followed by the sound of bodies crashing through the undergrowth, yowling and screaming in the most painful manner. A silence descended as instantly as the bedlam had started.

'Sounds like a female being chased,' Big Feet's friend said. 'Or a couple of Toms arguing about who owns what around here.'

He was right of course. I knew exactly what was happening. Tigger's change of chemistry was creating a scent that was inviting to Tomcats, but Tigger was not exactly sure yet what had made her the centre of attention. The attentions of the few Tomcats on the site were not appreciated as yet. This sudden pursuit by these Toms created a lot of fear in her, so her natural impulse was to escape their clutches as quickly as possible. She had done so by reaching the topmost branches of a tree, from where she stared down fearfully at her ardent admirers.

Tomcats soon get fed up with a standoff, and wander away a short distance, but Tigger would remain at the top of that tree for ages. When she did finally descend the tree with great caution, she would hit the ground and run for dear life.

It was days before Tigger came back to the plot. My humans discussed her constantly, fearing that something awful had befallen her. I just lay around wallowing in the sublime knowledge that I had my humans completely to myself again. I was the matriarch of this place, and God forbid anyone who didn't keep their place. Perhaps her new found adulthood would encourage her to find her own humans with whom to develop a relationship.

No such luck! I should never have even considered the possibility that she would strive to find a home of her own. She appeared from nowhere one day, standing in the entrance to the plot, tail high in the air full of her own importance, seemingly having come to terms with the knowledge that she is female and therefore has certain responsibilities in life.

Big Feet was in the road playing with a visiting TC. 'Hey!' He cried, poking his head around the plot entrance, 'Tigger's found her way back.'

Brown legs came running to the entrance, the reunion was yucky to behold. I yawned and rolled over on my other side, so as not to witness this moment of joy for both of them.

When she was satisfied with the attention my humans had given her, she strutted up to me and rubbed an ear on me. I totally ignored her and turned my head away. Not to be shunned she plonked herself down beside me and gave my fur a few cursory licks, which was her way of saying, 'Love you mum.' What could I do? I just gave her a few licks back, and resigned myself to the fact that this daughter was here for the foreseeable future.

She rolled over contentedly; it was then that I noticed she had been hurt. A piece of flesh had been torn from her throat. It looked like a gaping hole, and was not visible until she laid her head back, stretching her neck. I immediately set to work licking it clean; she winced but made no attempt to escape my cleansing tongue.

My humans had been watching her actions as she sniveled around me, they did not know whether to be amused or soppy, but their expressions changed immediately they noticed the gaping wound,

'Good Lord!' Gasped Big Feet, the first to find his tongue; 'Some things torn her throat out!'

Brown Legs made a move towards Tigger, her hands outstretched in front of her as she bent forward. Tigger flinched and made as if to rise. Brown Legs backed off immediately, she had sensed that Tigger would never allow herself to be picked up, or even held long enough to assess the amount of damage done. I think she fully understood that the healing power of my saliva was probably more important at this moment than anything she could do.

It could possibly cause more damage to catch hold of, and force Tigger to submit to any kind of human intervention. It is not easy to catch a feral cat if it does not want to be got hold of, even by a trusted human.

'Do you think a dog got hold of her?' she asked staring down at Tigger, who remained a little wary while I continued licking.

Big Feet moved around us, keeping his distance so as not to alarm Tigger. He gazed at the wound from a distance, talking quietly to Brown Legs at the same time,

'We know that foxes hunt in the hills around us, because we have seen a dead one on the road.' He paused for a moment, and then continued as if deep in thought,

'Tigger would be up a tree in a flash, nothing canine around here can get within fifty metres of her.' He paused again.

'No, I reckon something she did not immediately associate with danger got close to her; and whatever transpired then resulted in a forceful attack.'

He was not far from the truth. A local Tomcat had been attracted by her odour, and had started making advances. Tigger, not quite ready yet, had rebuffed the Tom, he in turn had grabbed her roughly by the throat causing Tigger to tear herself away regardless of the pain, hence the scream of fear mixed with the agony of fur and flesh being torn open. Once free of her admirer, fear lent speed to her hasty retreat up a tree.

It had taken five days for the fear generated by the attack to subside. During this time Tigger would be avoiding any contact between herself and her own kind; male or female. Finally she had plucked up the courage to get back to a place where she knew she would be safe, hence the tail in the air as she approached the entrance to the plot. Even in this safe haven, it took Tigger a few days to settle down to the extent where she would allow my humans to stroke her gently.

Very carefully they coaxed her, giving her little titbits, and holding them up so that she had to stretch her neck to take them.

'It's not infected,' Big Feet said, 'It looks very clean, in fact it seems to be healing at the edges-yes it is healing very well; good old mum,' he added as an afterthought.

He reached out to pat me, but I dodged his hand; well I can't allow that sort of familiarity, can I?

'Proud, isn't she?' Brown Legs said with a grin, as I dodged the grubby paw

Big Feet huffed, 'I think I'll rename her "The Duchess", she has the sort of haughty aloofness that fits the title.' I returned his gaze with casual disinterest.

'Yes you! You stuck up little madam,' he pretended to scold.

'He's a rough one isn't he?' Brown Legs said laughing quietly and bending down to tickle me under the chin; I liked that.

'Oh isn't she the choosey one,' he said, putting his nose in the air, and flouncing away theatrically.

Brown Legs laughed at his antics, I can't think why.

Suddenly Cleopatra appeared alongside me, having jumped on my tail playfully. 'What do you want?' I hissed at her crossly. 'Off you go back to your own humans plot.'

She shrank back at my rebuttal, and watched disconsolately as I got up to walk away.

I decided to walk down the road and have a word with a fellow sophisticate, to while away the rest of the day. 'Good day Maria,' I nodded to an acquaintance, as I passed her plot. 'Ah you've had them I see,' I purred, noticing the four little tearaways playing with her tail. 'Mine are all out on their own now,' I added conversationally.

'Lucky you!' Maria mewed. 'I've still got these for a little while yet,' she added.

As I walked around the corner at the bottom of the site, I spied a crude brute by the name of Cyclops urinating on the bushes marking out his territory.

'Hello darling,' the crude brute shouted across to me, 'Stopping for a chat then.'

'Certainly not,' I scowled back at him. 'I have better things to do than hang around the bushes with you.' I gave him a direct stare, 'By the looks of you, a good wash would not be out of order,' I added curtly to deflate his overbearing ego.

'Suit yourself,' he growled back, and then continued urinating on his bushes.

'Ugh', I shuddered at the thought, 'Dreadful Tom!' I muttered to myself.

A few yards further on I stopped at my friends plot. I sat on my haunches at the entrance and mewed, 'Vouna'. There was no answer. I waited a moment politeness preventing me from just strolling into a mothers plot uninvited.

'Vouna,' I meowed, louder this time.

A distraught face appeared from under the caravan: 'I have lost them,' she cried. I ran across to her, instantly aware of the personal disaster that had happened. 'I had to eat, she sobbed. 'When I came back they had gone.'

Nothing I could do would help or console her. For a while her mind would be totally consumed with the need to search, and to call plaintively for her young to come and suckle. I left her to continue her fruitless search, knowing full well what the outcome would be. After a while she would force the memory out of her mind, pick up the pieces of her life, and start all over again.

With no kittens to rear, nature would hasten her hormones to become pregnant again. One thing was certain; her next brood would be better concealed.

The thought struck me, 'There are no stray dogs in the compound at this moment.' That thought turned my mind to my encounter with the brute Cyclops. Could he be linked to the disappearance? None of them would have been fathered by him, and he was always in the vicinity. Add to this that he is certainly a sneaky type always prowling from cover, and disappearing in an instant if any good Toms appeared on the scene. All of this gives good cause for suspicion, the small territory he has is not wanted by other Toms, because no humans live there. It is unused space with thin hedges therefore little room for concealment. None of the more perceptive cats want to live there, particularly the females, it is no place for baby kittens.

Cyclops had become an outcast. His flat, ugly tabby face was further marred by a huge split in his upper lip. The two flaps of flesh hanging over his teeth, combined with his hawkish eyes and flat ears, gave him a look of impending evil. Not one female in the whole site liked him, and subsequently resisted any advances should we be unfortunate enough to bump into him. For certain none of us ever laid foot on his patch; the scent of him filled us with loathing.

The news of Vouna's loss spread quickly round the site. Mothers of new born became extra cautious, even mothers of kittens a month old kept a closer eye on their adventurous youngsters.

Brutes like Cyclops had no qualms about grabbing any size of kitten. Once pounced on from behind those sharp little claws could not be brought round into the attacker's face.

Cleopatra lived close to Cyclops patch in her new home, when she heard the news, she found TC, and joined a group of us staring into Cyclops territory. They were big enough now not to have to worry about the cannibal, but just like us all, they were curious to see what sort of beast ate its own kind.

This was the equivalent of a horror story that humans might enjoy, it raised a basically similar curiosity in us. I advised my now mature offspring never to go near to this beast.

'Avoid him like the plague,' I insisted.

My worries about these two were unfounded really, they both had loving humans to care for them, but a stern warning can do no harm, particularly with cats who had been handled by humans from birth, so had been protected from some of the nastier elements of being totally feral. Both of them still visited Brown Legs, but she did not feed them now, that encouraged them to go back to their own humans whenever hunger or thirst set in.

The meals provided by my humans had the effect of making our fur glow with health; we all had a sheen to us that stood out whenever we mixed with our not so fortunate brethren; all except Tigger that is. She was very healthy, always active and alert, but her fur was all over the place, which gave her an untidy appearance. Not that she worried; just lately her time was taken up with the male of the species. It was her idea now so she went in search of them full of the confidence of intended motherhood. Her neck was healed, so that incident was behind her, and only her present hormonal condition was uppermost in her mind. Nature had finally taught her that she was the boss when it came to events that affected her in the feline world. Her neck had healed so well, all the ideas concocted by Big Feet to trap her without frightening her terribly, and taking her to see a veterinary surgeon had been put aside, although I am sure he would have found some way of giving her a knockout mixture, if the healing process had not come about naturally.

'It's that good licking her mum gave her that has done the trick,' he said. 'Never underestimate the curative effect of an animal's tongue.'

****

Time moved on, and winter came to an end. By mid-March the Seasonal rains which had been much improved this year, gradually reduced in ferocity.

The Troodos Mountains had been blessed with a heavy carpet of snow, allowing an exciting skiing season. The snow melt from the thaw would be trickling into the many dams for some time to come.

By the end of April, midday temperatures along the coast were hovering around the thirty degrees Celsius mark, with inland temperatures slightly higher, they would reach forty six by the height of the summer.

All the small patches of fertile land along the seashore, and scattered between rocky outcrops along the coastline were glowing bright gold, as the wheat planted there became ripe for harvesting.

This was a time of plenty for all of us feral cats. The small rodents which we preferred were plentiful in the fields of wheat. We did however have dangerous competition for these tasty morsels.

Whether by instinct, or local knowledge of seasonal events, the various types of slithering reptiles started moving out of the rough hilly areas and heading towards the grain patches, to begin their mating season.

The traffic along the main highway, and the local roads took a heavy toll on these migrating snakes, all sorts of shapes and sizes could be seen flattened out on the tarmac, their squashed skins hardening as the strong sun dried them out.

This was also a time of plenty for the crows that inhabited the coastal areas their sinister black forms rose into the air or hopped casually to one side when menaced by an approaching vehicle; then, with a tenacity driven by hunger they quickly returned to their carrion.

The caravan site was surrounded by these small patches of wheat, so quite often the inhabitants would be treated to a visual example of a snake slithering quickly across human and feline territory, certainly more scared of us than we were of them.

Most of them were non-poisonous, or mildly poisonous, only very rarely did one see the "Blunt Headed Viper" whose venom could be deadly.

Cleopatra and TC were about to get their first real experience with a mildly poisonous reptile. They were lying on their sides in the road enjoying the mid-morning sun, when a slim object about a metre in length broke cover from a nearby hedgerow bordering the road in the next plot to ours.

Cleopatra was on her feet back arched in an instant. TC was just a fraction slower but her instincts told her to attack immediately. Her front paws landed in the middle of the snakes back just as Cleopatra jumped forward on stiff legs, joining the attack.

The snake continued to try to slither along the roads surface, and my two children were frantically trying to stop it by sinking their teeth into its scaly hide. The snake squirmed, and then began to fight back.

With jaws wide, and fangs protruding, its head made several lunges at its tormentors. They managed to dodge the lunging head, but it became obvious that if one of them did not make a grab for that position just behind its head, one, or maybe both of them would get a bite from those fangs which would certainly lay them out for a time, or if they had a weakness even kill them.

I could wait no longer; I dived into the fray, and sank my teeth in the area just to the rear of its head. The snake now had no chance at all, it writhed helplessly for a while under the attack from three sets of feline weapons; this was soon to become four as Tigger rushed from our plot and dived into the melee of savagely biting cats.

Big Feet and Brown Legs came rushing out into the road having become aware of all the snarling and growling, just in time to witness the final demise of the reptile as I ripped away at the flesh just behind its head. They looked a little shocked as they stared at their little darlings showing their true nature, and living up to that basic tenet of raw nature: "Kill or be killed."

I started dragging the carcass towards the hedge on the other side of the road. Cleo and TC had other ideas, and started pulling the other way. Then Tigger started pulling from the middle, so for a moment it was stalemate. I growled as them savagely through my closed teeth without letting go, and started jerking the body in my direction.

Three hours later, the carcass had been torn to pieces by an ever increasing number of neighbours sharing in the kill. As one of us became full, and backed off, so another one would push forward and tear at the carcass, it took a while, but it was all devoured and not a morsel remained.

'Wonder where the heads gone?' I heard Big Feet ask, and then state the reason,

'I would have liked to have kept that as a trophy.'

He would have to clear the bottoms of the hedgerows to find it, it was tiny and the lower jaw had been separated from the skull as the head bone was torn clear of flesh.

Cleopatra and TC had been blooded, they were now fully fledged carnivores, and had devoured the product of their kill. They would never go hungry while there was wild food around for the taking.

This fact, added to their natural appeal to kind humans would ensure their survival, and all this before they were one year old; isn't nature wonderful.

My friend Vouna came and joined in the feast, the loss of her family now just a ghastly memory. News of a big kill spreads quickly, and, almost as if drawn by some telepathic signal, all the local cats arrived for the feast, hanging on the perimeter until it became their chance to grab a mouthful and then fall back a safe distance to eat it.

Brown Legs often commented on our ability to be in a certain place at the appropriate time, when something of advantage would occur.

'These cats are psychic,' she would say. 'I only have to think of opening the fridge door and they suddenly appear, how can they be aware of unscheduled events when they are nowhere in sight, then suddenly appear as if I had called them?'

Humans will never understand us completely, but it's great for us while they try and unravel the mysteries of our psyche.

I took Vouna over to meet Brown Legs. She was a bit of a shrinking violet, but more cautious than shy. The terrible loss of her last litter of kittens had not helped to make her any more companionable.

However, after a kind 'Hello' from Brown Legs, followed by, 'Who are you then?' she settled down without any reservations, and acted like one of the family.

Brown Legs looked at me, and said conversationally; 'Brought a friend around for lunch, have you? Are you thirsty now?'

My lips moved in a silent meow, which meant, 'Yes please' to both of us, but nothing to anyone who did not have our rapport.

'Here you are then,' she said kindly, as she placed a large bowl of milk on the floor. Vouna joined me, and before the bowl was empty we had drunk our fill. Tigger polished off the remainder greedily.

We stayed a while, and watched Brown Legs pottering around with her pile of rocks, until we got bored, then we sauntered off to find something interesting to watch, or do until the night games started.

Cleopatra and TC were flat out, exhausted after their first kill, and the resulting full belly. TC's legs were twitching as she dreamt of her successful snake kill.

Vouna and I padded softly down the road that led to the part of the beach that belonged to the camp site, and the Taverna at the end.

We caught sight of the beast Cyclops squatting on his haunches just inside his territory. His evil eyes followed our progress. I stared at him balefully, my eyes showing the depth of contempt I felt for this cannibal. I nudged Vouna; she followed my lead and squatted down with me, gazing across the road straight into the eyes of the vile stealer of life.

Stand offs like this were a normal part of a cats existence. We always stared long and hard at a patrolling Tom near to our nests when we had kittens, and if he got a bit too pushy, or came too close, we would throw ourselves at him with great ferocity.

The Tomcat knows just how savage a protective female can be, so rarely faces us eyeball to eyeball for any great length of time. After testing our stare for a while he will sensibly move on. They knew we could be on their backside in an instant, tearing away with tooth and claw. The enemy is always at a disadvantage with his back to you.

The brutal Cyclops soon gave in, and with a growling rattle of the throat, slunk back into his territory. Vouna and I shared a self-satisfied glance, and went our separate ways. She would soon be starting another family, because the early loss of her last litter speeded up the cycle of fertility a bit. Nature did not like us cats to be lazy for too long.

The following weekend saw the first day of May arrive. It was a beautiful warm and sunny day, enhanced by a light breeze from the south. The humans started arriving in droves, and in the cheerful uncomplicated way that Cypriots seem to find so natural, the site was soon buzzing with laughter as barbecue smoke began to flavour the atmosphere, tinged with the enticing smell of cooking pork spare ribs, chicken, and fish.

The joy and laughter surrounding our plot was infectious, and very soon my humans had joined everyone else in adding to the delicious aroma's that overhung the happy site.

Needless to say the occasion had to be blessed with a few glasses of wobbly water to enhance the pleasure of this freedom from their labours for a while.

The Internal road that ringed the site soon became full of young humans enjoying themselves. This was a time we cats kept to the hedgerows close to the barbecues. It was a time of plenty, and this interest in food kept us away from the road.

Young boys were a disturbing factor, but their mums and sisters made up for the boys naughtiness by being nice to us and enticing us to stay by offering us tasty titbits that could not be refused.

With humans, vehicles, cats, and all the fauna associated with this site all crowded together for a carefree day, accidents are bound to happen. Truthfully, it is most rare for anyone to suggest that an accident can be beneficial to an area, or its occupants. However this can sometimes prove to be the case, whether one views an accident in a religious, or a philosophical context, or even cynically, in this case it could not have happened to a more deserving creature.

The fact of the matter at this point is that Cyclops had found another litter of kittens left on their own for a moment. Being a born opportunist, the horrible creature had grabbed one of the young, and darted from under the caravan with the poor kitten still clutched by its hind quarters mewing pitifully. In his haste to escape with his ill-gotten victim, he ran from the hedge straight under the back of a passing beast with round legs. Cyclops was instantly dispatched from this earth in a gory splatter of innards. The kitten miraculously escaped injury, falling from Cyclops jaws as he screamed his final breath.

The mother, totally ignoring the flattened mess, grabbed her kitten, and dived back under her caravan. She placed it in the nest and groomed it vigourously. She then suckled her whole brood as if nothing had happened.

The loud death scream had echoed around the site, and very soon a crowd of spectators had gathered to gaze in sickened awe at the remains of the flattened Cyclops.

Some ran away the instant they observed the gory remains, with a hand covering their mouth, either in horror, or fear of being sick. The few cats who were in the vicinity walked over to the body, gave it a cursory sniff, whilst they absorbed the meaning of what their eyes told them. Could anyone deny that this vile beast had got his just desserts? For a fact, all mothers in the area would breathe a sigh of relief. This terrible; sneaky, vile looking cannibal had plagued this area for some time, now that we had seen him in action, all our suspicions had been proved, we were well rid of him. Lord knows how many kittens he had snatched since he discovered this comparatively easy way to feed himself, which saved him from the rigours of the hunt while he pursued his grizzly feeding pattern with relish.

The body lay splattered on the road long enough for all to have a good look, and a good sniff. One relieved feline was heard to mutter.

'There is a god after all!'

Very soon the eaters of carrion started to circle above the spot where Cyclops flattened body lay. All heads suddenly flicked upwards as their shadows hovered across the ground.

All my site neighbours were ready for flight until they realized that the birds gently circling overhead were jet black crows which were no danger to us. One made a landing, and tested the remains, but he had to depart hastily as a Tom made a quick dart for him.

Big Feet and Brown Legs came upon this scene whilst out for a stroll. He quickly dashed back for his shovel, dug a shallow grave, and scraped Cyclops, or what was left of him, off the road, and unknowingly buried the beast in his own patch.

Big Feet of course had no idea how much we all hated Cyclops, but he said to Brown Legs, 'I think that is the Tomcat we have always thought looked so evil, since we saw him with a dead kitten in his mouth.'

'Oh come on, let's get away from here,' Brown Legs said, shuddering as she spoke. The sight of the squashed Cyclops had not been pleasant for her; she would not wish that sort of death on any living creature.

Big Feet washed the gore from his shovel at one of the site watering points, then wiped it in chalky soil, Looking apparently satisfied, he continued his walk with Brown Legs, but it was noticeable that he now had a comforting arm around her shoulder.

The hideous sight of the corpse, with the head untouched, and the mouth gaping wide had quite naturally unsettled her.

****

Later that spring, I began to get the feeling that my rest cycle had been a bit long. I should be preparing for my next family by this time. I of course do not know what, but something had disturbed my fertility cycle. My humans had also noticed this fact, and of course Big Feet just had to comment on it.

'She's usually as round as a dumpling by this time,' he commented, nodding my way in a most uncomplimentary manner.

'Oh it's just a female thing, even nature has a hiccup now and again,' Brown Legs answered him, and then pointing to Tigger added, 'See how she's thickening out just lately, I don't think we'll be without kittens for long.'

She was right. My prima donna daughter was getting very close to motherhood. That will take the wind out of her sails. She will not have as much time to strut and preen around when they are on the scene. I wonder where she has chosen to have them flashed through my mind. Like all of us she would have a particular spot in mind by this time in her pregnancy.

Two weeks later my thoughts had substance: Tigger had apparently disappeared off the face of the earth, not hide nor hair could be seen of her anywhere.

After a week of absence Brown Legs started calling for her during her evening walks, always to no avail. Wherever Tigger was hiding with her family, it was her secret, and not even my humans were going to know where until Tigger was good and ready.

Two weeks had passed; then one morning Big Feet came through the awning flap, and nearly went sprawling over the figure of Tigger standing there looking up at him expectantly as if she had never been away.

'Good Lord Tigger!' He shouted his tone a mixture of pleasure and surprise. 'Where on earth have you sprung from?'

Brown Legs appeared from behind him. I turned away, jealousy searing my mind. The reunion was saturated with soppy sentimentality.

Tigger wallowed in it; she preened and purred, rubbing her ears against my human's ankles in a most possessive manner. I could not stand the sight of it any longer; I sauntered out of the plot, and sat in the middle of the road viewing all the early birds with casual interest with one ear tuned into what was going on in my plot.

A squeal of: 'O! Aren't they pretty,' came from behind the caravan. Tigger had just showed them her two babies which she had put in my nest behind the caravan. Brown Legs was right, yes, they were pretty. One was a gorgeous pure white, with two barely discernable smudges; one above each eye. The other; a beautiful little mite, was a paler copy of me.

My first thought when I saw them earlier on that morning was, 'What, only two, is that all she had given birth to, or had she lost some?'

Only Tigger could answer that one. I think my suspicions were justified by the fact that she had brought her remaining two back to the plot. She instinctively knew; as I had known; that her kitten's chances of survival were increased a hundredfold when brought to the area of caring humans.

Fully aware that Tigger and her kittens would be drawing all the attention this morning, I went for a stroll down the road. The morning sun was warm on my back, and a slight breeze ruffled my fur now and then.

Indigenous and migratory birds who had not returned to cooler climes yet were singing and prating, chirping and whistling in the bushes and trees lining the road. The sight of me put them on the alert, but it did not stop the cheeriness of their morning chorus.

A few scaly black lizards were sunning themselves in the road, their long tails stretched out behind them, and their heads pointing towards the sun to gain the full benefit of its rays. These lizards had long legs that splayed out sideways from their body when at rest, but when galvanized into action, propelled them along at fantastic speed to get out of danger. They were just as fast running up trees into the very topmost branches, they could not be reached here by any land based animal because of course the twigs were too thin.

Young cats learn very quickly that these speedy reptiles are almost impossible to catch unless out in the open, giving a cat chance to build up speed before the lizard reached safety. Once grabbed of course they stood little chance of survival.

These worshippers of the Sun God did not dart away as I approached. They fixed me with their beady eyes, but would not expend energy unless I pose a threat. I, of course would not expend energy either, unless there was better than a half chance to make a quick kill. These scaly lizards would be up a tree at the first flex of a muscle, so in true feline style I appeared to ignore them, whilst inwardly ready to make a grab if the opportunity arose.

Every plot I passed had a beast with round legs standing patiently outside. They made wonderful shady areas in the heat of the day, but were very frightening when their humans made them roar. This caused any cat sheltering beneath one to run for its life.

Further down the road I sniffed at one of these beasts, the one human's call a "Pick-up Truck". It had its mouth wide open, and one ear stood out from the side. The other ear was closed tight to its head. Nobody was about, so I took this opportunity to have my very first look inside the head of one of these beasts.

The inside seemed unusually comfortable, so I curled up on the soft seat at the back, and dozed off. The internal smell of humans did not bother me at all, because every time I saw one of these beasts moving, it was always carrying humans.

My eyes had only been closed a moment when the sound of laughing children disturbed me. A quick glance told me they were running towards the beast. I looked around for somewhere to hide and saw that the front seats had enough room under them for me to fit in. I chose the one on the right hand side, and just managed to disappear beneath it as the children hurled themselves inside closely followed by their parents.

Suddenly the space I had crawled into became less as the father dropped heavily into the seat above me. The ears slammed shut with a bang, then the beast roared and started running down the road with me inside cowering under the front seat.

The roaring of the beast rose and fell many times, then settled down to a low rumble. I remained frozen with fear. Had I been eaten? If I had it was certainly not painful; just very frightening. Oh! How I wish I had not been so nosey. What was going to happen to me now? Would I ever see my beloved Brown Legs again? Is this what humans mean when they say, "CURIOSITY KILLED THE CAT!!"

DOWNTOWN ADVENTURE

The angry beast ran down the road on its round legs growling deeply all the time. It swung from left to right, and sometimes it growled very loudly as it ran to where it was going. Every now and then it seemed to be in a herd of similar beasts, and frequently some beasts hurtled past that must have been of monstrous size judging by the noise they made as they rushed by.

Suddenly it stopped running; so sharply that I nearly lost my place under the man's seat. It frightened me so much I made a rude smell. The children gasped, and went pfwaaaw all at the same time.

'What is it?' their Dad asked, not aware of my rudeness

You know!' the children answered, their little noses clenched meaningfully between forefinger and thumb.

'Oh you mean the Cow farm and the Pig farm at Moni, I'm afraid I can't smell a thing.'

The children looked at each other and grinned, then turned their eyes back to their father, their grin turning to a knowing smile.

The beast growled loudly and began running again. Faster and faster it went as if racing all the others. It swung sharply to the right; it then seemed to run forward in short little bursts. Finally it did a few more little turns and then came abruptly to a halt.

The big ears swung open and all the humans jumped out. I rushed from under the seat, and the man nearly fell over me as I got tangled up between his legs in my hurry to escape that very tight space.

'What on earth?' the man yelled, just catching himself before he fell. 'Hey!' He shouted, noticing me run for a clump of bushes, 'I know that cat, it's from the caravan site, and it's often in the British couples plot.'

He thrashed about in the bushes for a while in the hope of catching me. The children, thinking this a highly amusing game, joined in, and made a jolly pretence of being helpful.

Their mother, being of a more practical mind in such situations got on with the job of unloading every ones bits and pieces.

'Come on you lot!' She shouted: 'I'm not carrying this lot by myself.'

I had watched all this going on from behind a huge waste bin; and then, with the humans out of the way I started to survey my surroundings.

The area was full of these strange beasts with round legs, huddled together in groups, or lined up nose to tail on the pavements and the roads. The thought occurred to me that the humans had nowhere to walk; unless it was in the middle of the road where the beasts rushed up and down. They did make very good hiding places though. But it was very puzzling that they only came to life when a human was inside them.

Now that my initial fear had disappeared, I began to notice all the different smells and sounds that gave this area an ambience of its own. Surely all those lovely food smells meant that I would not be hungry for very long. The sound of humans enjoying themselves was much the same as the caravan site, except that the music seemed to throb to a different beat than the beautifully melodious Greek music.

I moved closer to the music, and the sound of voices. I jumped, startled as something landed beside me; it was a bone with meat on it. Without noticing who had thrown it, I snatched it up and scurried back to cover. The meaty bone only served to increase my desire for more. It must have been the excitement and the apprehension of recent events that had increased my appetite.

I crept towards the noisy tourists scattered around the tables in front of the Taverna where all the gorgeous smells came from. Everybody was eating and drinking, talking and laughing, and those humans inside the Taverna were gyrating their bodies to the rhythm of the wild music. These humans seemed to expend a lot of energy, they writhed and wiggled their bodies in all sorts of contorted shapes, and strangely, their bodies were in time with the music no matter what contorted position their bodies were in at that moment.

The younger humans were happily playing on those strange machines that have lights flashing all over them. Some people were knocking balls around a table with sticks in their hands, and cheering with enthusiasm when a ball disappeared down a hole; they were even happier when no balls at all were left on the table-strange beasts.

Someone noticed me and waved a bone at me.

'Here pretty puss,' the woman said kindly, dropping the titbit on the floor not far from me. I edged towards the bone, unsure, and very cautious.

'Come on then don't be afraid,' the voice said gently, and something about her reminded me of Brown Legs so I went closer.

Suddenly, a black streak appeared from nowhere, grabbed the bone and was gone just as quickly. The black phantom crouched under a beast with round legs, and tore away at the flesh on the bone. I could not help but notice he was a beautiful jet black panther; strong and lithe and well fed. His coat glistened brightly, he obviously groomed himself fastidiously.

'Never mind then,' here's another one.'

This time it was the other lady at the table who dropped a bone for me. This time it landed right in front of my nose, so I grabbed it quickly and ran for cover.

'You will have to be quicker than that if you want to survive around here,' the black Tom said in a pleasant low growl. I turned to face him, then became aloof and returned to my bone.

'There is plenty to eat, but there is also plenty of competition,' he said, strolling nonchalantly over to me as he spoke. He saw my instant unease, and stopped a couple of metres short of me, and spread his beautiful form on the pavement.

He had a proud and noble head and just oozed confidence.

'You are new to this area aren't you?' he asked matter-of- factly, and then, because I made no effort to reply, his tone became a little friendlier. 'If you are going to stay around here you had better learn the area very quickly. You will need somewhere safe to sleep where you will not be harassed by some of the not so nice characters that find their way here from time to time.'

Outwardly I continued to ignore him, but inwardly I had digested his every word. I finished the bone, and rising to my feet I stretched and arched my back, yawning at the same time.

'Suit yourself,' he said without malice, taking my yawn as lack of interest, he rose to his feet and padded away.

'I will need somewhere to stay,' I broke my silence, and tried to appear less haughty. He turned his head, and fixed me with those penetrating yellow eyes.

'Follow me then, and stay close behind me, not all the Toms around here are as gentlemanly as me,' he said, once again in a very matter-of-fact manner.

He led me through a maze of tall hotels and apartment blocks, powerful buildings the likes of which I had never seen before. Smells of cooking and sounds of laughter issued from all around me. This is surely the happiest place in the world.

'Hi Mario,' A gruff voice growled from the shadows.

I swung round to face the voice, instantly prepared for Action.

'Hey steady babe,' the gruff voice purred, then a broad faced, bulky ginger Tom became visible.

'Hi Achilleas,' Mario purred evenly, then leaned his head to indicate me, 'This is my new friend; er, what's your name?' He hesitated a moment staring directly at me.

'Fluffy,' I answered him, 'that's what I have always been called.'

The ginger Toms face creased. 'What sort of name is that?' he asked, his face puzzled.

'My humans call me Fluffy.' I answered lamely.

Achileas wanted to pursue the matter of my unusual name, but Mario broke in, 'Come on then Fluffy, I will show you a safe place to stay. Cheerio Achilleas, see you later,' he added in the same breath.

'Achilleas is a rough diamond,' he went on conversationally as we continued walking through this massive built up area. 'He will always help you, if needed, generous to a fault. Many a young cat has been grateful for his intervention in a sticky moment.'

I followed him in silence, paying attention to all the different smells round me. I had never seen so many high buildings joined together before. After a while the buildings came to an abrupt end, and we were walking on rough ground strewn with rubble and piled up soil.

Next moment we were walking through bushes and mature Mimosa trees. I became aware of the noise of a lot of beasts with round legs rushing along somewhere ahead of us.

'You can make a home for yourself in there, nobody will bother you,' he nodded towards a pile of rubble as he spoke.

'My patch is over there,' he indicated another pile of rubble with his nose. 'Lots of us live here in little dens we have scratched out of the brush and rubble, we all have our own space and only meet when we have to.'

He walked away without another word, leaving me to my own devices. The pile of rubble was pushed up against some bushes as if by one giant paw; the pile had the effect of stopping the top of the bushes curling over, so when entered from the bushes side it was almost like a cave. I very soon had myself a very snug nest to live in.

Compared to the caravan site this was a very noisy place, a huge path that beasts with round legs ran along was just above my new home, so I had to get used to trying to catnap with the loud growling of these monsters in my ears constantly.

The day had been such an eventful one, that I soon forgot the growling monsters above me and dozed off to sleep. Brown Legs came into my dreams; she would worry if my absence was too long. What a mess my nosiness had got me into.

After a fitful but reasonable sleep, I was up and about early next morning. Some lizards scurried away swiftly as I came out of my den, and two or three sparrows quickly vacated the top fronds of my bush roof. My neighbours were beginning to stir in the early morning sun; they all stared at the stranger in their midst.

Mario was away to the tourist area early,

'Good morning,' he said pleasantly as he padded by. In typical female fashion I did not answer, but admired his purposeful style as he strolled past the other watching females, and disappeared into the not too distant built up area.

'He's a great guy, isn't he?'

I turned to face the friendly purr. 'Hi, I'm Effi, and I know your name is Fluffy,' she purred nicely as she introduced herself. 'News soon got around that Mario was seen with a pretty feline last night.'

'He just showed me where I could sleep,' I answered defensively, but not unpleasantly.

'Oh, we all know that,' she replied with a twinkle in her eye. 'Mario is ever the gentleman, most of us here can be grateful to the Black Knight for our safety at times.'

'The Black Knight!' I exclaimed, not quite understanding.

'Oh it's just a name an old wise cat gave him once and it stuck. We use it because it describes his glossy fur, and his willingness to always react to the call of a feline in distress.'

Effi sounds educated: the thought passed through my mind. It was then that I noticed her truly magnificent colouring. In human terms she would be describes as "Silver Tabby", the "M" like mark on her forehead was quite pronounced with silvery surrounds. She was sturdy of build, and most delightful to look at. I had already warmed to her nice nature; perhaps we were going to be friends.

'Will you join me for breakfast?' Effi asked, gazing at me expectantly.

'Yes, I'll be glad to,' I answered, visibly showing my appreciation of this gesture with a friendly smile.

We strolled out of the rough ground, and were soon in the built up area. Everywhere I looked my surroundings were full of the requirements necessary to give tourists from any part of the world a great holiday. Everything I looked at was designed for the sole purpose of making people forget work for a couple of weeks, and have a good time instead.

'This is a great place for food,' Effi said. 'In the mornings it is best to go around the back of the restaurants, last night's leftovers are being put in the bins for collection, and the chefs always throw a tasty morsel to any cat that is there. You will soon discover that everybody is very kind, and if we do not crowd a place, we are looked after very well. If you learn to sit quietly watching a tourist with an intelligent look on your face, they just cannot resist giving you a little something off their plate.'

Effi's appraisal of life amongst the tourists was suddenly shattered by an uncharacteristic scream of anger, something one did not associate with the pleasantness so far encountered. The angry scream was accompanied by another deeper and gruffer growling.

We both reacted simultaneously, and cowered beneath a large waste bin. A streak of white fur hurtled past us as a young Tom scrambled for safety, closely followed by Achilleas cursing loudly.

'This is my territory,' he growled. 'You go and look elsewhere.'

He noticed the two of us under the bin, his face suddenly changed, and he appeared to forget all about the young trespasser. 'Ah, good morning ladies,' he gushed. His face split into a catty grin as he went on, 'You have come to join me for breakfast, have you?'

Effi had regained her composure,

'We certainly have not!' she answered, just as haughtily as I could have done. 'Fluffy and I will find our own breakfast thank you very much.'

The haughty rebuff did not affect his demeanour one little bit. The cheeky grin remained just as broad, 'Perhaps another time then,' he mocked in a most false manner. He then said,

'Ladies,' and sauntered off proudly without a backward glance.

'He's a confident one isn't he?' I found my tongue at last.

'Oh he's a great guy really, good to have around in troubled times,' Effi replied, and then elaborated, 'in human terms he would be known as a right "Jack the lad". He is however inclined to be a bit smarmy when dealing with us better bred ladies, so it is best to let him know immediately that when he talks to us he is talking to class, and should act accordingly. Good manners never hurt anyone.'

Her haughty but sincere statement brought a catty grin to my face. I turned from Effi in case she mistook it for rudeness. Her statement seemed more than a little out of context considering the fact that we were living a feral life, but perhaps that's what pedigree status does to a proud feline.

We walked along the seacoast road of the tourist area of Limassol. The early morning walkers; runners, and swimmers had finished their exercises for the day and were gathering at the cafes for breakfast. I soon learnt that English breakfasts were very popular, and proudly advertised in large capitals, including a long list of items. No wonder all these people looked so happy in the morning.

Two old ladies were enjoying breakfast outside a pavement café as we strolled by. I recognized the language she spoke, and for a moment Brown Legs rushed into my mind.

'Good Lord!' One old lady exclaimed looking at Effi with astonishment, 'That's a pedigree Classic Silver Tabby if ever I saw one.'

The other old lady, not to be outdone by her knowledgeable friend replied, 'And the other one looks very much like a "Leopard Bengal", how on earth do such special breeds happen to be on the streets here.'

Effi looked at me, 'Do you understand what they are saying?' she purred quietly.

'Yes, I have humans who speak the same as them,' I replied, my mind once again creating a picture of Brown Legs.

The first lady spoke again, as she cut a sausage in half and put it down for Effi and myself. 'Britain administered Cyprus as a colonial power, from something like 1878 until 1960, so I presume that cats of a type that one would only expect to see in Britain will have been imported by colonial office employees, military, and business executives.'

'They look well enough don't they?' the second lady interrupted her friend in a manner that suggested she was inclined to ramble on a bit.

As if her friend had not spoken, the first old lady continued, 'I'm not sure you're right about that darker tabby: Leopard Bengals are still pretty rare you know, and anyway the colouring beneath her black parts does not seem to have an orangey texture.'

'I'm not saying she's pure bred,' the second old lady stood her ground determinedly. 'She is an older cat now, and the coarseness of her youthful fur has turned to a beautifully sleek short hair light tan particularly round her muzzle.'

'I still say she's an ordinary tabby,' the first old lady continued to insist, 'Probably has a bit of Brown Mackerel Tabby in her genes I'd say.'

'Oh come on Ethel!' The second old lady argued, warming to the debate. 'That head is nowhere near thick enough, and there are too many black spots and stripes; look at her eyes, if they are not greenish then I'm a Dutchmans aunty.'

'Oh all right then!' she conceded, 'It's got a bit of Leopard Bengal in it.'

Effi and I sat licking our chops, looking up at these two pleasant, and apparently knowledgeable English ladies. I was looking from one to the other of them while they were discussing me. I did not understand the names that they used, but the gentle banter indicated that they were cat loving ladies who probably had their own feline friends at home.

'Maude, is there any milk left in that jug?' Ethel asked, and then without waiting for an answer, grabbed the jug and poured the remaining contents into an as yet unused ash tray perched in the centre of the table. 'Here you are then you pretty pussies, a nice drink of milk to wash your breakfast down.'

Effi and me poked our heads into the ash tray and lapped up the milk gratefully. I was beginning to like this tourist area very much. All along the road, cafes and restaurants were beginning to fill up with holidaymakers enjoying the breakfast of their choice.

The carefree nature of their attitude was catching; I began to take on a more cheerful view of my situation, things were not too bad after all; my stomach was full, and I had found a good friend.

Even so, this unusual feeling of euphoria did make my mind wander back to Brown Legs, and strangely that prima donna daughter of mine, I never thought I would miss her; it shows how wrong a cat can be when she has lost her familiars when she herself has been dispersed through her own foolish act of nosiness.

My friend brought me back to the present, 'Would you like a good walk before it's time for lunch? I will show you the new McDonalds, and the huge pleasure ground called the water park.'

'Oh I like water,' I replied enthusiastically, at the same time noticing the odd glance that Effi threw my way. It did not bother me, I was the only cat I knew so far who did not mind a frolic in running water.

The old ladies waved to us as we walked away from them. 'See you for breakfast tomorrow,' Ethel shouted after us. The tourists around them could not see us, and one cheeky young imp screwed his head with a forefinger indicating his thoughts. Then, noticing Effi and me, shouted with childlike hilarity, 'Oh it's the cats they're talking to.'

'Shush Tommy,' his mother nudged him, glancing at Ethel and Maude red faced.

The knowing smile from the old ladies eased her embarrassment. 'Can't take them anywhere can you?' Ethel said nicely.

'It's nice to see children being so jolly,' Maude added.

That broke the ice, young Tommy was soon learning some very valuable lessons as the two old ladies and his mum and dad found common ground in a nice light hearted family discussion.

Walking up the pavement, we soon learnt another nice thing about humans; they actually walked around us and gave us space. They did not barge us, or kick us out of the way. Many humans, noticing Effi commented on her beautiful markings.

'I don't think I've ever seen such a pretty cat,' one woman was heard to say. Effi could not understand what she said so I translated.

A cross roads halted our passage, and Effi shouted, 'There it is!' pointing her nose at a building with a large "M" etched against the background of a clear blue sky. 'One of my favourite places for a snack,' she added, smacking her lips with imagined relish.

'That "M" is almost the exact shape of the M in the middle of your forehead,' I informed her.

'Is it?' she replied, with heavy emphasis.

'Yes, honestly,' I assured her. 'It's almost exactly the same.'

Mario suddenly appeared beside us, coat glistening, and poise full of confidence. 'Hi girls,' he said politely, 'What-on-earth is so interesting up there?'

'Fluffy has just told me that I have a mark on my head exactly like that big "M" up there.'

Mario looked from Effi to the big "M" and back, his mind deliberating. 'Yes it is,' he confirmed. He looked at Effi in silence for a moment, then with a cheeky grin cracking his handsome features he said, 'We will all have to call you Mac the Cat from now on; having said that, his face took on a brighter countenance. No, no, he went on laughing, I've got a better idea. You will now be known as "Big M"', he grinned widely, as only a cat can do at his own inventiveness. Effi looked a bit miffed for a moment.

'That's a beautifully realistic name,' I voiced an opinion with a pleasant and not too catty grin.

'Do you think so?' Effi's face brightened a little, and a grin began to spread slowly across her lips, and then her whole face as she saw our convincing grins.

'Okay then let's eat, will you ladies join me this morning,' Mario said, then added in a confidential tone, 'The day chef likes me because he thinks no vermin will visit his yard whilst I protect it. He doesn't realize that vermin can never reach this far with the number of felines hunting in the bushes out there.'

Minutes later we arrived at the back of McDonald's.

'Just wait a moment,' Mario said confidently, 'he will soon come through that door to the waste bins.'

True to Mario's word, minutes later the back door opened, and out came a lovely human in a sparkling uniform.

'Mario!' The human shouted loudly, a big smile stretching his face muscles. 'You are late today.' Then noticing us said, 'Ah hah,' his voice lowering to a gentle lilt, he went on with a twinkle in his eye, 'I see you have two pretty guests with you, wait there, he gestured affectedly. 'Today we will have something special for you.'

He disappeared, and in a very short time burst through the doors flourishing a tray overflowing with all sorts of delicious bits and pieces. 'Mesdames et Messieur, votre dejeunon est ici.'

I hadn't a clue what he meant, but his enthusiasm was infectious, and without any hesitation I joined the other two diving into the food he had tipped off the tray, chops slavering.

The nice human laughed, 'Bon appetite,' he said nicely, and then leant down to me, 'vous ette un tres beau chat,' he said, his tone very pleasant, so I did not cringe back as I would have done with many a strange human.

Mario glanced up from the tray, 'He's French I think, so that makes him very chivalrous with the ladies,' he explained, his tone indicating he was proud to call this nice man his friend. The chef, as if in reply, bowed politely, and with the words, 'Mon pleasure, tout-a-vous,' he disappeared back into his kitchen smiling broadly.

We spent ages demolishing these tasty leftovers, and then spent time thoroughly grooming ourselves. Because we were now familiar with each other we licked each other as well.

Mario suggested that it was time for the afternoon siesta, so we all strolled back to the rough land for a rest, and to digest that magnificent lunch.

I had never seen so many cats together in one place before this living space was really a "Cat City". Cats of all shapes and sizes were sprawled all over the place. I noticed Achilleas standing at the front of a tunnel that went under the path that the beasts with round legs raced along. It suddenly dawned on me that I had seen another cat in exactly the same place this morning as big M and me left the living area. Mario noticed my quizzical glance towards Achilleas.

'We have to keep a constant guard on that tunnel,' Mario said, 'the other side of the human path leads to the wild mountainous area of Troodos. There is a band of very savage wild cats that have made the foothills leading to Troodos their refuge. Sometimes they send raiding parties down here, particularly when food in the mountains becomes scarce. They are called "The Trods", and they are led by a king called Zavosianos, who has a very wild daughter called Zavosena.

It puzzled me, so I asked, 'Why don't they come over the human path?'

'The beasts with round legs flatten them, but strangely do not stop to eat them,' Mario answered, and then explained further. 'We have to guard these rainwater flood tunnels to stop the Trods reaching the food rich tourist areas. These wild cats have lost the art of living with humans, and would not treat them nicely like we do. They would jump on the tables and snatch the food from under the human's noses; that would not be good for us because the humans would not come back, and then we would go hungry.'

'Does everybody have to guard the tunnel?' I asked, watching Achilleas rise to his feet and stretch himself as another cat took his place.

'Yes, we must take it in turns. Each of us knows who is on guard before us, so when we see that cat on duty, we know that it is our turn next. When a new cat comes to stay, I put them in just after me, that helps them to remember, so when you see me at the end of the tunnel you will know that you are next,'

I let what I had heard sink in, and then asked, 'So you tell everyone when their turn is?'

'Yes, he answered, and without being boastful added, 'I am boss of Cat City.'

We all slumped down in some shade for our afternoon catnap. High summer would be upon us before long, and that gave us some respite from the flies and other insects that were not at large when the temperatures soared for the summer months. I dozed off listening to the happy cries of tourists on the beaches not far behind me. Their cries of happiness intermingled with the roar of the beasts with round legs racing along to the front of me.

All of these sounds were not uppermost in my mind though. As I dozed off I thought to myself, 'I hope I don't meet any of these wild cats.'

My dreams did not stay with the wild cats though; they were of Mario. For some reason my reproductive cycle had been delayed, but my chemistry was changing now, and the urge to procreate was coming on fast. Only Mario was good enough to be the sire of my next brood, and nature would guide him, just as surely as it was taking charge of my body now.

Later that evening, Mario led the way to the water park. It was very large and stretched all the way up to the very fast human path. It was a beautiful evening, and the park was full of youngsters enjoying themselves, and the older humans enjoying a steadier time watching the antics of the young humans. I became aware after a while that most of the humans were strangers to each other, this was made abundantly clear by the number of different languages being used, only two of which I recognized.

I tired of languages and just watched the children, who, thankfully had too much to occupy their young minds, to pay attention to a few cats. Older teenagers seemed to have gravitated to the upper reaches of the park, where they were hurtling down water chutes from a great height, and doing all sorts of clever things in the water.

My companions seemed to spend much of their time dodging great splashes of water, but I did not mind the torrents of spray. They really thought it quite odd that a cat should enjoy water as much as the young humans.

The cafes were doing a roaring trade in the fast foods that young humans seem to enjoy so much, probably because the prices were at a sensible level for young pockets.

We had to get used to some of the sauces that humans used to flavour their food, but when people are so generous with their titbits, it would be a sin to turn ones nose up.

It was a great evening, but as darkness descended, people began to drift away to spend the night in many of the pubs, clubs, and cabarets that made up the nightlife of Limassol. There were also a few specially licensed places called gambling casinos where people got a thrill taking chances with their money. That seemed strange to me, surely the certainty of something in your hand was far safer than the certainty of losing it. Or did these humans who gambled have so much that losing did not matter to them.

Mario led us down the tourist strip to an area that was mainly disco clubs. The cafes were still open, and people who were not too fond of the continual throb of disco music, were having a good time in the small pubs and bars. Here they could enjoy pub games including backgammon which is very popular in Cyprus. I had seen most of these games in progress before in the Tavernas along Governors Beach, but here there were far more people, much more noise, and far bigger disco clubs.

The thought of my old hunting ground brought on a fit of nostalgia, and Brown Legs sprang to mind once again. How would she manage to keep all those young cats in line, most of them my daughters. I bet that prima donna Tigger is lording it all over the place now that she thinks she is boss, I would hate to be one of her sisters.

As the night wore on, we all became aware of a few jolly people who had been drinking that human liquid that makes their legs go wobbly.

Some human girls were in front of us squealing and giggling; their toes, in those shoes with high pointed heels going one way, and their wobbly knees going the other way. Each of them was trying unsuccessfully to help the other to walk straight. Suddenly all of them fell down at the same time, laughing and squealing in a big bundle of arms and legs.

'What a funny way to enjoy oneself?' I thought as we skirted round them.

'Oh look at those pretty pussies,' one girl squealed, then broke into laughter as if she had just told the world's funniest joke. Her friends apparently thought she had, they joined her rolling on the pavement, breathless with uncontrolled laughter, and enjoying themselves to the full, lacking in elegance or otherwise.

We continued our walk until we returned to the rough ground below the path of death, and then we joined the night games that are the equivalent of human social intercourse until we tired of play, and all went to our dens to sleep off a very good day.

****

'Allo, allo,' a voice shouted from the road.

'Is that someone calling us?' Big Feet said, looking across the breakfast table at Brown Legs.

'Allo eengleezi,' the female voice called again.

Brown Legs rose from the table, and with Big Feet hot on her heels went out to the road. A Cypriot lady from down the road greeted them.

'Kalimera,' she said pleasantly. 'Endaxi?' (Good morning, are you okay in Greek)

'Kalimera,' Big Feet and Brown Legs replied in unison.

'Your cat, she jump in our truck, and go to Limasasol,' the lady explained, her English slow and precise. 'She jumps out at our flat close to McDonald's.'

Brown Legs clapped her hands together under her chin. 'Oh thank you,' she bubbled, failing to hide the relief that flooded through her.

'Is that the big area of apartments on the right, just further on than McDonalds going towards the Old Port?' Big Feet asked, wishing to be clear in his mind just exactly where it was.

'That is right, she jumped out of our truck in the car park at the rear of the pub, we could not catch her, and she ran into the bushes.'

'How long ago was that?' Brown Legs asked.

'We have been in London for four weeks, so it is nearly five weeks.'

'Well thank you for taking the trouble to tell us,' Brown Legs said sincerely.

'No problema,' the lady replied, smiling in that pleasant way Cypriots have when they have done the helpful thing.

Brown Legs and Big Feet bade her 'good morning' again, and retired to the awning to finish their breakfast.

'Thank God for that!' Brown Legs said, dropping into in her chair as if drained by the sudden feeling of relief. 'At least we know now that there is a better than even chance of her still being alive.'

Big Feet nodded, showing his agreement as he poured water into a bowl. 'Let's clear up, and then we'll go and have a look at the area. You sort out a couple of photographs of her while I get everything ready. She has the sort of markings that people remember.'

Big Feet finished the washing up while Brown Legs searched for the photographs. When she had picked her favourites, she put on some lipstick. By this time Big Feet had started the car and was drumming his fingers on the steering wheel impatiently.

'You don't look any different,' he smirked, as she got in.

'Cheeky thing,' she retorted, thumping him on his left arm.

'Ow-ow-ow! Pain,' Big Feet screwed his face up, taking the micky out of her.

They drove west along the coast road to Limassol, found the area they needed, and parked amongst the blocks of apartments.

A big ginger Tom cast his eye over them as they vacated the car. Big Feet, ever the fool, flashed a photo of Fluffy at the ginger Tom, 'Excuse me Ginger,' he said, assuming an American accent. 'Have you seen this dame anywhere in the neighbourhood? She is wanted for crossing state lines for no reason at all.'

'Oh come on, stop fooling around,' Brown Legs scolded, trying hard not to be amused by his antics.

Achilleas had glanced at the Photograph held out to him, and had instantly recognized Fluffy, but of course he could not get this fact across to this human.

Brown Legs and Big Feet strolled around the area. Many cats showed interest in them as a possible source of sustenance, but none of them were Fluffy. At lunchtime they stopped at the pub on the corner and ate Moussaka, washing it down with a pot of tea for two.

'Have you seen this cat around at any time in the last five weeks?' Big Feet held a photograph up to the pretty waitress who had served them. The lovely girl took the picture and stared at it intently.

'Yes, yes! this cat, very many times I ave seen her here.' The accent was Russian; the English delivery confident.

Brown Legs eyes shone with expectancy, her voice slightly querulous as she asked, 'Do you see her every day?'

The pretty Russian girl thought for a moment, 'Maybe not for one week now, but I see her getting bigger, I think she have babies inside her.'

Brown Legs eyes clouded over as the memory of helping Fluffy with her last brood sprang to mind, but then she brightened as the realization hit her: if Fluffy is pregnant, and she came here often to feed, then she must be alive and in good health. Her face broke into a broad smile, 'Thank you very much,' she said to the pretty waitress.

'Glad to elp you,' the waitress replied politely, smiling pleasantly as she continued wiping the tables.

'Well that's a good start,' said Big Feet. 'But the act of searching for a cat in a built up area this size appears a little daunting at this moment.'

'We have got to try,' Brown Legs replied, a look of appeal accentuating her statement.

For the remainder of that day they strolled up and down the tourist area, but they did not make contact with Fluffy. During the following four weeks they became a usual sight walking the back streets and the shore areas. They quickly became aware that Fluffy was a very popular cat around this area. Many had seen her that day, and that added greatly to the frustration of not actually seeing her, but having the feeling that they were close behind all the time.

****

Brown Legs and Big Feet could not know it of course, but I was looking for them also. Not long after meeting my humans, and seeing the picture of me, Achilleas had told me of the silly human he had met.

'He had a small image of you,' he said importantly, knowing he was passing on something of great meaning to me. His revelation had the effect of making me stare at every human I passed whilst in the tourist area.

Four weeks had gone by since Achilleas had surprised me with his news. My three babies were ten days old, and well hidden from prying enemies. I had chosen to give birth well away from Cat City, because wherever there were hungry Toms around, the first few days of my kitten's lives were extremely hazardous.

For the first time in two weeks I had met up with Big M, so we made our way to McDonald's. As we passed the corner pub the pretty waitress waylaid us, so we stopped. She leant down and stroked my head, something I always looked forward to whenever we met, she always had a kind word to say as well, but this time her statement had a great deal of meaning to me.

'Ah pretty one,' she said. 'I ave not see you for so long, I think your people find you.'

Her words gave me cause for thought. Could her statement mean that my humans had been here searching for me? With this thought still bugging me we passed from the road to the back of McDonald's. We always felt comfortable here, the back was spotlessly clean, and the waste bins clean and tidy with lids closed and no horrible smells. Anton, the French chef took one look at us as he opened the back doors, and quickly disappeared inside again. I looked at Big M and she looked back at me, both of us a bit puzzled by his actions. His face had not shown anger, or any other human emotion. He had just glanced at us and gone back inside very quickly.

Both of us continued to look up at the door expectantly. A few minutes later the handle turned and Anton stepped through the door. As he stepped outside he spread his hands saying, 'Et voila, votre chat est ici.'

I gazed up at the two figures that came through the door. Big M's reaction was to run behind the waste bins.

'Fluffy, oh Fluffy!' Brown Legs squealed, unable to hide her joy. She picked me up and hugged and kissed me, her tears wetting my fur. I rubbed my ears against her, for I too was enjoying this reunion. Both of us were oblivious to anyone else at that moment. Big Feets hand reached out and stroked me gently; did I detect a tear in that big oaf's eye?

Big M crept out from her hiding place having seen that my humans were not to be feared. Big Feet gazed at her; amazement tinged his voice as he exclaimed, 'Good Lord! that's a pedigree British cat, in fact it's a classic silver tabby", look how pronounced that M is in the middle of her forehead.'

Brown Legs glanced at Big M but was far too involved with me to pay much attention to anyone else. Finally, still clutching me to her bosom, she looked into Antons eyes and said simply, 'Thank you very much my dear man; you have no idea what this moment means to me.'

Anton's features showed that he also had got caught up in the emotion of this reunion. He blurted out with quivering voice, 'Ees nothing madame, ees nothing.' The inadvertent gallic shrug emphasized his words.

'Goodbye,' Brown Legs said, and then they shook Anton's hand in turns. 'We shall see you again very soon.'

Anton smiled through misty eyes, and went back to work quickly lest we see just how sensitive he really was.

They turned to leave the back of McDonald's with me possessively clutched in Brown Legs arms. 'Let's go home now,' she whispered to me, hugging me to her face.

The statement had the effect of jolting me out of the nostalgic torpor I had slipped into.

'My babies,' I thought suddenly, and struggled out of her grip, landed on all fours. She immediately tried to pick me up again, but I backed off.

'What's the matter baby?' she asked, a hurt expression clouding her face. Once again she tried to pick me up. Once more I cringed back; I was torn between two loyalties. On one side was the love of Brown Legs tugging at my conscience, and on the other side maternal loyalty to my kittens. Big Feet, who was not so emotionally tied to me was first to understand my reticence.

'She's got kittens!' he said bluntly.

Brown Legs immediately straightened up, not taking her worried eyes off me.

'If she comes with us now, her family will not survive, that's what's in her mind,' Big Feet said in a convincing tone.

'What are we going to do?' Brown Legs voice sounded desperate. She had found me, but now realized that I could not go back with her.

'Well we know where to find her, don't we? She's been gone for a few weeks, so her kittens will not be that old, I think you are going to have to let nature take its course for at least two months.'

As he was speaking I started moving away. Big M followed me. I had no idea if Brown Legs would get the message and follow me, even though our bond was so close.

'She wants me to follow her,' she shouted excitedly. She had instantly realised the meaning of my backward glance.

With Big M by my side, I led them through the back alleys to the fringe of the scrubland. I disappeared under a thick bush, the base of which was strewn with rubble. They could not follow me under the bush, so they had to wait expectantly while I carried my babies out one by one.

Brown Legs gazed in awe at my little black bundles of fur.

'My God! The all blacks,' Big Feet muttered.

I did not leave my kittens there for long; I could see she was just aching to pick them up, so I hurriedly returned them to the bushes; the smell of humans on them could be dangerous at this stage, and invite curious enemies.

'Well there you are my dear,' he said. 'You now know why, and you now know where, leave it like that for a few weeks; we will pop down in the hope of seeing her now and again.

Brown Legs saw the sense in his reasoning, and looking back at me dejectedly, she shouted, 'Take care Fluffy darling.'

The future was unforeseeable, but I think we both felt convinced that now we had found each other again, the not too distant future would find us united in our old home again.

Fate however, had other plans for me. Fate intended to take full advantage of my act of nosiness, and map out a few difficulties for me to overcome; or otherwise.

****

My kittens were a month old when my turn for guard duty at the tunnel came round. I took over from my mate Mario as the sun peeped over Larnaca to the east of Limassol.

In the way that all territorial cats do, Mario ignored my sons, which were his sons also of course. He rose from his vigil, and without a purr, stretched his sinewy body, and strolled away head held high, showing all and sundry that he was master of all he surveyed.

I looked after him as he swaggered away, and the comments of some old ladies as he had passed them came to mind: 'Oh look! a lucky black cat, what a nice sight to start the day.'

He knew he was a beautiful example of a lucky black cat, and that added to his supreme confidence.

The kittens suckled and then I washed them thoroughly, including their little backsides as they rolled over and splayed their legs into the washing position. Interspersed with feeding and washing times, their lives were one long wrestling match, so I had to be fastidious about their cleanliness, they got into all sorts of mucky situations.

While my youngsters played, I poked my head into the drainage pipe that went under the path of death. The rumbling of the beasts with round legs had a different tone echoing around the side of the tunnel, and I could see light at the other end. The top of the circle formed a perfect arc in the light, but the bottom of the circle was broken up by the jagged outline of small rocks that had been washed into the tunnel by the torrential winter rains.

I shuddered momentarily; there was an eerie depth to the shadowy cragged outline of the bottom of the tunnel. It occurred to me that the whole of the floor was designed with perfect hiding places for any small predatory animal, even those as big as a cat.

I turned from the tunnel and cast my eyes around Cat City. Not a soul was in sight, not even Big M. Everyone had gone to the tourist area for breakfast. Without exception, Cat City looked like a ghost town.

Turning back to my guard duties, I stared long and hard down the length of the tunnel, knowing in my heart that I could not defend Cat City on my own. Perhaps the system was not that well thought out after all.

Suddenly, as if in answer to my worst thoughts, the sound of rushing, scurrying bodies reached my ears. I stared hard into the tunnel; shadowy forms became visible leaping over the rock strew floor of the tunnel. I screeched, terrified, as six sets of teeth sank into my skin. I writhed and shrieked, and tried to fight off my attackers, but they were already hauling me along the tunnel towards the other end.

The screams of my babies gave added strength to my struggles, but I was no match for the six brutes who hauled me ever closer to the light at the other end of the tunnel.

Suddenly we all burst into sunlight again. I fought to turn my head, to catch a glimpse of my kittens. They were all firmly in the jaws of females who had obviously been chosen for this assault on Cat City, but they had come to no harm. Realising the futility of my continual squirming to free myself, I submitted to the superior strength of my six captors.

My body was smarting from the rough treatment; no doubt I would carry the scars for the rest of my life. Encounters like this usually left the victim with torn ears, scratched eyeballs, and in the worst instances blindness.

The Toms gripping me were obviously fighting Toms. They feared nothing in the cat world, and only superior animals in other species.

Feeling my body relax a little; two of my tormentors let go of their grip on my neck fur, but remained close at hand. We were climbing steadily now, and my increased freedom of movement made the climb easier.

Human habitation started to get sparse, and as we reached the top of a great hill we looked down on a long valley which had a huge wall built at one end. Water had built up against the wall and formed a big lake. The hills all around the big lake were dotted with the large villa type homes that humans seemed to favour.

As we traveled it became obvious that we were going round the lake to the other end. We went up and down two more hills, and across two human paths, and then climbed a very big hill that was covered with bushes and stubby trees.

The climb began to get rocky, and soon my kittens and I were being hauled over large outcrops of rock which seemed to have broken from the side of the hill, leaving holes that made wonderful dens.

I had begun to notice that our progress was being monitored by rough looking felines perched on the rocks that we were passing. They all had the appearance of straggly unkempt fur, not an ear was intact on any of them.

As we rounded a huge boulder, its surface covered with rough cats staring at us impassively, a voice shrieked from somewhere ahead, 'Bring them to me, I want to see what these fine cats look like from the well fed side of the path of death.'

As we were dragged forward, I glanced up a tree to the position from which the harsh growls had emanated. My gaze was met by the most savage; the most glaring feline eyes I have ever seen.

'Let them go you fools!' she shrieked.

The order was obeyed instantly. The raiding party released us and scurried away into the anonymity of the crowd that had gathered, forming a huge half circle at a respectable distance from the tree.

'Welcome to Zavosena's court,' the savage female cackled. 'Not quite as nice as where you come from, is it?'

I returned her gaze in silence, unsure as to what attitude to assume at this moment. My sons scurried to my side, and sought solace by trying to suckle. I realised their need, and remained upright on my rear haunches, and let them nuzzle into my fur.

'Oh isn't that a pretty sight,' Zavosena sneered sarcastically. 'Mummy is feeding her little brats, isn't that a moving sight?' Her eyes scanned the onlookers demandingly. The nervous titters and the strained howls that rippled round the straggly crowd fed the massive ego that was the hallmark of this brutal female.

The nervousness of the crowd told me that this harridan ruled by fear, that meant that none of her subjects could act without being led by this female despot. Her people held more fear for her than I did, and given the chance would shake free of her.

My eyes dropped to the six fierce looking Toms at the base of the tree. Their stance; and their eyes glaring into the crowd told me they were her bodyguards, and also her enforcers. It was their presence that ensured the right response from her onlookers. By the looks of their chunky build, they were more capable of blocking tactics than the agility needed for an open cat fight.

The enemy surrounding me reflected the harshness of their existence; these were truly feral cats, devoid of any feelings that would make them appealing to humans. They may have had some appeal at one time in their lives, but that had been driven from them by the harshness of their surroundings; and the leadership of this female.

The underlying dislike of their leader showed in their apprehensive appearance. If Zavosena had cared to look into her subjects, rather than at them, she too could not have failed to notice the undercurrent of hate that lay just below the surface. Becoming aware of this I found my voice, and fearlessly posed the question uppermost in my mind, 'Why were we captured, and brought to this place?'

A deathly hush fell over the onlookers. They held their breath waiting for the termagants answer.

'Why!' She shrieked. 'Why! You think to ask me why?'

Her jaws were slavering with the force of her anger. Her eyes bored through me, the venom in them transforming the already cruel outlines of her features into those of a totally devilish; demonic, out of control feline. I had never witnessed such spitting fury as hers. Her mindless; frothing, ranting, cursing tirade was obviously fueled by some inner hatred indelibly etched on her heart and mind.

The crowd shrank back; fearing whatever ailed this mad-cat may transfer to them. Even the bodyguards, who until this moment had appeared as statues, shuffled uneasily.

She panted heavily showing the strain of her uncontrolled rage, and while she remained silent for some moments, the convulsions that had racked her body eased a little and slowly she quietened to the point where she could speak again.

'You dare to ask me why we on this side of the path of death should capture a well fed, pampered prima donna from the land of plenty,' she said, her attitude changing dramatically. Her eyes still glinted, but more with menace than madness now.

A terrible thought flicked through my mind, stirred by the words "well fed". 'Are they cannibals? Are they going to eat us? Is that why we were captured?'

As if reading my mind Zavosena continued; she had cooled considerably, and her voice now had an edge of control about it as she detailed her intentions, 'You—and they,' she indicated my kittens, 'are hostages; we are going to force that pompous leader of yours Mario, to give us some concessions in the areas where all the different peoples of the world come to have a holiday. If he does not concede to our demands, you will be removed to my father's domain high in the Troodos Mountains, and Mario will never set eyes on you again.'

She stopped speaking abruptly, her eyes searching my face for a reaction to her statement.

I sighed with inward relief; at least we were not going to be eaten. She took my pause as an indication that I had no answer, so she went on, gloating now.

'You see, we knew you were Mario's mate, we knew you had three sons, we also knew when you would be morning guard, not all of your Cities inhabitants are as happy with Mario's leadership as you think. All of us on this side of the path of death are the rejected ones. The ancestors of many of the cats who you see around you here, were disposed of by their humans, that makes us different than you cats from the other side of the path of death, your ancestors all had homes, and just chose to have their kittens where their humans could not find them, that way they kept their human home and were well fed, and able to go away and nourish their kittens properly.

All of us Trods are the offspring of rejected pets, thrown out of our villas because we had become a liability, or an inconvenience. It is not easy to grow up reasonable when the truth becomes obvious to you. It is not easy to be unwanted; it is most awful to be discarded much like a bag of rubbish. All self-worth disappears; leaving just an empty shell of what could have been a loving friend for life.'

She peered at me intently over the edge of the branch that was her throne. Her words had made me sit up and pay attention; this was certainly not the screeching mad-cat of a while ago.

The crowd were no longer fearful and fidgety; they were all up on their haunches giving Zavosena their undivided attention.

'It's the truth!' One of them shouted encouragingly. Others nodded their heads slowly, agreeing, but unsure how to react to this other side of their leader. This transformation was astonishing to them.

She had paused, so I found my voice, I could not let this moment slip away now that she had revealed another side to her complicated psyche.

'Have you suffered like this?' I asked loudly, meeting her gaze as I posed this most important question.

The look in her eyes made me enquire further: 'Were you thrown out unwanted?'

Her head dropped and her eyes moistened as memories came flooding back. She looked down at me, and then spoke softly as she laid to rest the devils that had haunted her for so long.

'I had a lovely home,' she began. 'I had a brilliant but lonely childhood. I was the only kitten my human took from the litter of the cat of a friend. I was nursed, and cuddled, and stroked; there was always food from a special tin put into my very own food bowl, and I had a huge garden to play in.

My humans took me to a veterinarian, and he poked needles in me; which I did not like, but were meant to keep me safe from terrible cat diseases. One day they took me to a veterinarian surgeon, and I suddenly found myself waking up from a deep sleep, and I had a cut in my stomach. The cut healed up quickly, and very soon I had forgotten all about this event in my life.

My world continued to be a very enjoyable one in the happy playful way that is the birthright of any domestic cat who has been taken as a friend into a human abode. I wanted for nothing; they even bought me my own toys to play with in the garden.

The time came when I was one year old, and familiar with all the actions and movements of my humans. One day some unusual events began to take place. Lots of workmen were hurrying around putting things in boxes. The boxes were put in one of those large beasts that speed along the path of death.

I remember my humans giving me an extra-long and warm cuddle, and then they put me down and were gone forever. I could not understand it, the big house that had always rang to the noises of playful children, and loud night parties suddenly became completely lifeless. The full food bowl which I had never seen so full lasted for days, and nobody came to refill it.

For the first time in my life I knew hunger. The very real effect of that hunger eventually forced me to leave the villa grounds and seek sustenance in the outside world. It was a jungle out there.' She paused, and gathered herself together as the memories began to hurt.

'That's right!' Someone shouted from the crowd.

'It's hell on your own!' Another voice growled.

'Finish your story Zavosena,' a quiet voiced old female urged.

Zavosena licked her lips and continued,

'For weeks I survived on a diet of lizards, shrews, and scraps from village houses, but I seemed to be hungry all the time. Before long I was fighting everybody for any scrap of food that became available.

Being savage for the least reason became a habit, but the worst realization was yet to come. I had noticed by this time that other females of my age were heavily pregnant with a second family of kittens, yet the Toms had never bothered me. This had puzzled me greatly until one night I was sharing some chicken scraps with a dear old female who also had no humans.

"I have never had babies either, she confessed to me".

She really looked the motherly type, so I just had to ask her why, like me, she had never become a mother? "They had me snipped, she answered simply" I did not know what she meant by "snipped"; this fact must have been obvious by the dumb look I gave her.

"You know", she said to me. "They took me to an animal doctor, and he cut out the bits that would have allowed me to have babies".'

Zavosena looked round her audience, everyone; me included, was gazing up at her, already knowing in our heart of hearts the diabolical reason for her passionate hatred when it emerged.

Only my kittens were completely immune to the emotional impact of this unfolding story. Her audience had completely forgotten the frightening episode that had led to this moment, and were waiting for the end of the story agog with interest.

Meanwhile my three sons had decided that all this was too boring and had resorted to a threesome wrestling match.

'Was that the reason Zavosena?' the old woman called up to her, 'had the animal doctor spoilt your chance of having kittens?'

Zavosena answered that question by taking up the thread of her story again, 'When my old friend mentioned that the animal doctor had cut the bits out of her that rendered her infertile, my memory shot back to a time when I had awoken from an induced sleep, to find that my stomach had been cut. I remember the sad look in her eyes when she looked at my stomach and said to me, "yes, the cut is there in exactly the right place, you also will never know the joys of motherhood".'

The crowd shuffled nervously; Zavosena had risen on her hind legs, her front paws crossed over her chest, her face contorted with the agony of the moment, tears cascading down her front.

The crowd gasped, they were used to her tempers; but now they were witness to a far deeper emotion. The transformation of their savage leader into this version of deprived female was too much for the younger females. They joined her in howls of anguish as some of the more mature cats hung their heads as a sign of mutual sorrow.

'The only thing that saved me from myself at that moment,' Zavosena sobbed, 'Was the fact that this old female had become my friend, she knew who my mother was, and she confessed to me that my mother had mated with Zavosianos, King of the Trods. You already know that when I was brought to him, this great old Tom gave me a place in his Kingdom, and a job to do. All of you know, I have tried hard to achieve the wishes of my father.'

Zavosena sat down on her branch, seemingly at peace with the world. Now that she had shared the great tragedy of her younger years with her followers, the venom had gone from her eyes. She looked towards me, I, who had been the catalyst that had brought this alarming incidence of human casualness with the feline species out in the open. No matter what the expense, these humans who had moved house should have taken Zavosena with them, or at the very least given her to the humans who look for another home for animals who cannot go with their humans. It is terribly cruel to make an animal totally dependent, and then abandon it so callously.

Fortunately we cats are a very resilient species, and fight hard for survival, but that in no way excuses any human who treats us as objects of momentary affection and then deserts us.

I took the opportunity to speak.

'That was a very moving story Zavosena, perhaps we should talk for a while about my capture, and what we can do about this situation. Perhaps we can build on this, and create a future where we can at least talk to each other.'

A bit of the old hardness glinted in Zavosena's eyes. Speaking firmly now, and with a distinct aura of diplomacy, she said, 'The events that brought you here are the express orders of my father; we must force a dialogue with Mario.'

She paused, then in a less forceful tone continued, 'All we want is access to that part of the area where there are benefits enough for all in this territory. We wish to do away with the path of death as a barrier between us cats from the mountains to the sea.'

This side of Zavosena spoke sense; I must reciprocate in similar style, lest the momentum of this conversation is lost. The wish to live in peace is a universal trait, not to be crippled by those who share a bent for warmongering.

I looked directly into her eyes. My look was not that of a hostage of only a few hours, but rather the look of an equal; an equal who showed no fear or awe of the present company.

'Let me try a diplomatic approach,' I said firmly to her face. 'Let me and my sons stay on this side of the path of death, until I have arranged a meeting between you and your father on one side, and Mario and Achilleas representing the shore side community of cats.'

She did not answer for a long time. The crowd could feel the tension in the air, and were hanging on with bated breath to see which way Zavosena's thoughts would take her.

After what seemed an age, her head raised to face me, and the pensive crowd behind me. She smiled for the first time, 'You do that,' she answered with meaningful stare. 'You go ahead and arrange this great debate. You may be just the one we have awaited for so long; someone with the wisdom to get things moving.'

The crowd roared its approval, and for the first time, a ray of sunshine entered the bleak lives of these mountain cats on this desolate hillside.

THE NEGOTIATOR.

Zavosena stared directly into my wide open eyes; she saw the surprise that her last statement had caused. "You do that"! She had uttered, the first smile that had cracked her face for many a year emphasizing the weight of the statement.

She eased her body slightly on the branch as she continued, 'We know you are called by the name of Fluffy, we also know that you understand the other language that is prevalent on this side of the Island; the one they call English. Now we see that you are a fair and fearless feline, and you have wisdom in your make-up. I believe you could speak for us with a strong and honest voice.'

She paused, and then appeared to be deep in thought. The crowd began to shuffle and whisper to each other as the pause dragged into seconds. She was oblivious to the impatience of her subjects, and continued sorting out her thoughts in silence. After an indeterminate length of time she looked up, 'Dimitri,' she called. Her subjects flinched noticeably as her voice startled them.

A scrawny, lithe limbed young Tom sprang to his feet and hurried to her presence. He sat upright on his haunches, looking up at her throne he said determinedly, 'Yes majesty, what is it you wish of me?'

'Dimitri my fine runner,' she said, her tone now commanding. 'You are aware of everything that has gone on here today?'

'Yes majesty.'

'Could you relate everything you have witnessed here today to the great king Zavoseanos?'

'Yes majesty, I have watched in awe.'

'Then you travel as quickly as you can to Troodos and tell my father that this brave feline we captured is also the right feline to present our feelings, and arrange a meeting of great consequence with the leaders of Cat City. Tell him we are going to arrange talks immediately, and other runners will keep him informed of progress. Off you go Dimitri, and be lucky, you must beware of the wild mountain dogs that the humans no longer want.'

Without a word Dimitri streaked out of the encampment, and disappeared into the folds of the hills high above the human lake. Zavosena turned to me saying, 'Dimitri will be gone six human days at least, if he does not meet any wild dogs, and does not have to hide from them for a long time he should be back with the Kings orders in a week.'

She stood up on her branch and stretched, giving vent to a wide yawn, 'It has been a long eventful day; I think we all need some sleep.'

Without another word she stretched out on her branch, laid her head on her front paws and closed her eyes.

'Come with me.' I turned to find the old lady who had encouraged Zavosena to finish her story looking at me in a kindly manner.

'It's a bit rough up here,' she said conversationally, 'And the mornings are inclined to be a bit chilly. You and your sons can share my nest for the night; it has fresh bracken on the floor,' she added, to make it sound a bit more appealing.

I followed her to the nice little nest she had made in a hollow between the rocks. I laid down where she indicated, and my three sons immediately started to suckle. 'They are fine boys; they must have a fine father,' the old female chuckled.

'Mario is their father,' I answered directly and honestly. Her question made me look at her a bit more closely. 'Do you have any children?' I asked.

The old female looked up shaking her head, 'I cannot have kittens,' she said sadly.

'Are you another one?' I asked gently.

'Yes, my story is much the same as Zavosena's. I was loved and nurtured, completely humanized, and then my humans sold their villa and left the Island. During my life with them I received many kindnesses; I was a member of the family, but they did take away from me the nature that made me acceptable to Toms. It meant nothing to me at the time because I shared all the love of a family; but then they deserted me, and now I can never know the love of something that is my very own, and something that needs me in return.'

She gazed fondly at my sons, now fast asleep. Her look of longing saddened me as I watched her ruffle up her bedding, and prepare to settle down with her memories. Only her breathing indicated that she was not asleep, but laying there thinking of what could have been if her beloved humans had taken the trouble to find her another home, rather than take the easy option. I nodded off still musing over how unfair life could be when people don't bother to do the right thing by their animals.

The following morning I arrived at the meeting place just in time to see Zavosena leaping up to her branch. She hurriedly settled into her perch, almost as if she was embarrassed to let a stranger see that she had to carry out the basic needs of nature just like all the rest of us.

Ignoring me completely she set about grooming herself with great attention to detail. Looking around, I could see by the emptiness of the camp that everybody was out hunting.

My kittens had joined a bunch of other young cats rushing from bush to bush, chasing anything that crawled; quite successfully by the crunching sounds coming from the bushes. These cats did not afford themselves the pleasure of tormenting a catch cruelly before eating it. Once caught the victim was gobbled up immediately lest it escaped and became a meal for a fellow hunter.

The morning wore on; and then as if by some telepathic signal everyone started gathering at the meeting point around Zavosena's tree.

My sons had pestered me, so I was lying down on my side letting them suckle when, without warning Zavosena called my name. Everyone looked up expectantly, and then all eyes turned on me.

'Fluffy,' she called, and then paused until she had my full attention. 'Dimitri will not be back with my father's orders for a long time, so I think we will start preparations immediately. Are you prepared to go back to the shore-side, and tell your friends what is happening, and convince them that all we want is dialogue at the moment? It is in the interests of both sides to resolve our differences.'

She paused, looking at me intently, hoping my eyes would betray any contrary feelings I may be harbouring. Seeing nothing but total attention in my eyes she carried on, this time her tone was more conciliatory.

'Considering the roughness of your capture, and the stress caused you and your sons, I think we should applaud your courage and presence of mind; in the light of what you are about to do for the purposes of peace.'

She stopped talking as the crowd shouted loud growls and purrs of approval. As the din subsided, I confirmed my willingness to act in the cause of peace, and try to bring the two sides together to resolve this long standing territorial division.

'I have only been a member of the shore-side community for a short time,' I reminded her. 'It is only recently that I have become aware that there is another community on this side of what has become to be called the path of death. Perhaps my newness to the community makes me the ideal cat to draw both sides together, I have no personal agenda to cloud my mind, and,' I emphasized, 'I have become Mario's mate, so that lends some weight to my credibility.'

Zavosena and her subjects were impressed by my honest and straight forward reply, and it showed as she joined them in their purrs of approval.

'You cannot go back alone with your three sons, there are dangers between here and the path of death,' she said, cautious for my safety.

'One set of teeth and one set of claws is not enough to fight off a determined attack by a hungry wild dog.'

She stopped talking to me, and without hesitation called out a number of names from memory, and gave them the responsibility of escorting me and my sons to the water tunnel under the path of death. She then surprised me by asking, 'Is there anyone else you would like to accompany you?'

'Yes there is someone else, the lady who shared her nest with me and my sons last night.'

Zavosena quickly recovered from the moment of surprise that my request had caused. 'Avoula,' she called loudly. 'Where are you?'

The old female crept forward and crouched before her leader.

'Yes majesty,' she answered with hushed voice.

'Do you wish to accompany Fluffy on this brave mission she is attempting?'

'Oh yes majesty,' Avoula replied eagerly.

'So be it, you are now the official companion of Fluffy and you will remain at her side at all times.'

Zavosena had given her orders, and by way of dismissal stretched herself out on her branch.

Avoula came alongside me and my sons, and immediately they rubbed themselves against her. The pleasure that this moment gave her shone brightly in her eyes, the moisture that appeared at the corners added a sparkle to them. This pleasant old female who had never known the joys of motherhood had now become an adopted grandmother; she could now retrieve the memories of belonging, and live happily once more.

Ringed by our escort we began the journey that would return us to Cat City. Many times we had to scurry up trees as the escort warned us of wild dogs ranging the hills in front of us. Several times they bit at the bark of the trees we had sought sanctuary in. They did not waste their energy for long, a hard fight or a long chase further sapped the meager strength of their scrawny bodies. These dogs had been trained to flush game for their human masters, they never had the chance to make the kill, this was achieved by the blast of a shotgun; now at the end of their useful lifespan they had been abandoned to a life of slow starvation, having been rejected by their former masters in favour of younger dogs that would more readily earn the food laid out for them.

The country air was often tinged by the fetid stench of a rotting body; having breathed its last under some bushes; or in a gully, or ditch.

By late afternoon we had reached the water tunnel. The escort stayed on the hill overlooking the path of death; they did not wish to risk a confrontation at this most important stage in the proceedings.

I shuddered involuntarily as I approached the tunnel; its eerie darkness caused the hairs on my back to rise. 'Hello!' I screamed into the tunnel. 'Hello! Can you hear me?'

'Is that you Fluffy?' The gruff voice of Achilleas echoed down the tunnel.

'Yes it's me!' I screeched back, relief evident in my tone. The welcome voice of Achilleas was far more reassuring than the voice of a timid immature young guard.

'I am coming through,' I shouted, not quite so afraid now. 'I have a friend with me,' I warned.

The five of us broke cover into Cat City, me leading. Avoula cowered as she peered at the hostile crowd facing us.

'Who's this?' Achilleas glowered menacingly.

Before I could answer, Mario came bounding across; his attitude showed he had only just become aware of a group coming through the tunnel.

'It's me! It's me!' I shouted, showing how glad I was to be back. We rubbed our ears against each other affectionately. He completely ignored his sons, and they kept at a safe distance crouched down beside Avoula.

'Who's this?' Mario echoed Achilleas's first question, the hairs on his back rising as he sniffed at this strange old female from the other side.

'Stop! Stop!' I screeched, putting myself between Avoula and Mario. The kittens sensing danger ran off, losing themselves in the crowd, who were also eyeing Avoula aggressively.

'You don't understand,' I screamed into Mario and Achilleas's stern faces. 'She is my companion, she has been ordered to bring me back and stay beside me.'

'Who ordered that?' Mario asked; his gruff growl remained menacing. He dropped down on his haunches glaring at me, 'Come on,' he growled, 'who ordered her to be the companion of my mate?'

Although in fear for her life, Avoula broke her silence, and steadfastly answered the question.

'Princess Zavosena ordered me to be Fluffy's companion.'

Mario turned to me, growling, 'You mean a Trod has given you orders. A filthy wildcat from the hills is giving orders to the mate of Mario, leader of the shore-side community, never!' He went on fiercely his eyes burning into mine. 'Never, will I allow one of my subjects to be under the orders of a savage from the hills.'

'You don't understand!' I screamed into his face. 'I am not under the orders of the Trods; I am free to remain here. Zavosena ordered Avoula to be my companion, because I am to arrange talks between you and Zavoseanos,' I glared into his face; now that I had steadied down a bit I was beginning to get angry with his male ego, and pig headed stubbornness.

He noticed my change of expression from apprehensive female to angry opponent.

'Do I here you right?' He asked, his voice tinged with incredulity.' Only yesterday you were brutally captured and made prisoner, and today you return as an emissary of the Trods?'

'I can explain it all; let us forget the heat of this moment; let us sit down together, and I will explain everything that has come to pass over the last two days,' I said, still looking straight into his yellow eyes, my eyes fervently looking for understanding.

Mario broke away from my steady gaze. He turned his head to Achilleas, whose savage glare at Avoula had now turned to a look of bewilderment, as the weight of what had occurred gradually filtered through his thick ginger haired skull.

'Have we ever talked to the Trods?' he asked.

'Not in my living memory,' Achilleas answered.

A quavering old voice from the back of the crowd spoke up: 'Old Nicos has.'

All eyes turned to an old female. Unabashed she continued, 'Nicos, the wise one had talks with Zavoseanos seven human years ago, only a few of us are alive now who were here at the time, and remember the events leading up to the talks.'

A few nods and murmurings from the crowd indicated that there were other ancients alive who were very aware of the history of Cat City.

Mario halted conversation while he doubled the guards on the tunnel. He then led everyone to the clearing in the middle which was also his patch.

High on the hill, on the other side of the path of death, the leader pointed out the gathering to his subordinates.

'Georgeo,' he said to a lean young Tom. 'Hurry back to Zavosena, and tell her that all the felines of Cat City are gathered together, and are talking. Emphasise that Fluffy is in the middle down there, and it looks as if they are preparing to listen to her story. Oh, and tell her to send a replacement for you while you rest.'

Georgeo disappeared into the gathering gloom as his companions turned once more to events in Cat City. Andreas, the leader of the escort group, and his remaining Toms were grateful for a beautiful moonlit night which allowed them to see the talking felines down below them all clustered around Fluffy the central figure, who was obviously relating a story.

The assembled felines of Cat City listened enraptured as Fluffy related the events of the last two days to them. When she had told her story, she was met by a wall of silence. Then, as if by some invisible cue, a buzz of conversation erupted simultaneously all around the meeting place.

Mario remained deep in thought, oblivious to the chattering cats surrounding the small central group. Achilleas glanced at him, and cleared his throat as a sign of impatience. This brought Mario out of his thoughts, and back to what was going on around him. He rose up on his front legs sitting on his haunches. The crowd fell silent in anticipation.

'I will not call for a decision from you all regarding Fluffy's story until we have heard the words of Nicos.' He paused for a moment casting his eyes around all there, and then asked, 'How many of you have known the wise one called Nicos?' At least ten faces from the crowd indicated that they knew Nicos.

The old female who had first raised the name of the wise old Tom spoke up, 'Nicos will be fifteen years old now; this is a great age for a cat that lives here. The reason for his great age and his great wisdom is that like his father and his grandfather before him, he has always lived with the same family of Cypriot humans who have lived in this area for generations; therefore he has the accumulated wisdom of his forebears, a wisdom that we cats who have no humans can hardly hope to attain.'

Mario interrupted a little impatiently, 'Yes, but does this wise-cat keep in touch with what's happening now?'

'Forgive me Mario,' the old female reacted to Mario's interruption. 'I am old and perhaps a little slow. To answer your question; all of us older cats keep in touch with Nicos; one or more of us keep company with him every day. You younger cats have your own thing to do, your own lives to lead, that is why you are not aware of the history that surrounds you. Nicos has never been a leader in Cat City, but during his time, he has always given help and guidance to us all in times of crisis.'

'But is he the only cat from the shore-side community who has arranged a meeting with Zavoseanos in the past?' Mario continued persistently.

'YES I AM!' An old but still strong purr came from the back of the gathering.

As one, the inhabitants of Cat City swung around to get a glimpse of the owner of this authoritative voice. They all gazed in awe at this old Tom being assisted by his two constant companions as they made their way to the centre of the throng.

'Ah!' He exclaimed; a glint of humour in his eyes as he gazed at Mario and Achilleas, 'So you are the two young Toms of whom I frequently hear. Your exploits are well known to me; and you must be Fluffy?'

He turned his wise old eyes on me without waiting for acknowledgement from Mario or Achilleas.

'I have not heard your story yet my dear, perhaps we should sit down together and you can tell me all that has happened to you. Oh what fine young Toms you have,' he said, glancing at my three sons, his old eyes appreciating the sturdy forms of the future generation.

He turned to face Mario, 'I think you should dismiss everybody until you and I have had a chat, we have much to discuss, and it would seem; some decisions to make.'

Mario reacted instantly to the old Toms suggestion. The gaze from the old Toms eyes showed intellect, and commanded obedience, without an air of superiority.

The crowds dispersed, and the small group of felines who were the main cast in this drama settled down to talk in Mario's patch.

From high on the hill, on the other side of the path of death, Andreas, the leader of the escort group took note of all that was happening below him. The bright moon illuminated the main characters drawn into a tight circle. He saw Nicos assisted to a position in the centre of the group and knew immediately that great importance was being applied to the return of Fluffy, and the purpose of her mission.

'Yiannis,' he called to one of his mature Toms and feeling the body draw up beside him continued, 'That is a very important old Tom, the one supported by those helpers in the middle. I want you to describe this scene to Zavosena. Off you go, make good speed, and ask her to send a replacement for you while you rest.'

Yiannis surveyed the central group on the other side. When he was satisfied that he had consigned the scene to memory he disappeared into the moonlit hills to the rear of their vantage point.

By the time Fluffy had related her tale once more, it was early morning. Mario called a halt to the proceedings until they had all had a catnap, and scoured the cafés for breakfast.

After his nap, Nicos, supported on either side by his loyal friends, went back to his home. His humans put out a bowl of food for him, and seeing his two companions threw out some scraps for them, which they devoured greedily.

'So your friends have found you again, have they?' The old female human said. Nicos rubbed his ears against her old fashioned stockings affectionately. She stroked his tatty old fur in return.

'If you are staying out all day, don't be late this evening, you know how we worry when we cannot find you,' she chided lovingly.

The sun was high in the sky by the time the populace of Cat City returned to the shade of the bushes. The central figures were stretched out under the Carob tree in the centre of the meeting place. Everyone knew it was the old wise-cat Nicos who was going to speak, so all the shady places under the trees and bushes were soon packed with drowsing cats waiting for the wise one to speak.

When there was no room left under the foliage, latecomers climbed up into the branches, and to all intents and purposes appeared to be more comfortably positioned than their peers on the ground. Soon all the trees were festooned with cats who allowed their tails to hang down below the branches like huge catkins from the trees further north on the Island.

Nicos glanced at Mario. Mario acknowledged the unspoken question. The crowd stirred expectantly as Nicos rose from his belly, and sat on his haunches facing the crowd. Some of the youngsters who were a bit boisterous got a cuff around the ears from their mothers. The scowl and low growl that accompanied the cuff brought instant obedience. Young ones lay back submissively, but with their ears flat against their heads, and paws up in the defensive position.

Nicos waited patiently for silence.

'Fellow citizens,' he began. 'Compared to humans we are an uncomplicated species. Therefore I say to you that only one thing stands between the shore-side cats and the mountain cats, and that one thing is civilization. Whenever a mountain cat has survived crossing the path of death, he has been discovered as soon as he offended a tourist by jumping on the table or fighting for a scrap of food. It has always been the policy of the shore-side community to evict these ill-bred monsters, to ensure that the humans who feed us are not disturbed during their holiday. Our livelihood depends on happy people having a good holiday. For that sole reason we guard against intrusion by any uncivilized types.

Seven years ago Zavoseanos came down from the mountains, and shouted to us from the hill on the other side of the path of death. He said he wanted to talk, and asked if we would allow a party made up of his more civilized felines to visit us and put a proposal forward.

We finally agreed that ten felines would be allowed into Cat City to talk. They did not know of our water tunnel at the time, and we did not give anything away. Sadly, not one of the party got across the path of death alive. Without exception they were all flattened, not having the sense to wait until the path was clear to cross.

Zavoseanos raged at us for a whole day from the top of that hill. Because he could see humans in the beasts with round legs, he accused us of setting up the humans to kill his delegation. He would not be pacified; he threatened us with all sorts of terrible revenge. His final words before he departed summed up his total abhorrence of the death of his delegation, and in one way gave us an insight to the way this so called King thinks.

He screamed at us, "Your friends have flattened my people, and left them there. They do not even want to eat them. What sort of animals kill, and then do not eat their kill"? That was the end of the proposed talks.'

Nicos shook his head sadly, the memory of the disaster still clear in his mind. After a moment's contemplation he continued, 'Now thanks to our recent arrival Fluffy, we have another chance to talk. If we are to gain peaceful co-existence with the mountain cats, this time there must be no mistake, we must at least give the talks a chance. We must get our views across immediately; these cats from the other side will need training if they are to be given the freedom of the shore-side.'

He paused for a moment. 'We must not allow free access without some reciprocal form of agreement. Therefore I recommend that all initial talks take place on the other side of the path of death.'

A murmur of approval rippled through the gathered throng. Nicos had finished his speech so sank down onto his belly, his head stretched out on his forelimbs, his eyes closed as he rested. A hubbub of conversation rose from the crowd. The thought of mixing with the wilder element from the other side had an air of excitement about it. The older cats however urged caution.

Mario rose on his haunches, 'That will be all for now,' he said authoritatively, 'but if any of you have doubts about the coming talks, give me your objections now. I assure you,' his face took on a serious air. 'No concessions will be made whatsoever if the other side is not honest and totally straight forward in their intentions. They must be totally prepared to stand by the rules that we live by on this side.'

The crowd roared their approval. Old Nicos opened one eye at the noise, grinned knowingly and closed it again. All the cats started dispersing chattering noisily as they made their way back to the tourist area in small groups. The central figures of the shore-side hierarchy remained where they were for the time being. 'Where is your companion Avoula?' Mario asked.

I jumped to my feet, suddenly remembering my sons. No need to worry, they were sound asleep, draped all over Avoula. The sound of my call brought them bounding to my side, their noses nuzzled me to allow them to suckle. I walked over their probing heads and guided Avoula to the presence of Mario. She stood a little apprehensively in front of him, her nervousness making her purr quiver as she said, 'You want me?'

'Are any of your friends on the other side of the path of death at the moment?'

'Yes, Fluffy's guard is at the top of that hill,' she answered truthfully. 'Her safety is their concern on the other side of the path of death.'

Mario frowned for a moment. The realization that the enemy had made allowances to ensure the safety of one of his subjects would need time to sink in properly. He shook himself free of the feeling. 'You have safe conduct to take a message to them, and then return immediately,' he said with an air of pomposity, and then continued, 'Tell them that today we will form a group of felines on this side, whose first duty will be to join a similar group on that side to start preliminary talks. I confirm that I hope these preliminaries will lead to a meeting between me and Zavoseanos. The final outcome will depend on we two finding common ground on which to form a basis of unity.'

He paused mulling over his dictat. 'Tell them also, that I concur with Zavosena's orders that there must be no fighting Toms in the discussion group, and that the group must be made up of motherly females.'

He turned to Achilleas, 'Take her through the tunnel, and wait there for her to return.'

Andreas and the rest of the escort group listened carefully to Avoula's words. Her speech was halting, caused by the need to catch her breath after the exertions of the climb.

'I must return quickly,' she added, having gasped out her message.

'Miros, do you understand all of what Avoula has said?' Andreas pointed the question at a young Tom who had been listening intently to Avoula.

Miros confirmed that he understood completely, and then with a nod from his leader bounded lithely down the hill into the surround brush, relieved to be active once more.

Achilleas escorted Avoula back into Cat City and had just stretched out to catnap with his pal Mario, when a terrible commotion coming from the edge of the city disturbed them.

Both Achilleas and Mario sprang to their feet, prepared for immediate action.

What is it?' Mario shouted as a young Tom broke into view surrounded by a loudly chattering group of youngsters, and a distraught female heavy with kittens.

'Two mountain cats have got across the path of death further up the tourist area; they are running amok amongst the cafes.'

The young Tom paused for breath, 'Lala here tried to scold them and make them behave, but they just roughed her up quite unnecessarily.'

'I'll sort this one out!' Achilleas made to race away as he spoke.

'No, hold hard Achilleas!' Mario halted him. 'You are needed here. Send a group of young felines to bring them this way, we will make an example of them; then they can run the gauntlet of the path of death again.'

Achilleas quickly dispatched a mixed gender group to sort out the problem, and drag the perpetrators back to the city for punishment.

'Can you imagine that?' Achilleas voiced his exasperation. 'Going to all that trouble to get us to talk to them, and then allowing two of their young Toms to cross the path of death; can they be serious?'

Mario grinned widely at his friend's outrage.

Achilleas frowned saying, 'I don't think it's funny!'

'No my old friend,' Mario pacified him. 'It just occurred to me; here we are thinking we are on the road to peace, when all the time there are probably hundreds of mountain cats running around the hills out there, who haven't a clue as to what is going on. Ironic, isn't it?'

Achilleas lightened up, a grin splitting his face, 'I hadn't thought of it that way,' he said sheepishly.

An hour later the air was rent by terrible screeches and caterwauling. The battle group that Achilleas had dispatched was gradually forcing the interlopers towards Cat City. The inhabitants formed a great circle within which to detain and hold them securely, until a decision had been made concerning their punishment

High on the hill, Andreas watched the drama unfolding before him. 'There's something going on down there,' he said, to no-one in particular.

The two young mountain Toms broke cover as their tormentors forced them through the brush. They burst from the brushwood into the circle, and as they frantically searched for a way out, the circle closed around them.

Realising that they were well and truly outnumbered, the two young mountain Toms shrank to the ground, ears laid back, all defenses primed for the final attack.

Andreas, watching intently from the other side, read the situation immediately. Whatever was going to happen to the young mountain cats, he could not just sit there and watch it happen. He sprang to his feet shouting as hard as he could, 'Mario, Mario,' all the time hoping his voice would carry across the noise of the path of death, and reach the ears of those below him.

Those who heard the frantic shout turned in that direction. Mario had heard, and shouted at his subjects, 'Quiet!'

As a hush descended, he turned his face upwards towards Andreas. The young mountain cats seeing the face of one of their territorial Toms, grinned with relief.

'Let me have them Mario,' Andreas called. 'Do not punish them for being ignorant, they do not know what is happening, they do not know that we talk of peace.'

The two young Toms glanced at each other, disbelief in their eyes. Mario glanced at them at that moment, and seeing the astonishment in their eyes knew that these two young cats were only guilty of doing what scores of Trods had done before them.

'Escort them through the tunnel!'

Mario's sudden loud order caught Achilleas off guard. 'I vote we give them a good beating first,' he growled, and was instantly supported by the surrounding throng.

Old Nicos spoke up, 'No, no;' he appealed to the crowd, and then as all eyes turned on him he continued, 'you cannot hope to have successful peace talks if you have just given a severe beating to a couple of young Toms who know nothing of what is afoot.'

His words quelled the belligerence of Achilleas's supporters. Still scowling, they dropped their gaze and deferred to the superior wisdom of old Nicos. Mario repeated his order to Achilleas, adding, 'Make sure they reach the other side safely.'

The crowd pressed around the entrance to the tunnel as Achilleas indicated to the two young cats where they should go. They edged cautiously into the tunnel still prepared to fight should the need arise.

'Up here,' Andreas shouted as they burst into the sunlight again on the other side. They scrambled swiftly up the hill, and rubbed their ears against Andreas's flanks. Andreas was in no mood for platitudes, and it showed in his stern attitude.

'I've got a job for you two scoundrels,' he said tersely. 'How many of your group is still poised to cross the path of death?'

'Very many,' the nearest one replied cautiously.

'Then both of you go quickly,' Andreas urged. 'Tell those that you meet to come and join me here with all haste. Assure them that there is a possibility of peace, this may be our prize after all these years.'

Still not understanding the enormity of their new knowledge, the young Toms streaked away to do as they had been bidden.

Nicos, who had watched from the other side, had to ask Mario what was going on because he could not see events clearly. He nodded his wise old head as he took in Mario's description of the action on top of the hill. He was now fully confident that Andreas at least was determined that nothing should interfere with these talks.

When all the excitement had subsided, Mario called, 'Quiet!'

He waited for the buzz of conversation to stop, and then began. 'All of you must decide who the four felines are going to be who will act as the shore-side delegation. You must pick them from all of the females in our city who are mothers, regardless of how young or how old. I think it would be best if you choose those who have just weaned a brood, they will not be disturbed by the needs of their young and the attention of Toms during their rest period.'

Nicos opened one eye and interrupted, saying, 'May I speak to the mothers when they are chosen?'

'Sure Nicos,' Mario answered, not in the least bothered by the old Toms interruption. He turned back to the crowd, 'We will meet again after we have fed tomorrow morning.'

As the crowd dispersed I looked around. 'Avoula,' I called, suddenly realising that we had only fed from the surrounding bushes. She mewed at me from where she was sitting with my three young Toms. 'Come along!' I ordered, it is well past time for us to eat.

She fell in behind me obediently, patiently accepting the frolicking little demons who were my sons. They were getting more boisterous day by day. The time was fast approaching when I would start cuffing and scolding them whenever they tried to suckle.

This evening we had enough time to be selective about where we ate, and soon Avoula was in awe at the splendour that was the tourist area. Never had she seen so many happy humans of all kinds and languages enjoying themselves, and being so generous. Because she is a meek and obedient female, the humans soon began to like her. Some of them commented on her appealing round eyes and open face. Most of them noticed that she was not a young cat any more, and before the evening ended, Avoula had allowed quite a few friendly hands to stroke her.

Finally, absolutely bloated by the handouts she could eat no more. I lay down beside her, and together we watched my three sons practicing their begging techniques; who could resist them? Their baby faces looking upwards without fear were too much for the average human diner to resist. They too were soon full to bursting.

On the way back to Cat City the kittens became quieter at every step. All of us in fact, were suffering the effects of a long tiring day; not to mention very full bellies.

As soon as we reached the bushes on my patch, we all fell asleep where our tired bodies first touched the ground. Cat City was bathed in moonlight; it would have been a lovely night for socializing with all the other inhabitants; however they, like us, were also early to bed. Cat City echoed to the sounds of felines living out the day in their dreams.

Early next morning, as a light breeze rustled the leaves on the trees and bushes, Cat City sprang to life. It was much too early to descend upon the shore-side yet, but this start to a glorious day must be celebrated with play and socializing, and generally having a bit of fun at anybody's expense for a couple of hours.

The young kittens of Cat City, after a good night's sleep were up to all sorts of mischief; tormenting their mums and anybody else who was fair game to be on the receiving end of some playful surprises.

None of the territorial Toms were pestered though, they had far more important things to occupy their minds than boisterous youngsters. Any kitten that made the mistake of including a senior Tom in his playfulness got a swift good hiding and a serious lesson in untouchableness.

I noticed four mature females joining company and rubbing their ears against each other in friendly greeting, then stroll away together towards the tourist area. These then were the four mothers that all other occupants of the City had cajoled to represent them in the preliminary talks. Neither I nor Avoula had been approached for our views concerning the selection because of course we were comparative strangers, with little knowledge of the individual personalities that formed the community of Cat City.

My part in what was to take place had already been decided; in human terms I was to be Piggy-in-the-Middle. On one hand I would have to make sure that Zavosena's dearest wish was properly presented by her own delegation, and on the other hand, that my sisters in the Cat City delegation understood how fervently Zavosena wished for a unified solution beneficial for both sides.

I had mused over my job several times, and the sight of four mature females had stirred my brain into action. The full weight of the duties that had been placed on my shoulders was slowly sinking in. Naturally, one of my dearest wishes was that the two sides when they met would become friends very quickly, God knows what I will do if eight females suddenly decide that they can't stand the sight of each other.

I forced the thought out of my mind, 'Think positive,' I urged myself.

Midday found Nicos and his two constant companions hobbling into the City. They dropped down on their bellies in Mario's patch, and rested their old bones for a while.

The four chosen females on seeing Nicos arrive ambled over to Mario's patch and dropped to their haunches at a respectable distance, until the wise one had rested. I too had been told that Nicos wanted to talk to us all before we met with the delegation that Zavosena would send. We did not have long to wait.

The old Tom had a good cat-nap and then started the proceedings by rising on his front legs, whilst remaining comfortably seated on his haunches. Mario and Achilleas remained stretched out their heads lying on their front paws apparently totally at ease; only their eyebrows betrayed the fact that they were alert to everything that was going on.

'Hello ladies,' Nicos purred, having first cleared his throat. The purr was strong for an old Tom, and instantly demanded attention. 'Before you meet with your opposite numbers I would like to tell you about some of the recent history of this Island that we share with our human friends.'

He paused, looking around at the faces in front of him. It was then that he noticed that the inhabitants of Cat City were edging along the ground on their bellies to get closer to the group so that they could hear what was being said. They too had a healthy interest in all that was about to begin. Mario and Achilleas raised their heads and looked around the congregating community, but seeing only curiosity in the intent looking faces relaxed again heads on paws.

Nicos raised his purr slightly, inwardly glad to see the community taking a keen interest in what he had to say; history was passed on this way.

'My father, and his father before him, and now me, have all lived with the same Cypriot family. My forefathers and I grew to understand what humans are, and how they live. Our family associations with humans led to my forefathers and me being called wise-cats. We have not only seen how good humans can be, we have also seen how bad humans can be. All of us shore-side cats have had a long territorial battle to ensure that the barbarian element from the hills do not disturb our way of life. If we were human we would kill to preserve our territory; but we are felines, and nature has provided us with a much more subtle approach to defence and attack. Many of the mountain cats have been killed crossing the path of death. Not one mountain cat has been killed by a shore-side cat. This comes about because of the natural instinct for survival amongst our species. If the other Tom is stronger, and is winning the fight the loser, knowing the superiority of his opponent will concede the fight before any terrible damage is done, it is not our nature to fight to the death. We are imbued with the right territorial instinct and will run away if we are caught in another Tom's territory. We are clever enough however to know that if that Tom is not strong enough to defend his territory, then a hard fight is worth the effort.'

He paused, searching the upturned faces of his audience: 'The point I am trying to make will surprise you. The very humans who feed you, and are so friendly to you, are capable of fighting to the death in their own defence. There are also those humans who will purposefully take another humans territory, and kill each other in their thousands to achieve their territorial aims. This has happened to the people who share this beautiful Island with us. In my great grandfather's time, the two races that populate this Island spilt each-others blood, so now other peoples of the human race have come to this Island to keep the two races from killing each other again. All the time there are talks going on to solve this problem and try and get the two peoples to live together in harmony, because the average people of Cyprus would like total peace.'

He paused for breath again; the effort he was putting into this speech was beginning to tire him but, he went on, determined to finish.

'Over a quarter of a century later, the two races are still kept apart by a great divide. The 'Green Line' is part of that great divide, and is policed by selected nations of the world so that the peoples of this Island will not kill each other again. The whole of the sensible world is trying to help the Cypriots to overcome their differences and form a united Cyprus once more. Nothing is easy, there are many doubts and fears in some people's minds, and only dialogue, and constant effort will help to dissolve the fears of the doubters.'

He turned to me and the four chosen females, 'Now you know what has happened amongst the humans of this Island, you will realize that our problems are as nothing compared with theirs. Just as the humans must break down their divide, so we must abolish the path of death as an obstacle to peace. We must bring the mountain cats into our community, and teach them to survive amongst humans just as we do. That is the task that is at hand. It is a task that we must not let ourselves fail to carry out; for the benefit of all Tom-kind.'

Nicos finished his speech, his old voice beginning to croak. The audience remained silent for a moment, his words still sinking in, then as if by some silent command they all purred loudly, 'Bravo, Bravo Nicos!'

I watched him sink to the ground; his eyes closed as he laid his head along his front paws, and as he dozed off into a catnap his loyal companions stretched out either side of him. I looked at the three of them, and wondered what in the past had created such loyalty between them. My own feelings of deep admiration for this wise old Tom provided the answer to my inner thoughts at that moment: Nicos always put his learnt wisdom to practical use in the service of his species.

Hunger pangs told me that I had not fed for what seemed like hours. A pang of guilt added to the sensation; my sons and Avoula would also be suffering the same need for sustenance. I found Avoula sitting alone in my patch; my sons were nowhere in sight.

'They are young and impatient,' Avoula said. 'They have gone off to hunt by themselves.'

A moment of panic showed in my eyes.

'Don't worry Fluffy,' Avoula assured me gently, 'they are becoming big young Toms now, they are only doing what you have taught them to do, come, I will show you which way they went. They will not stray far from the route you have shown them.'

I followed Avoula, her calm manner reassuring me. We quickly found the young devils tucking into a piece of sausage provided by an old human they had met before. Without hesitation this kind old human included me and Avoula in his generosity. He recognised me as the mother of his three admiring beggars and bought another meal just to ensure that we kept him company. I think he had his own feline friends at home, and was missing them terribly, so we filled that need in his old life, and he showed his gratitude for our company in a practical manner.

We did not return to Cat City immediately. All of us lounged beneath the bushes and trees along the pavements, and stayed close to the water receptacle.

Some young human male tourists were having a great deal of fun in a bar across the street from us. They were playing a game we had watched humans play many times before. When the last ball on the table had disappeared down a hole it caused great howls of appreciation and slapping of hands on backs.

Still laughing loudly, the young men sat side by side on tall stools and proceeded to drink more of the wobbly water that seemed to increase their happiness. We watched them visit another three bars, then disappear into a large building with loud music coming out of it with some human females they had met.

Watching these young humans intent on pursuing the good life, and having a jolly good time, it was hard to believe the words of old Nicos which were still ringing in my ears.

Surely, these humans could not be so happy with each other one day, and then fight each other to the death the next day. If that is what they do, then they are complicated beyond all reason.

My sons broke my reverie; they stirred, yawned widely, and moved to my side rubbing their ears along my flanks. I washed them instinctively, joined by Avoula. Her instincts also forced her to join in a good communal licking session.

After topping up at the water receptacle, we strolled back to Cat City. The revelry of the young humans around us would go on through the night to the early morning, where they got the energy from I do not know.

Two days later, the sun was just about to vanish beneath the hills to the west, when a shout came from the hill overlooking the path of death.

'Mario!' Andreas called loudly. But by the time the sound wave had been diluted by the roaring of the beasts with round legs, it could hardly be heard.

'Mario! Mario!' he meowed, straining his voice harder this time.

Mario raised his head as the faint sound reached his ears.

'Mario, it is me, Andreas.'

Mario moved from his patch and gazed up towards the hill.

'The delegation is here!' Andreas said.

'Are they all adult females?'

'Yes, all of them are mothers.'

'We shall start the talks tomorrow then,' Mario replied, and turning away, effectively brought the shouted discussion to an end.

'Fluffy,' Mario called across to me, 'You will start the talk's tomorrow morning after our delegation has eaten.' He looked around him, 'Where is Achilleas?'

'Here!' came the gruff response, as the ginger body appeared from behind a rock.

Mario grinned at the disheveled appearance of his pal. 'Send a runner to inform Nicos the other side has arrived, and talks will start as soon as we have eaten tomorrow.'

Achilleas obeyed, growling under his breath, annoyed at being disturbed from his catnap.

Cat City began to settle down for the night, little groups of family or friends huddled together for warmth during the coolness of the night. Youngsters all around were enjoying the hour of dusk. This was a time for hiding, and stalking, and pouncing on one another, as they practiced for adulthood.

They played footsy with each other through the lower bushy branches, and then hurtled up the trunk in mock escape, their little claws giving good purchase on the coarse bark of the Carob trees, and the smoother Mimosa.

Gradually all movement ceased, and not a soul could be seen. The brilliant stars; and the full moon illuminated what seemed to be a lifeless patch of trees, bushes, and building rubble. But behind every rock, and every bush, and in every conceivable hidey hole feline life laid sound asleep, safe in the knowledge that they were quite secure in their little haven.

Not so for those on the hill. During their whole lives; be it in daylight or in darkness, they had to be prepared for the rushing attack of a wild dog. For this very reason Andreas had sentries posted everywhere, if he should lose but one of the female delegation; Zavosena would hang his fur out to dry.

Old Nicos arrived at Cat City early next morning. He would not interfere with the work of the delegation of either side, he had said his piece, and that was all that was required of him. His curious nature however, obliged him to be present.

I had gathered the four shore-side mothers around me, and we all awaited an indication from Andreas on the other side that they were prepared to receive us.

'Good luck to all you fine mothers,' Nicos purred. 'Your knowledge and your kind hearts will lead you to arrive at a fair conclusion.'

We all gazed back at him, greatly encouraged by his words.
I suddenly felt Avoula beside me. I was just going to say, 'Look after my sons please,' when she got her word in first, 'my princess has ordered me to stay by your side, so that is what I must do. Anyway,' she added coyly, 'I have grown to love you as a sister.'

Our eyes met as she spoke; In that instant I knew our bond was for life.

My young Toms were off play hunting with other young cats, completely oblivious to what I was doing so I cast my worries about them aside and concentrated on the job at hand as Andréas appeared at the top of the hill.

'We are prepared for you,' he shouted.

The six of us glanced at each other and then confidently entered the tunnel, the great job had begun. A whole new world could open up for us as these first firm steps were taken on the road to peace and harmony.

The eeriness of the tunnel subdued my confident mood slightly. It was not just the rubble on the floor that cast shadows, and made excellent hidey holes for snakes; there seemed to be an overbearing aura of evil that permeated the dark interior.

All six of us burst out into the sunlight our hackles raised as if being chased by demons. We quickly settled down and ran to the top of the hill, to be met by a truly motley throng. Rough looking cats of all colours and sizes gazed at us curiously. Tatty-eared old Toms, scrawny females, and some fierce looking young devils that had never had a brush with civilization, total wildness showed in their aggressive demeanour.

Andreas greeted us warmly, whilst showing he was prepared for a cuff around the ears if we thought him too forward. He pointed out the mountain cat delegation, Androula, Anna, Katarina, and Elena. From our side, I pointed out Soula, Alexia, Zena, and Effi....not the Effi who was my friend Big M this was another female who shared this popular Greek Cypriot name.

Big M had left the scene at Cat City to have kittens. Everyone knew me and Avoula, so the cats that were capable of showing a polite greeting did so, the remainder looked on scowling.

I looked closely at the mountain females; they were terribly alert to every movement, a nervousness, and lack of assurance showed in their actions. Their flanks hung down loosely from their sides, the contours of their ribs clearly visible through skin and fur.

All of them looked instantly ready to dash off after any lizard that broke cover. My instant assessment was that these four mothers were desperately hungry; in fact their bodies indicated that they lived constantly on the verge of malnutrition.

Patches of scabby skin showed through their fur, and not an ear was free of damage. Compared to us lot from Cat City, these poor females were in a dreadfully run down state.

Now the two delegations had met, Andreas, and the rest of his Toms withdrew and gave us space to start our job. It was noticeable however that the wild young Toms amongst his cats gave the comfortable figures of the Cat City females a thorough appraisal. I looked at the sorry state of the four nervous females, and realised that their minds were more concerned with their empty bellies than any conversation that would take place here.

'When did you last eat'? I asked all four of them bluntly.

The question surprised them, and they glanced nervously at each other. Katarina broke the silence, 'I have not eaten for two days.'

This encouraged her friends to speak up,

'Nor me.'

'Me neither'

'Just a small lizard.'

I looked at their sorry haggard faces and made a decision, 'Andreas,' I shouted.

'What's the matter?' he answered, bounded over to our company his face showing he was expecting trouble.

'Your felines have not eaten,' I said firmly, and then continued before he could reply, 'I am going to take them to the shore-side, and these talks will not commence until these four mothers have full bellies.'

All the delegation was now staring at me wide eyed. 'Follow me ladies,' I said insistently, starting of down the hill towards the tunnel.

'You can't do that Fluffy.' The worried voice of Andreas called after us. 'Mario insisted that no mountain cats could enter Cat City before some agreement has been reached.'

'I don't care what Mario said,' I answered tersely. 'These mothers are starving, and I am going to make sure they are fed, before any talks start.'

I strutted confidently down the hill, Avoula alongside me, closely followed by both delegations, four of whom were very apprehensive, but followed my lead hopefully. I shouted to the guard through the tunnel, 'Fetch me Mario immediately!'

Moments later, Mario, with Achilleas close on his heels appeared in the circle of light from the other end. 'What's the matter Fluffy?' He shouted; a hint of worry in his voice.

'I cannot start these talks with females who are dreadfully hungry; they have thoughts for nothing but food,' I answered loudly and firmly. 'I must bring them to the shore-side and make sure that they eat!'

My sternly delivered demand caused some consternation on the other side; Mario's and Achilleas's head movements showed that some discussion was in progress.

'Come on Mario!' I urged. 'It only takes an act of diplomacy, and after all, they are only four very deprived females.'

The head of old Nicos joined the heads of Mario and Achilleas framed in the circle of light. Moments later Mario shouted, 'Bring them through.'

'Follow me ladies,' I ordered.

Only the wise old face of Nicos held a smile of greeting as we regrouped on the Cat City side of the tunnel.

Mario and Achilleas gazed on with dark frowns, as behind them, a throng of inquisitive faces were assembling, some with hostile glares.

'How long will this take?' Mario growled.

The four mountain females cringed from the hostile glares, and the dark frown on Mario's face.

'Don't be afraid ladies,' I tried to reassure them, and then, glaring back at Mario just as hard I said, 'As long as it takes!'

The fire in my eyes visibly startled them all, and they took a pace backwards, knowing full well the damage that can be caused by an angry female. They edged back further, unsure now how to continue. Nicos smiled knowingly and let himself flop down on his belly. The gathered crowd seeing Nicos's act of gentle permission, opened up a pathway through their midst.

'This way,' I said determinedly to those behind me.

They followed obediently, the Cat City females mingling protectively with their less well fed sisters from the other side. Other females in the crowd gasped when they realised just how ill cared for their mountain sisters were.

'Oh the poor things!'

'Nobody should suffer like that'

'You are welcome sisters.'

'Eat well, and stay with us.' Was an example of other expressions coming from the gentler inhabitants of Cat City.

These welcoming gestures from the crowd heartened the mountain females. They raised their cowering bellies from the ground and stood upright raising their tails in response to the warmth of the greeting.

Only the thick headed Toms remained in the background, their dull looking faces showing that all this was way above their range of understanding

'How long will this take?' Mario asked again. 'I must know, I have to answer to the other side.'

I realised his predicament, and showed him so.

'Give me fourteen days to get these females fit and confident, during that time we shall all know how successful this bringing together of two cultures will be.'

His face showed the worry in his mind. He did not want the mountain cat regime accusing him of stealing females.

Avoula, realising his concern tried to reassure him in a quiet gentle manner, 'Zavosena trusts Fluffy,' she said. 'She has put her full trust in her, she knows that nothing untoward will happen to her subjects; that is why she accepted Fluffy as an honest negotiator for both sides.'

Avoula paused, searching Mario's face for some sign of understanding. Not finding it she added, 'I will go through and explain to Andreas, he will send a messenger to Zavosena telling her of Fluffy's decision.' Mario's face lightened visibly.

Andreas watched the drama being acted out below him. He too was worried about the outcome of Fluffy's determined stand.

Mario looked up and saw Andreas watching events keenly, and knew that his worries were similar to his own so he shouted up, 'Avoula is coming through; she will explain what is happening.

Some relief showed on Andreas's face. 'Send her through,' he shouted, running down the hill to the tunnel entrance.

Five minutes later he reappeared at the top of the hill, just as Avoula rejoined my group.

'Very well,' he shouted down, very much at ease again. 'I will get the message to Zavosena immediately.

Mario's face reflected the relief he felt. Both he and Andreas were more than a little aware that the success of these talks relied upon the diplomacy of their leadership as it relied upon my determination that these talks would be a success.

I gave Mario a female grin, and purred somewhat sarcastically, 'There there now, what was all the fuss about?'

He watched me as I led my group away. I glanced back at him victoriously.

I led the group towards the fringe of the tourist area. The mountain females gazed in awe at the multitude of human life stretched along the strip thoroughly enjoying their holiday.

'These people from many of the different countries in the world are our livelihood,' I explained. 'They come here after a year's work to relax and seriously enjoy themselves. Their kindness while they are here feeds us very well. The Cypriot humans who feed and care for the tourists also like to see us around, but not in great numbers, so we have learnt to live by a set of rules that is beneficial to everyone.

I quickly told them of the basic rules, and then sent them on their way in small groups of two; one shore-side female and one mountain female in each group. Avoula stayed by my side as we watched each group disappear.

I kept out of the way so as not to give the impression that I was watching them too closely. By tonight they would either return to me well fed, or very disappointed, and still desperately hungry.

As the last couple slipped from sight, I turned to Avoula.

'Fancy a McDonald's?' I asked, knowing full well that she had no idea what I was talking about. Before she could answer we were pounced on by three black furry bodies who had obviously stalked us to this position.

'You naughty little devils!' I scolded them, cuffing them around the ears with claws retracted. 'Come on then, you can have a McDonalds also,' I said. 'But don't you surprise us like that again.'

A puzzled Avoula tagged on behind; two hours later however, any questions she could have had were completely answered, which was obvious by the look of satisfaction she wore, and the protruding tongue licking her chops clean.

We settled in again at the agreed meeting place, my sons scampered off to find something adventurous to get involved with as darkness descended on the strip. The glowing street lights, and the bright neon lighting of the pubs and clubs cast an appealing glow on the area. Soon the figures of eight bloated females ambled their way back to us. They flopped down worn out, their bellies bulging with the success and excess of their first experience of the tourist area. Without so much as a sound, they all lay stretched out on their sides and fell sound asleep, their bellies rising and falling indicating their inner contentment.

It was late morning the following day before any of us arose. Immediately obvious, was the change that had come over the mountain group. The apprehension had disappeared from their faces; their movements were confident, and not ill at ease.

Noticing their improved manner, I decided that all of us would make this area of scrubland our home for a few days while we became familiar with one another.

As the day moved on, the mountain cats became more amiable, a sure sign that they were comfortable with their situation. Slowly, any differences between us were ironed out, and our association developed from being two separate groups, to a single group developing a real trust in each other.

After a week of good eating the mountain cats began to glow with health. Bodily functions took on a regular routine, and reproductive systems, now better nourished, began to bow to nature's demands.

We returned to Cat City a week earlier than I had at first thought possible, much to the relief of Mario and Andreas.

'Are you succeeding?' Was Mario's first question, and without waiting for an answer continued, 'What demands are they making?'

Katarina, the most comely of the mountain females, gave him his answer with a practical demonstration of where her present feelings were taking her.

Nothing could be more demanding than the insistence of nature in the wild. She strode boldly up to him, and rubbed her ears against his powerful flanks. For a moment Mario looked unsure and edged away, but Katarina was insistent. She continued her affectionate ear rubbing until Mario finally caved in and gave her head a couple of quick licks.

'Does that answer your question?' I said to Mario, grinning at his male flustering.

'The talks are over,' I continued. 'All of us females have become inseparable friends. Without exception we are all in favour of total unification between all of us Cypriot females, and,' I continued more fiercely, 'You Toms will not prevent us from joining together whenever we wish it so.'

From the top of the hill Andreas suddenly realised what had happened as he watched the seductive antics of Katarina.

'Hah- hah,' he yelled, grinning widely. 'Hey Christos, come and see this; look at Katrina breaking down the barriers.'

A sudden commotion from the northern side of the hill caused Andreas and Christos to swing their attention in that direction.

'That is Dimitri,' Christos said as he focused on the cause of the hubbub from the bottom of the hill. Andreas acknowledged his statement, 'It is Dimitri, and he has worked hard to get to Troodos and back, and then dash here.'

Dimitri struggled to the top of the hill surrounded by fellow Trods trying to urge some indication from him as to the reason for his hurried approach. He reached the top gasping for air; the Trods pressed closer, eager to hear his message.

'Zavoseanos will not be coming,' he gasped out. 'Zavosena will represent him when the time is right,' he went on, and then made the reason clear.

'The King is old now, he knows that a journey such as this would be too much for him; therefore, he has insisted that this new friend Fluffy must be trusted in her support of Zavosena's wishes. He has fully endorsed Fluffy as the chief negotiator.'

THE PEACEMAKER.

The shout of glee that emitted as a loud HAH HAH from Andreas, wafted over to the central group in Cat City. All eyes turned upwards to the top of the hill. More than one pair of eyes in Cat City showed concern at the increased number of mountain cats that had gathered under the command of Andreas.

Even though he had dispatched a large number of the itinerant cats back to Zavosena, a large number had been retained to act as couriers. It was this rag tag and bobble of rough looking cats that caused concern to the inhabitants of Cat City because they were made up from the roving gangs who constantly patrolled the other side of the path of death in the hope of dashing across unharmed.

Not all of the mountain cats were as elated as Andreas at Katarina's methods of breaking down barriers. The neutered and the spayed joined the hostile growls coming from the fighting Toms. This was not lost on the shore-side Toms, they had watched keenly from the background, and were perhaps more than a little annoyed that Katarina had chosen the alpha Tom to express her feelings to, without giving any of them so much as a glance.

On the top of the hill Andreas was completely unaware of the bad blood that was beginning to boil in the younger elements of his group, joined by the deprived and dispossessed. His eyes could only see the advantage that Katarina's amorous advances towards Mario had given to these initial talks. 'Christos,' he called to his companion.

'Go to Zavosena and tell her what you have seen here, tell her, it looks as if our mountain mothers have won the day, and much friendship abounds.'

Below them in Cat City, Mario strolled off his patch closely followed by Katarina, who by now was becoming quite brazen with her show of affection. Old Nicos raised an eyelid, and the sides of his mouth curled up in a knowing grin.

Avoula, who had paid no attention at all to Katarina, moved over to Achilleas. After a few short purrs had passed between them, Achilleas escorted her through the tunnel, and waited while she passed a message on to Andreas.

'The mountain mothers will be staying in Cat City now to learn how to be shore-side cats, so that they can teach their mountain sisters how to control the rougher male element of the mountain cats. It is they who will need more instruction in the art of living in civilization.'

'What of Katarina?' Andreas asked with a sly grin.

Avoula caught the meaning in his tone and replied bluntly, 'Katarina will do exactly what nature has decreed female cats are born to do, and so will the others no doubt.'

Andreas accepted her retort Tomfully, and nodded agreeably. 'Maybe it is for the best,' he called after Avoula, who, having said her piece trotted back down the hill to the tunnel. She joined me minutes later, and after a glance at my three sons playing with a group of Cat City youngsters, closed her eyes and enjoyed a catnap with me. The remainder of the day passed on quietly around us.

****

For the next two human months, peace-making duties kept all us females busy. Many more females from the mountain cats joined us for a few days at a time, many of them bringing their young. Civilization was now making inroads beyond the path of death.

All four of the original delegation from the other side became mothers again, and it was noticeable that the majority of the offspring were pure black, and many were a deep ginger in colouring. This meant that the territorial Toms in Cat City, had exercised their prerogative within their own territories, and passed their superior genes on to the next generation.

All of this activity had been keenly watched by the young Toms from both sides, who, as yet had won no territorial recognition. My sons, of course, were now strongly entrenched in the pecking order of their peers, and were happily engaged in all the things that young Toms do; practicing to be old Toms.

Autumn came and the temperature dropped a little, bringing on the first rains of the season. The heavy downpour, and the thunder and lightning were a new experience for this year's brood in Cat City. Young ones scurried for cover everywhere, crawling over each other in panic to escape the pounding rain, and the startling effect of a thunder storm.

Slowly, just like cats everywhere, they realised that they were just wet, and not in any real danger. Their terror quickly changed to playful pawing at the streams of water dropping from bushes, trees, and rocks. Terror however, quickly returned to scar their young minds.

The sun had barely shown the top of its shiny head in the east, when the still dark morning of the next day was shattered by hundreds of loud bangs from the hills overlooking the path of death. Cats everywhere dived for cover. Self-survival became the order of the day. Cats of all colours and sizes clawed at each other in dreadful fear as they sought the safest hiding places. Even the old and experienced felines forced the young out of their places of safety they had reached first. The haunting meows of the kittens mixed with the fearful howls of the adults sounded like a scene from hell.

Old Nicos instinctively dived under a bush close to Mario's patch, then his experience took over, and gradually he relaxed. His long memory trained by years of awareness of the habits of humans began to recall the reason for the bursts of gunfire coming from the hills.

Today was the first day of the hunting season. Macho humans all over the Island donned khaki green camouflage clothing, and began the slaughter of any game creatures that were forced to break cover by the hunters dogs.

It was the time of year for feral cats, and abandoned dogs to run for cover lest they become an inadvertent victim. The ninety thousand partridges released this year to give the shootists some sport would not last long, then it would become the turn of the hares.

Nicos and his fellow elders began reassuring the younger element of the City, and slowly normality returned to the daily life of the inhabitants, although the reaction to cringe to the ground at every burst of gunfire would take some time to disappear.

High on the hill, the first bursts of gunfire brought an instant flurry of action. Most of the cats spread around the hill, and others closer to it, were less than a year old; they had no way of knowing that this annual event was not aimed at them.

Everyone except Andreas and a few adult females, fled away into the surrounding countryside, trying to escape this fearful noise. Inevitably some of the frightened runners became unintentional victims as the dashed from behind a rock or bush in a headlong burst of speed to escape a dog obediently flushing everything from cover.

Standing with Mario and Achilleas, staring up at the commotion on the other side of the path of death, old Nicos wore a worried frown. All of us females involved with the initial peace talks reacted to his worried look with some concern, he had never shown any sign of uncertainty so far in the proceedings. 'What is it Nicos?' I asked.

He did not reply immediately, his eyes remained fixed on the top of the hill, and it was obvious that his mind was working out the effects of the early morning gunfire on the Trods who were totally exposed on the top of the hill.

After a few moments he turned to Mario, and said determinedly, 'You will lose everything Fluffy and her friends have worked for if you don't act immediately. Go up that hill and bring all the Trods who have stayed there into Cat City.'

Mario hesitated, amazement showing in his yellow eyes. He looked at Achilleas as if seeking confirmation that his ears had heard correctly. Achilleas's face remained blank.

'You must do it now Mario,' Nicos urged insistently. 'Otherwise you will be accused of colluding with the humans to break up this effort for peace.'

The old Toms words brought Mario into action; he had not forgotten what Nicos had told them all about Zavoseanos' last attempt at talks. He streaked through the tunnel and up the hill.

Minutes later an entourage of mountain cats led by Andreas followed him back down the hill and into Cat City. Before he entered the tunnel, Andreas had one more order to give, 'Yiorgos my brave friend,' he said, turning to a companion of similar age. 'You must run the human gauntlet with haste, and tell her that those of her subjects who did not run at the first sound of the guns are safe in Cat City.'

Yiorgos smiled at his friend, and without a word obeyed his order.

My friends and I watched Yiorgos dash away, we knew without doubt the reason for his speedy disappearance. We purred with approval at Andreas's swift action to inform Zavosena of the latest crucial news. Approval however was not universal amongst the inhabitants of Cat City.

'There will be more Trods than locals,' a voice growled from the rear of the watching crowd. A few murmurs from the crowd indicated he was not alone in his worries. All of this was not audible to the central cast, who were now involved in greeting the cats from the hill.

The first priority was to get them fed, and then spread them along the fringes of civilization. Fortunately we had a few Trods already trained who would pass on their knowledge to their fellow newcomers.

****

Yiorgos bounded through the rocks and scrub overlooking Germasogia, Agio Tychonas, and Amathus. He was heading for the high hills overlooking the huge Dam of Germasogia. This was the only source of water Zavosena and her people had before the rains came; now, pockets of water appeared everywhere.

It was late in the evening when Yiorgos staggered into the camp almost in a state of collapse from his mighty efforts. Several times the spatter of buckshot into the bushes he had just vacated had added a burst of extra speed to his flight. He did not know it, but his light tabby colouring and his white underbelly could be mistaken for a hare by the not so careful hunters in the vicinity. Trigger happy hunters rarely took a second glance. Fortunately he had escaped the accidental death toll of the day, which was a good omen considering what was at stake.

The camp was in an uproar. One of the young Toms who had run from the hill at the first sound of gunfire was causing great outbursts of growls from the crowd with the lie that Mario had called the humans in to once more break up the attempt to unify. Not all the crowd were convinced, they were a few years older, and had witnessed the annual kill many times.

The younger element given strength of purpose by those who had an axe to grind held the floor. Zavosena looked on scowling darkly, listening to all that transpired, but not wanting to believe it.

'By now they will have killed Andreas and all those who stayed with him,' the young Tom howled, continuing to whip up the crowd.

'No cat has ever been killed by the other side,' scowled Zavosena. 'If what you say is true then there has been trickery at work here.'

Her growls were drowned by those who would prefer to believe the worst of the shore-side cats.

This was the scene Yiorgos burst in on.

'Silence!' roared Zavosena, as Yiorgos collapsed beneath her throne.

'Silence; all of you!' she glared sternly at the meowing crowd.

Her body guards began to edge forward menacingly, causing a hush as they glared into the crowd. No-one wanted to be singled out, and made an example of with a swift drubbing from the scowling Toms.

Yiorgos slowly regained his breath.

'Speak, my brave Yiorgos,' Zavosena ordered respectfully.

'Mario has saved your subjects majesty,' Yiorgos gasped,' He personally ran up the hill and took Andreas and all the others into the safety of Cat City.'

The crowd started murmuring as they heard the words of this highly respected territorial Tom.

'Stop that young Tom!' Zavosena screamed to her bodyguard as the slim shape of the young Tom tried to sneak stealthily away. 'Hold him!' She ordered. 'I will deal with him later.'

The young Tom was not going to give in quietly: 'They are stealing all the females,' he screamed at the crowd. 'Not one of us young Toms have been included in the groups visiting Cat City.'

Silence descended on the scene, they all waited for Zavosena's reaction to this disobedient outburst.

'Is that right Yiorgos?' She asked after a moment's thought.

'Yes majesty,' Yiorgos replied, then explained: 'I must remind you that the original agreement forbade the inclusion of fighting Toms in the group, that rule is still in force.'

'That is so,' confirmed Zavosena. 'But that rule was applied to the discussion group, and all messages brought to me proved that the delegation was successful, and that both groups had become firm friends. We also heard of how Katrina broke the ice with Mario.'

Zavosena lapsed into deep thought again. Minutes later she raised her head, her face showing she had reached a momentous decision.

'My brave Yiorgos,' she began. 'Tonight you are exhausted, and need rest, but early tomorrow you must go back to the hill, and there you will advise Mario to prepare himself for my arrival.'

A buzz of excitement rippled round the crowd; she had to call for silence before continuing.

'The talks have gone very well so far, but it is time they were taken a stage further. Already some of our females have mates in Cat City, and will have kittens that will belong to both sides. We must now bring fraternization onto an equal footing.' She glanced towards the young troublemaker surrounded by her bodyguards.

'I hear your words, and I understand how you young Toms must feel. Tomorrow you will return with Yiorgos, and from this moment on you are his Lieutenant. Your lie is forgiven, because you had assumed the worst, and not waited to find out the truth. In future you will be more cautious with your accusations.' She gave the young Tom a stern look as she finished her remonstration.

The young Tom stood dazed. To be scolded and then promoted in the same breath was too much for his one track mind to grasp all at once.

'Thank you majesty,' he uttered totally amazed.

'You are dismissed Yiorgos, sleep well, and you also young Tom; now you may go with your leader.'

With Zavosena's words ringing in his ears, the young Tom followed Yiorgos to a quiet spot, and settled in for the night.

'What is your name?' Yiorgos asked pleasantly, as he wriggled until he was comfortable in some dry earth between two large stones.

'They call me Vassos, they say my father's name was Vassos, and he disappeared on the path of death at the time of my birth.'

Yiorgos raised his head, grinning at the young Toms fervent explanation of his name.

'Well young Vassos,' he said. 'Your life has changed forever as of this moment. You are no longer a young Tom fighting for a position amongst your peers; your turn has come early. Realise this and act accordingly, everything you do from this moment on is in the public eye. Be brave and honest, and watch carefully.'

He laid his head back down on his front paws, and was asleep in seconds, leaving young Vassos to ponder over the night events until he too drifted off into a catnap.

Early next morning they stood before Zavosena. 'I shall set out in two days,' she informed Yiorgos, 'the human sportsmen will have begun to tire of their annual sport. Travel safely old friend, and teach your young protégé well,' she added, blessing him with a rare smile.

It was barely light as they made their cautious descent of the big hill overlooking the human dam. They stopped half way down; the light had improved sufficiently to be able to scan the edge of the waters of the dam on the western side.

They barely gave a glance to the few humans standing like statues facing the water with long poles in their hands; they were in no danger from them. Yiorgos's head suddenly stopped its searching motion as his eyes caught sight of four humans spread well apart, but all walking in the same direction.

Several dogs coursed the ground in front of the men, and successfully made a bird break cover. The bird's' dash for safety was short lived; seconds later it hung from a hunter's belt like some ghastly trophy of unequal combat.

When the coast was clear, Yiorgos led the way around the lake to the great buttress of concrete that held the water trapped. After gazing carefully down the valley on the dry side of the dam, he encouraged Vassos to run with him to the eastern end of the valley.

By midday they were approaching the path of death. This was a highly populated area, and most human families kept a dog. Several times they were startled and had to run up a tree to safety. Yiorgos knew that these domestic dogs only chased a cat for fun; unlike the deserted members of their breed, who were deadly serious about chasing a feline, and had but one purpose in mind.

One of the domestic dogs did manage to bowl Yiorgos over, but retreated howling with pain as Yiorgos's fore claws scarred his nose. He chased the fleeing hound, and for good measure sank his teeth into a quivering rump muscle.

Vassos got caught up in the excitement, and for a few moments clung to the hapless hounds back as it galloped along crying pitifully for its human friend to come and rescue it.

'Our first defence together,' Yiorgos grinned. Vassos raised his head and yowled at nothing in an act of sheer exuberance. The thrill of the chase, and the adrenaline charge made him strut with self-approval; this only served to make Yiorgos grin more widely. He was beginning to enjoy the youthful exuberance of this brave young Tom.

They were still highly excited as they reached the top of the hill overlooking Cat City. The City below them appeared to be deserted; it was obvious the inhabitants were away feeding.

Yiorgos decided they should rest after their rigorous journey, and inform all concerned of their news at first light tomorrow. The fact that not a soul could be seen in Cat City relieved him; this meant that both sides were feeding together.

Neither Yiorgos nor Vassos had missed the many pairs of youthful eyes that stared at them from the surrounding hillocks to the north of the hill, and to the east and west. They made no attempt to approach the two senior Toms; such an attempt would be an affront, and could result in a sound beating.

Vassos had noticed the curious glances and the low growls. His closeness to Yiorgos had confused them. Why was Vassos, himself a junior Tom, accepted by such a senior Tom as Yiorgos?

Yiorgos cast his eyes around the curious young faces.

'Spread out you lot!' He ordered. 'Cover every access point to this hill, and alert myself or Vassos if any humans come too close.'

The young cats did as they were told immediately, even more aware now that by some means Vassos had suddenly risen to a position of some importance.

The bang of the guns began to fade as darkness covered the land. Only the growls of the beasts with round legs served to remind everyone that danger was not too far distant.

'Andreas! Hey Andreas,' Yiorgos shouted as he saw his old friend come into view next morning. Andreas caught the faint sound of his name, as did the other early risers; as one their heads swung towards the hill.

'Yiorgos my friend, you are back so soon,' Andreas yelled back, but the offshore breeze and the growls from the path of death drowned his voice.

Andreas turned to Mario, 'I will go across to meet Yiorgos: he will have important things to tell me.'

Andreas bounded up the hill to greet his friend, their heads banged together in friendly greeting. After he had listened to Yiorgos, he went back through the tunnel and approached Mario and Achilleas. Mario recoiled slightly at the news that Zavosena herself would now join the ever expanding group of females at the unifying talks.

'I would like to talk to Yiorgos myself,' Mario said. 'Bring him through the tunnel and we will all go for our morning feed together whilst we talk.'

'He has a young fighting Tom with him, and by the looks of it the young cat is his lieutenant,' warned Andreas.

Mario thought for a moment, gazing up at the hill to the two faces staring down at them. 'Bring him too,' he said magnanimously.

Yiorgos, visibly surprised at being brought into Cat City, was even more surprised when he found himself chewing vigourously on a sausage at the nearest café. Young Vassos must have thought he was in cat heaven; a waiter had thrown him a handful of scraps from the night before. Still in a state of shock, but belly full, he followed his seniors back to Cat City.

Yiorgos quickly warmed to Mario as they sat down to digest their plentiful breakfast. He related all that Zavosena had decreed to the whole group sitting in Mario's patch; he diplomatically left out the part played by the eager young Vassos, knowledge of which would do nothing of any good to anyone.

Vassos breathed a sigh of relief. In the light of present events, his pathetic eagerness to think the worst shamed him somewhat.

Not all however, was sweetness and light. In the background the young Toms of Cat City were watching Vassos; amongst them were three very fine looking young Toms. Every one of these young Toms knew that Vassos was a fighting Tom who had not yet reached territorial status. Their curiosity verged on open hostility.

They were not the only envious and openly hostile eyes watching the proceedings. High on the hill several more pairs of eyes watched intently; they also glared with the look of envy that could quickly turn into hostile action.

A murmur of discontent reached Mario's ears. He broke off his discussion, and turned in the direction of the sound of bitterness. All the young Toms flattened to the ground under the gaze of the alpha Tom, but not before Mario had noticed the sleek black hides of his sons.

'Fluffy!' He turned as he spoke my name. 'There's trouble brewing over there,' he indicated the bushes. 'Your sons are among them, sort it out will you.'

He turned back to the discussion group, having delegated the problem to me. I too had heard the growls of antagonism against Vassos, but was somewhat surprised that myself, and not Achilleas had been ordered to "sort it out". Rising to my feet, I strode determinedly to face the young devils.

My sons looked at me warily; they still remembered the cuffs around the ears, and the savage scowls which encouraged their independence when I completed their weaning process.

'You lot be quiet while these talks proceed,' I ordered them sternly. One of my sons looked at me cheekily, 'Why is that young fighting Tom with them?' he asked, a sullen curl to his lip affecting his outburst.

'I don't know,' I said truthfully but firmly, then added, 'But he is there, and he is accepted by all the territorial Toms, so that means he has been ordered to be a part of the group, and the only person who could give him such an order is his leader, Princess Zavosena. So you lot hold back, have patience, wait and see what the outcome of the proceedings turn out to be. You know you will be told of events as they occur.'

My eyes scanned the young faces in front of me, their juvenile expressions gave me no reassurance, these young devils were eager for a fight, and as with all young Toms they sought every opportunity to achieve territorial dominance above their peers and their weaker elders.

'Do not try anything against the territorial Toms,' I warned, very serious now because I could foresee a major upheaval looming. 'They will surely unite against you, and drive you from the territories surrounding Cat City. They will give you a severe beating, and thereafter repeat the beating any time you dare to draw near, and that means banishment,' I emphasized, my eyes boring into any eye that dared to hold my gaze for any more than a second.

Finally, I turned on my heels and walked away from them, my only hope; that my words had been strong enough to avert a disaster, if only for the time being.

Mario glanced at me as I returned to the meeting, his eyes rested on me momentarily, taking in my worried expression, before returning his gaze to Yiorgos.

'Then she will be here tomorrow, regardless of the dangers of the journey?' he asked Yiorgos seeking final confirmation of Zavosena's arrival.

'The sounds of the guns are not so frequent now,' Yiorgos answered. 'So by tomorrow morning she may consider it safe enough to start her journey.'

'How many will come with her?' Mario asked, his practical mind considering how many extra mouths there would be to feed.

'Herself and her bodyguards, with a small number of fighting Toms to face any dangers on the way, other cats are bound to follow, because they always have done so.'

'What kind of cats are her bodyguards?'

'Yiorgos noticed the edge on Mario's purr as he asked the question.

'Well there are six of them, and they have been chosen more for their ability to form a defensive ring around her to fight off any assailant, rather than work out a strategy. By that I mean that they are totally obedient to her wishes alone, and will defend her to the death.'

'So that means they have a totally aggressive manner?' Mario asked, his eyes emphasizing the gravity of the question.

'Totally aggressive,' Yiorgos confirmed. 'But also totally passive until ordered to defend.'

The cautious answer did not give Mario the reassurance that it would be safe to allow Zavosena's bodyguards into Cat City without causing an all-out war.

He glanced over to the bushes where the young Toms had congregated. Heads ducked down out of sight as his glance covered the area.

He thought deeply for a moment, then, reaching a decision, he raised his head and spoke firmly, 'I cannot allow the bodyguards into

Cat City. You know, and I know; that could be all that is needed for our young Toms to react violently; the bodyguards must stay on the hill. My felines are now familiar with yourself, Andreas, and Vassos, you three will stay at her side if that makes her feel safer.'

Yiorgos and Andreas exchanged glances. Andreas, as the senior Tom now took over, 'That is very agreeable of you, a very good decision.'

He paused momentarily, 'I think it would be best if she is aware of this decision before she arrives here.'

Mario nodded his agreement. Andreas turned to Yiorgos, 'Can I use your lieutenant?' He asked out of politeness.

'Surely you can,' Yiorgos replied.

Andreas called Vassos closer and gave him detailed orders to carry to his princess, 'Now make sure that she understands the problem here, but don't overdo it. Impress upon her though, that just as there is on our side, there are also some more aggressive and warlike in the shore-side community, and it is best that we do not give them reason to tear apart the good work that has been done by the delegations of both sides.'

The face of Vassos showed how proud he felt at that moment. He, a junior Tom had been entrusted with a diplomatic chore of great importance. He had to convince Zavosena of the wisdom of the decision that had been made. His feeling of pride was not lost on the senior Toms.

They grinned knowingly at each other as Vassos bounded eagerly towards the tunnel. He burst through at the other side at the gallop, streaked up the hill and disappeared over the rim. What the senior Toms below did not see was that Vassos was immediately surrounded by the young Toms of the Trods who had no fear of stopping a fellow Tom recently elevated. They, not knowing the reason for his promotion, still thought him an equal.

'What is going on?' One savage little beggar snarled straight into Vassos's face. 'Why are we still excluded from everything that is happening? Why are we not invited to feed, and to mix with their females, just as they mix with ours?'

Vassos looked the angry young Tom in the eyes. His breathing was still a bit laboured from the rush up the hill, but he forced himself to speak with authority,

'Stand back, all of you,' he advised with forceful tone. 'I am taking an official message to our princess. Be warned, all I have to do at this moment is scream 'ambush', and a hundred cats will descend upon you, and many of them will be your own people.'

The savage little beggar recoiled slightly at this fierce delivery. A less aggressive young Tom whined, 'But we don't know what is going on, we are not included in anything, and why have you suddenly become so important?'

'Your problems are known, Zavosena herself will be here tomorrow to ensure your inclusion in this great effort for unification. Now, out of my way, and let me be gone.' His revelation silenced them all momentarily, and by the time their astonishment abated Vassos had bounded away to complete his mission; his self-importance now increased hundredfold now that he had exercised his authority.

Such was his determination to deliver his important message, that he had become a little careless in making sure the ground was clear before boldly dashing across open spaces. The result of this eagerness almost cost him his life. A shot from a hunter, who mistook his flight for that of a hare, spattered him with lead pellets.

Fortunately the wounds were superficial, but had drawn blood. One pellet had shattered the cartilaginous flesh of his tail, causing it to droop in an unsightly manner. He picked himself up and struggled on with his mission reaching the encampment before light failed that day.

He looked a sorry sight as he staggered into the camp and collapsed before his princess. She gazed down at his bloodstained fur, and recognised the young Tom she had promoted.

'Tend to him!' She called loudly to a group of females.

They dashed to do her bidding. For several minutes Vassos lay gasping as the females licked the congealed blood from his fur.

'None of his wounds are serious,' an old female assured Zavosena, then added sympathetically, 'But his tail will never stand straight again.'

Zavosena looked down at her young subject, and with regal gentleness said, 'My brave young Vassos.'

Her tone brought Vassos painfully to his feet.

'No young Tom,' she insisted, you lay there and relate your message.'

Vassos lay down, gratefully acknowledging her command. His heart swelled with the importance of a young Tom who knew he had done a good job, and would be remembered for it.

Should he live to realise it, his deed was now carved in stone in the minds of all who looked on at this moment. The memory of Vassos and his brave dash would be elevated in the feline world to equal the huge effort of Leonidas and his great run, celebrated the world over by runners who copy this classic effort.

Vassos relayed his message, purring clearly now, leaving his princess in no doubt as to the great importance of his words.

'You have given me plenty to think about, my brave Vassos,' she said, and then turning away called, 'Chistos.'

The mature Tom leapt to his feet, surprise etched across his features.

'Yes majesty,' he answered, still taken aback by her sudden demanding call.

'You are well rested now, and quite fit to make a night journey. Make haste to Cat City and tell them that Vassos has succeeded in his orders. You must then tell them that in the light of what has happened to Vassos I shall delay my journey one day. Off you go!'

Christos disappeared quickly down the steep slope of the large hill, his night journey safe from the loud guns, and the flushing dogs that fed them.

'And you my brave warrior,' she smiled at Vassos. 'You find a choice spot and rest peacefully, you are now part of my closest company, and are entitled to the rewards of the brave; sleep well.

Four young females escorted Vassos to a readily prepared nest, and did not retire until their charge was sound asleep. He slept well, but like all mammals closely associated with humans his body actions showed that part of his mind was recreating scenarios from recent events, and he was reliving some of them. Even when his body was still, it may be presumed that the pride he felt at his sudden promotion came flickering back to please him. Maybe his subconscious even went even further and told him that providing he obeyed the rules, and did not overstep the pecking order, his future was assured. Maybe very soon his offspring would be boasting, "My father is the great Vassos of Germasogia". Certainly the females he sired would be the creators of the new generations, for it is they who dominate the day to day life in the world of the feline.

Vassos awoke early next morning. He jumped up from his nest of bracken stretching and yawning widely. He tested his limbs; surprisingly, apart from a few aches and pains, he felt quite fit; he did however, feel a pang of regret when he observed the angle at which his tail was bent. He raised it high in the air, but the tip determinedly bent over like a handle.

'A battle scar to be proud of,' an old female informed him, smiling with affirmation.

'Yes, it is,' he purred, his pang of self-pity forgotten. He wagged it a few times, and found its floppy nature amusing; and then, with his back end confidently swaying slightly from side to side, he walked over and stood before Zavosena.

A smile cracked her face as she viewed his bent tail. Then, remembering her position she quickly wiped the smile from her face.

'You have something to say Vassos?' She asked pleasantly.

'Yes majesty,' he answered. I request that you give me leave to return to Yiorgos. My duties are with him, by your royal command.'

'Are you fit enough for such a journey?' She asked; her face creased with concern.

'Yes majesty, the wounds are not severe, they are just scratches.'

'Then you can take a message to Andreas: Tell him that my bodyguards will stay outside Cat City while I introduce myself and get to know a few cats in the shore-side community. But I foresee a time when my bodyguards and also the young fighting Toms must be included in the unifying process. We cannot have friendship blossoming among a favoured few at the expense of those who have not reached a sociably acceptable level in the feline hierarchy. That would surely be a recipe for great unrest.'

'I will make haste with your message majesty, and make sure that Andreas realises how wise it was of you to give this matter further thought.'

He had disappeared down the hill before he could see Zavosena's reaction to his tactful acceptance of her orders.

'My word,' Zavosena murmured watching his swift departure. 'He is learning quickly!'

Vassos was only intent upon showing everyone that his injuries were not bothering him at all. That was the brave intention he intended to give. In truth his body was very sore, but his rapid rise from fighting Tom made him ambitious, and he had no wish to let a bit of soreness and a bent tail hinder his momentum on the sure path to territorial Tom.

A few hunters were scattered around the country areas of his route, but he was well acquainted with his path now and was well practiced at making full use of any bit of cover. By mid-afternoon he stood before the entrance to the tunnel attracting the guard's attention.

'Come through,' yelled the guard; giving him a straight stare as he broke into daylight.

'I am Vassos, and I have a message for Andreas.'

'I know who you are!' The guard answered tersely, but making no effort to delay him.

As he reached the group, young eyes suddenly picked him out as he joined the main body of leaders.

'How did he get through without us seeing him,' the savage young beggar snarled. 'Why didn't he stop with us first?'

Vassos is an important Tom now,' the less aggressive Tom explained. 'His place is with Andreas and Yiorgos, and he obviously carries orders from Zavosena. He would not wish to confront us again with such an important mission to complete. Hey! Look at his tail, it is bent over at the end, something has happened to him, that bend is not natural.'

Andreas and his friends were just as surprised to see Vassos. They listened attentively as the young Tom relayed Zavosena's orders word for word. Old Nicos spoke to Vassos as he finished, 'What hit you my son?' He asked.

'There was a human and a big bang, and suddenly I was blown over by the force from the bang, and my tail was broken, Vassos replied very respectfully. To be approached by a Tom of such seniority and wisdom was certainly an accolade.

'Ah these young human hunters,' sighed Nicos. 'They are so eager to blood themselves they care little for the target. You are a brave young Tom to return so quickly after such an encounter.'

'Zavosena agreed that it was my duty to return,' Vassos answered politely.

Nicos smiled at the young Toms eagerness to be gracious in his presence. With the smile still on his face, he returned his attention to the leaders.

'You know,' he said deliberately. 'It would be a good idea to give all these young Toms on both sides something to keep them occupied.'

Mario and Andreas nodded in agreement, immediately realising that this was common sense. 'What do you suggest?' Mario asked.

'Well,' Nicos started thoughtfully. 'The devil soon makes work for idle minds, so if you want to keep the young Toms out of mischief at this very crucial time, why not consider giving them an adult job that they are mentally and physically capable of doing.'

'Such as?'

This time it was Andreas who posed the question.

Nicos gazed at Andreas, and then answered, 'Send your young Toms to meet Zavosena, and assist the escort group. It will take them off the top of that hill for a couple of days, and make them a part of everything that is going on. Send young Vassos here as their leader, it is a good opportunity to give him another job to do; he has certainly proved himself to be reliable.'

Andreas's face brightened up; this was a sound idea; keep the young devils occupied.

'What about our young Toms?' Mario asked. 'What can we possibly give them to do?'

'Ah-hah!' Nicos chortled. 'Don't keep them here dreaming up mischief, send them over the other side with a real job to do.'

'What!' Mario looked dumbfounded, and the expression on his face drew a grin from Nicos as he expressed his astonishment at the old sage's ideas. 'Send our young Toms over there with their young Toms; that's asking for a fight.'

'No-no it isn't,' insisted Nicos. 'Send our young Toms into the hills overlooking the travel route. Their job will be to run down and tell Zavosena if any danger is imminent, that will also serve to assure her of our best intentions.'

All eyes scanned the wise old face in front of them. Nicos ceased speaking, and placed his head on his paws as if to say, 'There you are I have done my bit, now you lot set about putting it into action.'

Andreas reacted first, 'Let's go,' he ordered Yiorgos and Vassos. You stay here Christos, just in case one of us is needed here.'

They disappeared into the tunnel, and those below waited for them to reappear climbing the hill. The watchers in Cat City took note of the body movements of Andreas as he rammed his orders home to his young Toms. They had been devouring a large whip snake that it had taken ten of them to overcome.

As soon as Andreas paused, they fell upon it again tearing large chunks out of it ravenously. They made it plain: First priority hunger, second priority sleep, third priority orders. Andreas continued giving his orders watching the primitive sight in front of him, 'Vassos will lead you, and you will be ready to leave at first light.'

The savage young beggar raised his head from the feast bits of snake hanging from his teeth.

'And what if we won't follow Vassos?' He asked insolently, his lips curled hideously, dripping bits of food.

Andreas did not hesitate; he flew straight at the savage insubordinate little beggar, and pinned him to the ground with his teeth sunk into one ear. His hind legs; claws extended, raked viciously at the young Toms back. The savage little beggar screeched in fear and agony, his body relaxed in submission. Andreas released his hold; the young Tom cowered back spitting defensively, holding his claws out to defend. This did not satisfy Andreas; he dived at the savage little beggar again, and chased him down the hill. The young Tom ran for his life, his momentary defiance dissipated. Andreas clawed at his hind quarters, making him turn and twist in his headlong flight. Andreas continued the chase until he was satisfied that the insubordinate little beggar had fully learnt his lesson, and sought refuge in the top branches of a tree.

'And that's how you deal with young Toms who do not know their place!' He muttered to his companions as he returned to the group a little short of wind.

Vassos looked at his leader with awe, respect oozing from his stare. A grinning Yiorgos growled, 'That insubordinate little beggar needed a lesson in respect for his elders.'

Below in Cat City, all eyes turned at the first screech. They had ringside seats for the first part of the action. Mario turned to Achilleas with a knowing grin as he realised what was going on. Achilleas grinned back, and by way of reply added, 'There's a good lesson in leadership.'

Mario's young Toms had also witnessed the disciplinarian in action, and looked suitably impressed. Old Nicos raised that knowing eyelid again and murmured, 'Discipline must be maintained.' And then the eyelid dropped again as he continued, 'That young devil won't be so eager to step out of line again.'

Andreas returned to Cat City with his companions. Nothing was said; no words were needed, actions spoke louder than words.

'Join me at McDonalds tonight,' Mario invited Andreas; then continued with a grin: 'Make it a victory feast.'

Nicos looked towards Vassos and asked, 'Have you ever eaten with humans?'

'No I haven't,' Vassos replied, just a little bemused.

'Well now is the time to learn young Tom. I am going to take you to meet my humans; you will soon learn to enjoy this new experience.'

Vassos did not know which way to turn; such was his awe of this old Tom. 'Thank you Nicos,' he said simply.

Mario did not give his young Toms their orders that day; he calculated it would be better to think on it overnight, and then call them to his presence after Vassos had left the hill tomorrow morning.

Zavosena would not arrive until the day after tomorrow, so he had plenty of time to prepare his young Toms. His main concern was to make sure that absolutely no contact was possible between his Toms, and the wild young devils led by Vassos.

Early next morning Andreas and Yiorgos accompanied Vassos to the top of the hill. Andreas impressed upon those present the absolute need for total obedience. He rammed it home that their essential duty was to act as escort for Zavosena, as soon as they met.

'Anyone disobeying the lawful orders of his leader will be chased away from this area and never allowed to return,' he stated with dreadful seriousness.

The savage young beggar knew that this statement was aimed at him; he looked suitably subdued. The pain of his good hiding remained to serve as a reminder that it is best to obey the orders of a territorial Tom, especially at close quarters, where escape was less possible.

His less aggressive sidekick however, looked forward to the job. He too had ambitions, but had the sense to bide his time.

Mario and Achilleas watched from down below, and when Vassos disappeared over the crest of the hill leading his escort group, he turned to Achilleas.

'I want you to lead our lot,' he stated bluntly. 'Not one of them has ever been over the other side of that tunnel, and,' he emphasized, 'You are the only one amongst us who has consistently patrolled the area beyond the hill, only you know the area sufficiently well enough to lead our young Toms.'

'Huh!' Achilleas grunted, a wide grin gradually spreading across his face. 'I knew it would be me as soon as the wise one said his piece yesterday. I agree,' he added pompously. 'I am the best Tom here to lead this group.'

They strolled over the rough ground together, to the area where the young Toms were allowed to congregate. Not one look of insubordination greeted them. Every face that stared their way was totally bemused as only the young and callow can express a certain vacancy.

Mario and Achilleas anchored themselves in front of some fifteen young Toms, their front paws firmly set in a sphinx like pose. The stance impressed the young Toms, they knew they were being confronted by two determined territorial Toms, and of course these two alpha Toms were the fathers of most of them.

'You are going over the other side,' Mario informed them firmly. The young Toms exchanged glances of surprise.

'Achilleas will be your leader,' he went on. 'Only he knows every hill, and every path from Agios Athanasios, through Germasogia, and on to Agios Tychonas. Your job will be to mount look out posts on the best vantage points overlooking the great barrier that holds back the water, the one the humans call Germasogia Dam. Sometime tomorrow, Zavosena will come into contact with the group led by Vassos; he will escort the entourage through the dangerous land between there and Cat City. There will be human hunters with their dogs, but worst of all there will be hunting dogs that have no master. I don't have to tell you the danger of getting caught unawares by one of these desperate dogs. Should an attack occur upon the entourage you are to dash to their defence. The absolute priority of your mission is to ensure that Zavosena arrives safely at Cat City.'

He cast his gaze over the young Toms facing him. It pleased him to see that every face held a look of expectancy. It occurred to him that Achilleas would have to curb their youthful enthusiasm, these young Toms were perhaps too eager for confrontation. 'You will leave as soon as you have fed.'

He broke off, turning to Achilleas: 'They're all yours,' he stated with all the authority of the alpha Tom.

Mario strolled back to his patch leaving Achilleas to get on with the job of organizing his group into a cohesive if somewhat totally inexperienced team of individuals, which means to say: a cat will do exactly what it wants to do, and it is only when cats feel the need to do something at the same time that a group action is possible.

By midday Achilleas and his young Toms had fed. He led them dashing through the tunnel watched by the astonished eyes of those in

Cat City who were not aware of the decisions made by the leading cast in this drama.

Mario watched the enthusiastic youngsters follow Achilleas's lead, as the last one disappeared into the tunnel he turned and called, 'Fluffy.'

I turned my eyes away from the tunnel, and seeing him looking my way ambled across to him. He waited until I had sat on my haunches and then began.

'You and all the females who are responsible for bringing this unifying action this far, will be responsible for Zavosena when she arrives. She is a female, who will pay no attention to me as a Tom. She will accept that she is in my territory, but she will do only that which suits her mind.'

I looked at him, not expecting these words of wisdom from a Tom. He noticed the approving look on my face and paused for a second.

I said nothing; so he continued. 'In truth, everything that is said will only be thought right if it is the females that come to an agreement. If any individual territorial Tom does not accept a Trod female into his territory, then patience must be exercised until familiarity becomes established.'

He looked at me again, so I said with understanding, 'No more could be hoped for.' I was grateful that he had not acted in the way of the egotistical territorial Tom. He watched me in thought for a moment, and was polite enough to wait while I sorted out my thoughts.

'I have told you that Zavosena favours a tree branch as her throne,' I said after a few moments. 'Her personal superiority is beyond question amongst the Trods. Her father had no hesitation in accepting her as his long lost daughter, so invested her with total power over those of his subjects under her command. She will come here as a proud princess, acclaimed leader, and a feline with great responsibility. In the past she has become infamous as the savage leader of her group of Trods. Her present acquiescent state is only brought about by the fact that she has managed to get some of the hate off her chest.'

'Come to the point,' Mario interrupted, not unpleasantly.

'This tree in the middle of your patch has a very good lower branch,' I nodded at the branch I referred to. 'Do you agree that it would be a great diplomatic coup if you offered her that branch as soon as she enters your territory?'

'But then she would be living with me,' he replied defensively.

I grinned at this streak of petulance; he was horrified to even consider such an intrusion into his male bastion.

'She is not like other females,' I explained gently. 'The parts that make her a demanding female have been removed by the humans a long time in the past. She is a female without the need to have kittens; she has been robbed of her female birthright that means she does not exude the scents that are attractive to Toms. If you are worried that she may attract the attention of all the other territorial Toms to your patch, that cannot happen, she has been rendered totally un-female.'

'Oh all right then!' He muttered, frowning deeply at my persuasive manner. 'But she must not interfere with my ways; she must not butt in when I am in discussion with the other Toms.'

He looked at me, keen to read my reaction, then, for no visible reason his face brightened and changed to a broad grin. 'I know what to do,' he said, looking quite pleased with himself. 'When we receive notice that she is upon us, you and the other females meet her on the hill. Make it look like a welcoming party, and then while you are greeting her, you can whisper that I have given her a very prominent thronal position, but warn her politely that she must not interfere with my running of Cat City.'

Having said his piece, he strutted away thoroughly pleased with himself; probably under the impression that his wisdom equaled that of Nicos. That was doubtful, although I must admit, looking at his black strutting frame stretch itself out with Andreas and Yiorgos, he did have a keen sense of timing when it came to delegation. I had not expected that job when I deemed to advise him on a diplomatic course. He had successfully dodged initial contact with this particular female. 'Ah well,' I thought; then muttered to myself, 'It's probably for the best.'

That evening, all of us females spread ourselves along the tourist strip. It was a beautiful night and the pavements were alive with happy tourists. We strolled past our usual return point up to a Danish Ice cream shop. As we reached the pavement outside this popular shop, I suddenly gasped with surprise. There under a table was Big M with her head inside a large ice cream tub licking away furiously at its contents. Two tourists at the table who had obviously handed the tub down to her were roaring with laughter at her attempts to get the very last lick out of the tub.

'Effi,' I called, using her real name.

Her head raised from the tub, 'Oh Fluffy,' she cried, rushing to me and giving me a welcoming ear rubbing, 'I am glad to see you,' she continued close to tears.

'My word you have put on some weight,' I said, appraising her ample figure, 'Why have you stayed away for so long?'

She sat down amongst us and told us her sad story of addiction.

'When I left you to have my kittens, I found a very quiet little spot just past the Theme Park. My kittens were born there, and I found enough lizards and mice to feed on until they could walk. I had never been this far along the strip before, until one day I stopped at this shop. There were many tourists eating the creamy white stuff that comes in those round tubs. One of them put a tub down for me with a mouthful left inside, from that moment I could not drag myself away from this shop, I even slept under that bush over there,' she indicated a spot just across the side road from us, before continuing, 'Every waking moment of every day I have spent here since that fateful day. I just cannot drag myself away from this beautiful creamy taste. Look around you, not another cat in sight. I have been so greedy in my need for this gorgeous taste, I have fought off all the other cats and chased them away, even my children left me early because they had to learn to catch mice and be nice to tourists. They were at least strong enough to fend for themselves because of the richness of my milk, but I had only started the weaning process when they left me.'

'Oh Effi,' I said sympathetically, struggling hard to suppress the grin that was twitching at the corners of my mouth. 'How awful, to like a thing so much you just have to stay near to it day after day.'

My colleagues by this time had grasped the meaning behind Big M's addiction to human ice cream. They turned away so that their faces could not be seen. It was only female feline politeness that prevented them from succumbing to purrs of laughter.

'You must come with us now,' I said as firmly as I could. 'I have some very serious work for you to help me with.' I paused for a moment, turning to my friends, 'This is Avoula,' I said, then introduced the others. The blank look on Big M's face made me add: 'You will get to know them as we go along.'

I tried to keep her mind occupied as we walked along. Very soon she was chatting amiably with the females from the other side. They in turn, because they were completely transformed to creatures of the civilised world, accepted her quite naturally as a sister. All of us now kept Big M involved until we reached Cat City.

Mario, upon seeing her gave her an interested sniff or two, but then, when she recoiled from his advances lost interest completely. None of us uttered a purr about her ice cream addiction; she would have to come to terms with that in her own good time. For now, I would keep her as close as possible, in the thick of the peacemaking.

****

Achilleas spread his young Toms over an area of hills where all of them could keep a watchful eye on the great barrier that held back the water. They could also sweep the hills all around because their slopes came right down to the waterside. Such were their vantage points that they could rush down into the valley in a matter of minutes if the need arose. Vassos and his escort group could not be seen anywhere, so obviously they had found some deep cover.

The entire Cat City group fed by chance that night. The recent rains had left pockets of water everywhere, so thirst was not a problem. Most of the hills in the area had a human villa perched on their summits, and during the evening, and going on to the early hours of the morning, the tops of the hills were illuminated by the light that the humans made themselves.

The sounds of music and revelry issuing from many hilltops indicated that many private parties were well patronised. Achilleas's young Toms, well versed in how to appeal to humans supplemented their country diet with titbits tossed in their general direction by humans who were used to the continual presence of felines.

All of the young Toms managed to catnap that night until the sun's rays stirred them into action. They yawned widely then stretched their lithe young bodies, before ambling off individually to seek out water and slake their morning thirst.

Achilleas spent a good part of his morning running up and down hills checking that all of his young Toms were at their posts, and had not forgotten the reason why they were here. By mid-morning all of them were casually watching three dogs coursing the scrubland reaching out to the path of death.

The young Toms did not know it, but this land was forbidden to hunters because of its proximity to human habitation. After a while it became obvious that these dogs did not have a human master; they were wild dogs.

The hill that Achilleas had chosen as his vantage point was also shared by five of his younger Toms who he had not wished to leave on their own.

'Watch those dogs very closely,' he ordered the youngsters, and then dashed off to ensure that the remainder of his troop was also aware of the pending danger. He left each group with definite orders.

'If those three wild dogs pass through this circle of hills, all of you meet me in the valley, and we shall form up at the rear of the dogs.'

Achilleas dashed back to his hill, glad to see that five young pairs of eyes were locked onto the forms of the approaching wild dogs. Every now and then the dogs would break into a mad rush as something edible broke cover. The mad rush would end with one of the wild dogs raising its head, the better to gulp down whatever it had caught.

Achilleas searched the area to the west of the lake; a movement caught his eye. A group of cats was moving furtively from cover to cover. His eyes swung back to the great barrier and the three dogs.

Vassos had also caught sight of Zavosena and her small entourage. He began moving his escort group along the barrier to make contact with her. Neither he nor Zavosena were aware of the presence of the dogs gradually coming their way.

Achilleas kept his eyes on the three dogs, and suddenly became aware that one of the dogs had picked up a scent. The dog's actions alerted the other two, and their large ears flopped against their heads as their noses tested the air, and then returned to the ground scent.

The lead dog started trotting along his nose close to the ground, as the trail led them towards the great barrier. Within minutes the three wild dogs had passed through the valley below Achilleas, this stirred him into instant action. 'Come on!' He yelled at his young Toms, hoping the other ten on the ridges opposite would follow his previously delivered orders.

He reached the valley floor just as ten panting young Toms fell in behind him. 'Spread out!' He ordered, as they ran, keeping a safe distance behind the three dogs.

The wild dogs had picked up the trail of Vassos and his Toms, and by its freshness knew that a meal lay ahead, if they could fall on their prey from behind in a surprise attack.

The group led by Vassos encountered Zavosena, and led them swiftly over the barrier to the south eastern side of the lake. It was then Vassos caught the sound of the dogs just as they broke cover, and came hurtling towards him. His young Toms met the dogs head on, with no chance of escape it was all they could do. Three of them were instantly grabbed by the small of the back, and tossed high in the air, to lie in a broken, crumpled heap of fur, lifeless in the dust. One of the dead was the savage little beggar.

At that moment Achilleas and his Toms broke cover, dashing straight into the fray and attacking the three dogs from the rear, instinct taking over as they sank their teeth and claws into the tatty hind quarters of the surprised dogs.

The dogs swung round to throw off their tormentors, but the momentum of their swing kept the young Toms clear of the snapping jaws, as they clung with tooth and claw to swinging rumps.

Vassos took immediate advantage of this diversion, and led his Toms into the thick of it. The dust rose high, disturbed by the writhing mass of bodies. The growls of the dogs and the screeching of the felines created a scene from hell as fur flew and blood flowed.

The conclusion was inevitable; the three wild dogs could not defend themselves against thirty five young Toms all furiously blooding themselves for the first time. They scurried away yelping with screaming cats dropping from them as they ran. The fur of all three dogs was in shreds, and blood spattered the ground as they ran whimpering through the bushes frantically trying to shake off the more tenacious of the young fighting Toms.

The three wild dogs would live to fight another day, but behind them lay a scene of carnage. Four young Toms from the brave Trods lay mangled and dead, and three from the shoreside had met the same fate. Both Vassos and Achilleas had received bites, and the gaps in their straggly fur showed the full scars of this vicious encounter; but overall there was a feeling of jubilation. The dead were left where they fell, as is the way with felines. A few cautious sniffs at the inert bodies was their only send off to cat heaven; no cat visibly mourned.

The entourage; now consisting of both Trods and shore-side cats, spread out, and continued the journey to Cat City. Differences between the young Toms of both sides no longer existed. They had united successfully against a common enemy, and come out victorious. Stories of this brave unified escort group would go down in cat history as the "Great Battle of Germasogia", and all the talking that could have taken place would never have the same unifying effect as the spilling of blood in a common defence by those who had now become comrades in arms.

Vassos dropped alongside his princess as they walked. Achilleas had gone to the head of the group, and had sent the young shore-side Toms ahead as scouts.

'Your arrival was unexpected,' Zavosena said. 'Who ordered this timely engagement?'

'Andreas gave me my orders, but I can only assume that Mario gave the orders that brought Achilleas and his Toms to protect our rear.'

'Well both of you have saved the day, none of my entourage would be here now without your intervention,' Zavosena said with gratitude, then added, 'Much glory has been earned this day, and many brave actions must be rewarded when the time is right.'

Vassos looked devotedly at his princess as her words caressed his already heightened self-esteem. She did not return his look, but she knew her statesmanlike words would draw this faithful young lieutenant even closer to her.

From the bushes on the edge of the hillside, three pairs of eyes watched the entourage and its protectors continue on their way. When sure it was safe to do so, three bedraggled and scarred hounds slunk back to the battleground and ate their fill.

———————

That same day, during the afternoon, I led my females through the tunnel and up to the top of the hill. As always, the trip through the tunnel brought the hairs on my back erect, and a cold shudder ran down my spine. We did not have long to wait, a group of young Toms came into view, and as we stared aghast at their torn young bodies, the remainder of the entourage arrived.

The bedraggled but proud young Toms made Avoula gasp, 'Good Lord!'

I too looked on with amazement at this awesome sight; but then, my wonderment changed to astonishment as I realised that all the young

Toms of both sides were closely intermingled together. Achilleas saw my look, and whispered as he drew near, 'It is done; all you have to do is make sure that it lasts.' His whisper held a note of triumph.

Zavosena reached the top of the hill panting from her exertions, and to my great surprise stretched her body out alongside me and rubbed her ears against me. 'Give me chance to catch my breath,' she gasped. 'This walk was made most strenuous by fear of another ambush following the battle.' She drew a deep breath: 'These Young Toms of yours acquitted themselves most bravely, as did my young fighting Trods; but that will come later,' she hastened to add, looking into my very quizzical face. 'First of all where do I and my entourage settle down on this not very comfortable hill, and, I also notice it has no trees.'

I caught my breath sharply, suddenly remembering my reason for being in this position. 'You are to be accommodated in Cat city,' I said quickly. 'Mario has made a tree available for you in his territory. He hopes you will feel comfortable there.' I leaned closer and whispered conspiratorially, 'You know what territorial Toms are like; let him feel that he has done you a great service, and that your presence will cause him no hindrance at all.'

She gave me a knowing smile, and replied, 'Fluffy, you are a female of great wisdom; I suspect I see your hand in this.'

I looked away saying, 'Follow me now.'

Her bodyguards made to come with her; she looked at me for a second intuitively then spoke firmly to her guards. 'No!' She said to them collectively, 'You remain here my loyal friends, I shall be in no danger, and we shall soon organize your entry into Cat City.'

Achilleas and Vassos, with all the united young Toms behind them made no move to enter Cat city with us.

'Why do you stay here?' I asked Achilleas

He turned his broad ginger head, and said firmly, 'We fought and won as one, so we shall enter Cat City as one: we are now united,' he added proudly. A loud meow from all the young fighters confirmed his statement.

Andreas and Yiorgos greeted their princess at the bottom of the hill and placed her between themselves to pass through the tunnel. Christos greeted them as they broke free of the tunnel's confines, Mario stood beside him.

'So we meet for the first time Mario,' Zavosena got her greeting in first. Her eyes appraised his lithe frame, and shining black fur, a moment of sadness seared her brain. 'If only I was the complete female.' The thought flashed through her mind, and then disappeared just as quickly as duty took over from personal thoughts.

'You are welcome Zavosena,' he said, his face set like stone. He had heard so much of this female over the last two years, as alpha Tom in this City he had never thought this meeting possible. Not really knowing what to expect, he suddenly realised that this female who met his eyes with the same steady unwavering stare was probably more than his equal. Through her royal heritage she was the ultimate territorial female, and he knew instantly that she would not bend an inch if anything was not to her liking. Mario did not realise it, but he had been staring at her for minutes. It took an embarrassed shuffling from those around him to bring him out of his thoughts with a jolt.

'Co..come this way,' he stammered, struggling to get himself together, but sounding rather foolish.

Zavosena glanced at me, a knowing grin flitting across her face, she had only been in Cat City a few minutes and already she had the upper hand.

Mario led her to his patch and pointed at the carob tree. 'This will be your throne for the present,' he said graciously, his self-assurance gradually returning.

Zavosena scrambled up the tree, and perched herself commandingly on the branch that appeared grown for the purpose of being a throne. Her gaze took in all the inhabitants of Cat City all sitting on their haunches staring up in awe at this figure whose reputation as a she-devil had been passed down from mother to daughter for the last few years. Not a sound came from the gathered throng. Not a cat amongst them had the slightest doubt that they were gazing at a female of great strength of will, who by some chance was the daughter of the self-appointed king of the Trods. Even though this City was ruled by territorial consent, every cat afforded this strong female the honour of her position, she had no enemies here. Whatever had caused the division all those years ago that made the path of death a dividing line between the two communities was now buried. Only old Nicos fully remembered that it was the building of the path of death that was the precursor to a separate community with a much harder existence.

A GREAT SURPRISE

Zavosena gazed down on the gathered population of Cat City. Many of the faces that stared back at her were her own people already integrated into the society of Cat City, everyone was there, not a soul was absent for this great event in the cat lore of Cyprus.

Old Nicos broke the silence, bringing all of us firmly to the task in hand. 'Greetings Zavosena,' he welcomed her. She returned the greeting politely, and waited for Nicos to continue.

'I only wish to say that I have waited many years for this moment, and I think now is an appropriate moment to remind us all that it is the good work of our new friend Fluffy, and her first contact with Zavosena that has made this day possible. Fluffy has proved to be a good friend of both communities, and it is her efforts in bringing the first group of females into a united force for peace that has enabled us to come together in this way. Let us not waste the good will that surrounds us at this moment. Let us go forward together and make this Cat city the cat capital of Cyprus. There is plenty of room for all of us now; we can all roam freely from the Troodos Mountains in the north to the tourist beaches of the southern coast.'

He paused, staring keenly at the crowd stretched out before him. Not one hostile stare met his gaze, so he continued in an instructive manner, 'It is the duty of all of us to assist our brothers and sisters now returned to us. We must teach them the laws that we have found necessary to live in harmony with our human friends. These laws are not hard to learn, it is merely a point of being nice to those who share what they have got with us. To a great degree they are our benefactors, so it is only right that we should return their kindnesses by being of some use to them in the way that nature intended of us cats. In other words we must keep the tourist area free of all vermin that could upset our annual visitors.'

His intense stare softened as he brought his short speech to an end with the words: 'Open your hearts felines of Cat City, go through the tunnel and meet your fellow felines, mingle with them, befriend them, bring them in to us and spread along the strip with them . Teach them what they must know, then let there be freedom for all Cypriot cats to pass freely through the tunnel, that way the whole Island will be open to each and every one of us who inhabit this beautiful Island together. Go now my friends show your fellow cats from the mountains the true meaning of Cypriot hospitality.' He slumped down, his emotive speech finished. I looked at him closely, it was obvious the effort had drained him, he needed rest.

So that he could see that his words were received with unanimous agreement, I led my females into the tunnel; as I expected several other females broke away from the crowd and joined us.

First to be escorted through was Zavosena's bemused bodyguard. I realised that this act would basically annul the orders that Mario had insisted upon, but since his orders a united battle had occurred so I judged that much of what he had ordered was not now relevant, therefore, if he had any objections I would face the music later.

Just as they had previously decided, the battle groups from both sides, led by Achilleas and Vassos all dashed through the tunnel one after the other in a mixed line. They ran straight to Mario and Andreas and banged heads together in Macho reception.

While all the Toms, both territorial and young fighters were joined together in mutual head banging, wallowing in their excitement of the aftermath of battle, we females, joined by Nicos, began to arrange accommodation areas for the new females in our midst. It was agreed that Zavosena and her newly redundant bodyguard would join my group of Trod females, and establish themselves to the east of Cat City in an area the humans were rebuilding.

Old Nicos had far greater knowledge of the southern coastline, both to the east and to the west, that knowledge would be put to good use in the next week or so.

'There are plenty of places to establish small communities of cats, all the way from here to Governors Beach,' he explained informatively.

My ears pricked up at his last statement. I knew that name. I had not heard it spoken for several months, but I certainly knew that name. Suddenly it dawned on me. Governors Beach was my birth place; it was the place where Brown Legs and Big Feet sometimes lived. My heart surged with joy- tinged with sorrow; suddenly I missed my dear humans. A lull in the conversation gave me the chance to ask Nicos tentatively, 'W... where is Governors Beach?'

'Why do you ask?' He replied, looking at me closely; he had noticed the catch in my voice.

'I believe it is my place of birth,' I answered honestly.

By now our group was on the edge of human habitation. From here I had to take the group east along the strip, and old Nicos had to go west a short way to his home.

'We must separate here,' he said. 'You have much to do before nightfall; we will talk of Governors Beach next time we meet.'

I bade him farewell my heart bursting with excitement. I would await our next meeting with great anticipation.

Including myself, there were eighteen felines in the group. Zavosena and her six bodyguards, the original eight females of the discussion group, Avoula, and Big M.

I had to coax the six bodyguards to leave Zavosena and spread out as individuals. It was not easy; they had been together as an inseparable group for so long they were almost like Siamese sextuplets. Finally it took a direct order from Zavosena, and the intermingling of the females to force them apart.

All of us shore-side females knew that it was most unwise for cats to be seen in large groups; humans could sometimes be very sensitive about a large number of cats, and take steps to reduce their numbers humanely.

I encouraged Zavosena to walk with Avoula and me in front. This made the bodyguards a bit happier because they could see the source of their loyalty straight ahead. We passed the Danish ice cream shop, and I encouraged everyone to spread out among the cafes, hotels and shops. I led the bodyguards to the open ground behind human habitation where they could hunt freely, and also be close to a tunnel that went to the other side of the path of death. Before leaving them I pointed out that the tunnel was clear, this fact proven by the puddle of water lying stagnant in front of the entrance.

'You are now free to use this tunnel in both directions whenever you wish,' I informed them. 'The hunting will be better on the other side, until you get used to living with us.'

The six gave me a grateful glance; it was painfully obvious that they were very uncomfortable this close to humans. They also glanced worriedly towards the building behind which Zavosena was learning the ropes.

'She will come to you when she is ready,' I assured them. 'She understands how difficult it is for you to change your way of life so suddenly,' I added, seeing their need for some reassurance.

Zavosena at that moment was endearing herself to a couple of elderly female tourists. It was the time of year when grandparents preferred to visit Cyprus and consequently a time of plenty for us cats.

'Hasn't she got a proud look about her?'

This statement of fact from an old grandma brought a critical response from her companion: 'Coats a bit rough though,' she replied, not seeing beyond Zavosena's unkempt appearance.

I returned to my friends, and grinned when I saw Zavosena enjoying her first human friendliness for many years, by the old humans to whom kindliness to animals was a way of life.

I waited while Zavosena milked her sudden friendship dry, and then turn with regal aloofness away from her benefactors and stroll over to me. I could not hide the wide grin on my face as she approached. 'Lovely humans,' she said, stretching out with a self-satisfied expression on her face beside me. I too stretched out as I told her, 'I have put your bodyguards on a big patch of ground that has no humans on it, I am sure they will be much happier there, they can pass backwards and forwards under the path of death as they wish.'

'It is harder for them,' she replied sympathetically. 'It will be harder than weaning cloying youngsters, getting those six Toms to lead a life of their own. I will have to stay close to them until they get the idea into their thick heads that they are now individuals, although I doubt the bond to each other will ever be broken. They have all been very loyal to me. As neutered Toms they suffered no distractions, which is why they were perfect for the job.'

I walked with her back to where I had left her six loyal Toms. Tagging along behind came the eight females of the discussion group, all of whom were now heavy with kittens. Their immediate priorities were to sniff around the many hidey holes and bushes that were strewn across the area. There were hundreds of ideal little birthing spots, and if all of these females had their kittens here, their young would grow up here, and help to keep nature in balance.

'Where is Big M?' I asked Avoula, after we had said our farewells to Zavosena and our old friends.

'I don't know,' she replied. 'I thought she had found somewhere to eat.'

I nodded my head knowingly several times. I knew where Big M was.

'Look there,' I said to Avoula, as we approached the Danish ice cream shop. Sure enough there was Big M, her head stuffed inside an ice cream tub chasing it around under the table, frantically trying to get at the last lick. Her benefactors looked highly amused; once again Big M was making a laughing stock of herself.

'M! Come away from there,' I growled firmly. Her eyes locked onto mine, a desperate wide eyed look across her face.

'Sorry,' she whimpered. 'I just couldn't help myself.'

She scurried off in front of us, belly dragging the ground in shame. Avoula could not suppress a low purring giggle. I too was on the verge of a huge grin as I watched Big M scurrying on ahead of us. If she ever went missing, we would have no problem finding her.

As we strolled along the strip we began to notice felines from Cat city showing the ropes to their new friends. The young Toms of both communities were enjoying themselves; some were eating, some were flat out relaxing, while others were cementing friendships and establishing a pecking order playing hide and seek, and tail chasing with youthful enthusiasm, much to the amusement of the passing tourists.

What a heartening sight, flashed through my mind; 'Keep them well fed, keep them friendly, give them a well-defined patch of their own and include them all in the grand scheme of things, and you have a rock solid base for permanent peace.'

Avoula glanced at me; I had been purring out loud.

'Have you eaten yet?' I asked her.

'No I waited for you to finish with Zavosena.'

'Then let's have a McDonald's,' I said, leading her determinedly around the back as I spoke.

The lovely Frenchman greeted me. 'Ah ma Cherie,' he said tickling me under the chin with a crooked forefinger. 'You cannot stay away from me, can you?'

He put a pile of chicken bones down for us, and then added some bits of beef burger, and we fed heartily on the scraps before they were destined for the refuse bins.

The kindly Frenchman looked at us through the back door with a gentle grin spread across his face as he washed his hands before returning to his kitchen.

The autumn sun was very pleasant, so after eating we stretched out in the backyard of McDonald's and soaked up the sun on this very nice afternoon. Nobody bothered us, they just stepped over us. While we were there no sneaky little rodents would dare to sniff around this clean yard in the vain hope of finding something edible.

Upon waking we strolled off to Cat City, the late evening sun casting long shadows across the scrubland upon which we walked.

The peaceful air of the evening and the loud chatter of the happily occupied tourists was shattered suddenly by a horrendous bang, followed by a grating, scraping noise, and long drawn out screeches. The three of us quickly realised that this awful sound had come from Cat City. We raced to the spot where the noise had come from; the sight that met our eyes was absolute carnage. A huge beast with many round legs was upside down on the edge of the city its round legs still going round as if it did not know it was upside down. Up on the path

262 reigned for the rest of the evening

of death, humans were running to and fro dragging other humans out of the beasts with round legs who had obviously been in battle. Two huge monsters were locked together head to head. It looked as if one monster had challenged the other to a fight then jumped over from his path to get at him. Neither of them had won, they lay there motionless while humans ran all around them. Lots of smaller beasts had joined the fight also; strangely they too had gone into the fight head on, and in their hurry to be at the front, they were locked nose to tail into each other on both sides of the path of death.

Pandemonium reigned for the rest of the evening, and well into the night. A great beast ran into Cat City, and with a huge arm sticking up from its back, turned the other beast back onto its round legs again. We watched in amazement as it then lifted the beast off the ground and placed it on the back of a third beast. Obviously it could not run any more so a friend took it back home. Similar scenes were being acted out of the path of death as all the other wounded beasts were carried off by their friends assisted by the humans. What a loving relationship this must be, some humans even stayed with their beasts to the bitter end, and they were taken away in another beast with flashing eyes and a loud persistent wail. I found it strange that the humans and the beasts with round legs were such obvious friends, yet such battles frequently occurred.

Many bushes were flattened in the city before all the beasts had gone. Felines could be seen sniffing around areas where their patch had been, unable to comprehend why their home had disappeared. Territorial Toms were running around sniffing out the boundaries of their individual domains, and then quickly spraying and re-scenting. Some females were also carrying out the same procedure, their tails quivering in the air as if to elaborate the process.

Fortunately no mothers ever purposefully had their kittens close to each other so there were no kitten fatalities. It would be a long time though before Cat City regained the bushy cover it boasted before the battle of the beasts. Thankfully the carob tree had survived, so our leader Mario still had his patch intact.

Before darkness lifted early next morning, another catastrophe descended on the city from the heavens. The wet season was well and truly upon us, and a huge storm cloud had emptied its contents on the whole of the southern area of the Island. Cats, which had just a few hours earlier scraped a new nest for the night found that they were washed out of their make shift shelters.

The torrential rain caused a maelstrom of water, brush, mud and rocks to be washed through the tunnel. In a very short time Cat City was a lake and rendered totally uninhabitable.

Homeless cats started leaving Cat City in droves, seeking more reliable shelter in all directions. Before the sun showed its head, peeping dejectedly from behind the black cloud that was now sweeping rapidly eastwards, all the felines of cat City had re-housed themselves in the comparative safety of the surrounding human structures.

Cats who had just joined us from the mountains did not know where to go for the best. They could not return to the other side because of the deluge pouring through all the access points, and they were not sufficiently familiar with the shore-side area to know when they were trespassing, and when they were in free territory.

Most humans had their own domestic cats that never came into contact with us feral cats. These posh cats however were just as territorial as we were, consequently the stormy start to the day was shattered by the screeches of escaping strangers running from the well protected territory of a domestically cared for feline.

As Avoula and I scurried for cover amongst the tall buildings of the humans I noticed that Big M was not with us. For an instant I was worried, but then calmed down. Big M was a mature feline; many times a mother, a heavy rainstorm would not have more than a temporary ill effect on her well- being.

The storm was now quickly easing off, as the dark cloud swept eastwards towards Larnaca. Avoula and I made no rush to move, the bush we shared was enclosed in the back yard of a block of flats.

Some-time later, the back door to a ground floor flat opened, and a kindly human female voice said, 'Off you go, and come straight back if it starts to rain again.'

The dark grey and black form of an old tabby Tom emerged into the open looked up at his mistress and mewed, 'Efcaristo.'

We instantly recognised the old Tom as Nicos. He noticed us under the bush and mewed, 'How is Cat City?'

Before we could answer he went on, 'Every year at this time we have great rain storms, and every year Cat City becomes a lake and everybody has to leave, I see with you two sitting here the same has happened again. Cat City is never prepared for disaster; all the cats new this would happen, but in the way of all felines they never prepare for the worst. It may be lovely to lead a life in such a purely optimistic way; thinking that everything will turn out for the best, but sometimes it pays to be like humans and learn from life that it is better to be ready for disaster when it comes.'

We both grinned at this early morning pearl of wisdom from this old Tom; he was not finished yet though as he took us into his confidence. 'My old mistress has taken a fancy to that brave young Tom Vassos. When this downpour started, the first thing she said was: 'Oh dear! I do hope that young Tom is out of the wet, if you find him bring him home with you again.'

He looked at us both with a query in his eyes; seeking some indication of where Vassos might be. I understood, so I told him, 'Vassos is still in Cat City, he has stayed with Mario and Achilleas under a great slab of rock on the slope down from the path of death. Yiorgos and Andreas are with them also.'

Old Nicos looked up at the sky, it was totally clear overhead now, but another large black cloud was approaching quickly from the west.

'My old companions have gone into hiding,' he murmured as he looked left and right before stepping out of the back yard, and then started walking towards Cat City. It was a tiring stroll for such an old Tom, but his mistress had showed affection for young Vassos, and even if it killed him, he would bring Vassos back to his home, just to show his old mistress that the young Tom was safe and sound.

A pang of guilt hit me, as I watched his old frame hobbling along. 'Wait!' I mewed loudly, rising to my feet. 'I can do this quicker than you, you wait here, I will go and tell Vassos to meet you here.'

A look of relief crossed his face; 'Thank you my dear,' he said gratefully.

I ran to Cat City and gave Vassos the message. Without an instants hesitation he was up on his feet and following me back to where old Nicos waited patiently. Apart from the respect he felt for the old Tom, he had thoroughly enjoyed his first contact with the old Cypriot grandma, and having a human shelter was far more appealing than sharing an outcrop of rock at the side of a noisy path of death with several other Toms.

A small part of the back door of Nicos' home had scratch marks in a bottom corner which coincided with the height of a cat. Old Nicos walked up to this part of the door followed by Vassos. We watched as he clawed the door a couple of times.

His old mistress opened the door and squealed with delight. 'Ah you clever old Tom, you do understand me when I talk to you, come on in now, I have your morning feed ready.'

'If only I could speak human as well as I understand it,' old Nicos purred to Vassos, grinning broadly as they strolled into the kitchen.

All of this meant nothing to Vassos; he had looked up at a smiling face which had immediately reassured him that he was welcome in this human abode. The words spoken were just a human noise, and he had not been with humans long enough to associate the noise with a physical meaning. What he could not know at that moment was that he had been adopted, and should he care to stay, was now securely in the hands of the two old humans who had liked him so much the first time they had met him. A few kindly welcomes, and a few meals from now, and he would feel assured of his position in the hearts of these two kind humans.

Before she closed the door, the old lady looked at the sky, in so doing her eyes fell upon Avoula and me still crouched under the bush, she paused for a moment staring at us, and then said, 'My word we do have a lot of visitors this morning!' She looked at me a little closer. Avoula shrank back, a natural reaction for her.

'Aren't you a pretty little tabby,' the old lady said, bending over slightly to get a better look. 'Your colouring is much the same as my old Nicos,' she added still smiling, and then went on with a wistful look in her eyes, 'His grandmother came all the way from America; ah what a beautiful wild looking cat she was. No wonder our first old Nicos fell in love with her. She stayed with us until her family moved to Nicosia, we kept her son here because we knew our first Nicos was his father, he was the image of him.' Her old face retained the wistful smile as she recalled Nicos' family tree. 'This old Nicos is his son; he was born of a stray young tabby who hung around here for a while. We have been very happy with all our Nicos'; they have all been good companions. They loved riding in our pick-up truck, and they really loved running free at our caravan at Governors Beach.'

Her face showed a hint of sadness as she went back through the door, having recalled old Nicos's ancestors with fondness. Minutes later the door opened again.

'Here,' she said, 'A little something to keep you going in this nasty weather.

She put the plate down and retreated through the door again; but not before she had observed us dive gratefully onto the plate of scraps she had so kindly provided.

While we ate, I reflected on the old ladies words. She had mentioned Governors Beach that was why Nicos used the name with such sureness; he had traveled there many times in his long life, and spent many happy hours there in the company of his humans; he probably knew the area as well as I did.

My thoughts returned to my own humans, and the bond we shared together; that only served to increase my longing to be with them again.

****

Several times during the rainy season, Cat City took on the form of a lake. Each time, Avoula and I evacuated ourselves to the bushes in the back yard of old Nicos' humans. We were always made welcome, and always fed.

In the first month of the next human year, I bade Avoula farewell for a while and moved to a pre-selected spot to have my next litter of kittens. Avoula understood, and moved permanently into Nicos' back yard where she knew she was safe.

I had six kittens, and sadly, two died before their eyes opened, and one was lost to a renegade Tom. The loss was not an act of negligence on my part; the surrounding areas were frequently passed through by itinerant Toms attracted by the scent of receptive females.

Whenever the territorial Toms caught one of these itinerants all hell broke loose, and the neighbourhood echoed to the shrieks of a cat being hounded out of the area bearing the scars delivered by a determined defender. Very often eyes would be lost, ears torn to shreds, and there would be no let-up of the chase until the offender had taken his chances escaping across the path of death. Not all chancers made it safely to the other side; the justice of chance is sometimes fast and punitive.

My new generation of kittens grew to adulthood with all their peers in a united cat community with total access to all the mountain areas, and the shoreside. This ensured that the tourist area was never overrun by a plague of cats, because there was now ample room for everyone. We had the extra space, and the Trods did not have to worry about shortage of food anymore, when times were rough, they now knew how to seek out a café, and quietly wait to be fed.

The rains decreased as spring arrived, wet places behind the building plots of the humans dried out. Fresh greenery brightened up Cat City, and old occupants started returning, and rebuilding their hidey holes. Nature had repaired the damage done by the battle of the beasts with round legs, although handy little puddles of water remained where the round legs had been.

With my youngsters off in the company of their associates doing their own thing, Avoula and I took a stroll down the strip in the hope of meeting old friends. The rainy season had dispersed many of them to find shelter wherever they were welcomed, it took a little while for them all to find their ways back. Nature had a say in the matter, so every year for many reasons, from death to forgetfulness, many cats did not return.

Nearing the Danish ice cream parlour, we bumped into Zavosena. She sat proudly on the pavement wallowing in the attention of many tourists who were taking pictures of her. The haughtiness she exuded had made her quite a celebrity, life amongst humans obviously suited her, and so being an intelligent feline she had taken full advantage of her new situation in life.

'Hello,' she gushed, her voice affected by her own self-importance. 'Jolly glad the rain has stopped, I have had a terrible time keeping my fur looking beautiful for my public, one tends to spend the whole day licking and polishing.' She preened poshly as humans pointed their little boxes at her, only relaxing for a moment between the clicking sounds that they made. Some of the boxes flashed with a very bright light for an instant. We had all seen it before, but we still stared in wonderment.

'This is my new home,' she indicated the whole block in one sweeping gesture. 'All my humans love me here, so I share myself around, they all belong to me, they are my new subjects.'

Avoula stared in amazement at the female who had been her princess. She could not believe the transformation of her royal highness from savage determined leader, to high society feline: it was a bit hard to come to terms with. For my own part, I was delighted to see this once terrifying creature now so completely civilised, and so totally confident in her new situation.

'Has Effi been to this area?'

My question took her off guard for a moment. 'Oh you mean Big M,' she finally answered, then a little off handedly continued, 'You will probably find that rather large feline under those bushes sleeping off her last ice cream binge,'

I rushed over to the bushes Zavosena had indicated. There buried in the dried brush underneath was a loudly snoring heap of a cat. She had truly become enormous; how those little cat legs carried such a body I shall never know. Her lips fluttered slightly as the expired air passed between them followed by the rattle of her palate vibrating. Her legs twitched in reaction to some command that had flicked through her one track brain. Probably someone had stolen her Ice cream, and she was chasing the thief.

Avoula looked at Big M and gasped, she had never before seen the terrible effect of too much human food. What, to a human, was an invitingly pleasant interlude as they strolled up the strip had totally taken over Big M's life. Without some concentrated help she would become a bloated reminder on the pavements that too much of a good thing is not essential for the general upkeep of a healthy lifestyle. Something serious had to be done in order to help this dreadfully overweight feline to kick a habit that had grown into an addiction.

'EFFI!' I shouted firmly in her ear. 'Wake up!'

Her eyes shot open, and she stared at me blankly for a moment, then her face took on a sickly grin. 'Oh Fluffy, and you Avoula,' she said lamely. 'I have not seen you both since the start of the rainy season; is it over?'

Her attempt at innocent blandness did not impress me at all, my forehead assumed a deep frown. 'Where are this seasons kittens? Where have you left them? Look at you; you are in no state for motherhood.'

My strict remonstration reduced her to tears. 'I haven't had any babies this time, I have been too fat to carry out my duties,' she sobbed, a real note of despair evident in her voice.

'Can you walk far?' I asked brutally.

'Oh yes,' she replied, 'but not very fast.'

Avoula turned away, she had to. The pretence of my harshness, and the pathetic reply had nudged her giggle button. She tried to turn her giggle into a cat cough, but it came out as a strangled howl of mirth. Her outburst affected me, I failed to sustain my act of disgust, and both Avoula and I united in howls of uncontrolled mirth.

This scene was worse than a slap in the face for Big M, the total weight of her lack of self-worth descended upon her like a crushing force. 'Help me,' she said pitifully.

Those two little words could not have been better chosen; our gurgling howls stopped abruptly. 'Oh you poor thing,' I said to my friend, thoroughly ashamed of my thoughtless outburst. Avoula also, appeared suitably sheepish, 'Sorry Big M,' she purred softly.

I quickly took hold of the situation. 'Come!' I said commandingly, 'We are going to find you a healthy place to stay until you have lost this desire for ice cream.'

'Oh it's not just any ice cream that affects me,' Big M said, in a manner that suggested that her craving was selective. Ordinary ice cream I can just enjoy, and then forget about it until the next time. It's just this ice cream at this shop, it is so beautifully creamy, and I just cannot help myself. I even dream about it never being there again, and the dream turns into a nightmare.'

The giggle muscle had reactivated; I had to get her moving before I collapsed into a fit of giggles again. 'Come on then,' I ordered, forcing myself to sound sympathetic. 'We must get you somewhere safe from this terrible addiction that has overtaken you.'

What a sight we presented as we strolled along the pavement together. One elderly maiden, still very fit. One regular mother still very fit; and one lump of lard wobbling up the pavement, wheezing and panting; stopping every few yards to catch her breath.

I had an idea in mind. It was very doubtful if anything Avoula and I could do would be effective in rehabilitating Big M. We could not stay by her side twenty four hours a day; it is not a feline's natural habit to stay interested in anything that long. What Big M needed was the constant care of a determined cat lover.

It took us all one human hour, but we finally reached the back yard of old Nicos' house. Cheekiness is not a thing that bothers cats, so I did a completely natural thing; I scratched on the back door where I had seen old Nicos scratch. Some moments later the door opened, and the old Cypriot grandma looked down on us. 'Hello,' she said, smiling fondly at us. 'You love me enough to come visiting now, do you?' Her eyes fell on Big M and her face changed at the sight of this abject looking female.

Avoula edged back as she noticed me creeping backwards, away from Big M. The old grandma frowned for moment at our actions, then realization hit her, she had grasped the reason almost instantly. 'You want me to help her? You clever ladies! That is it, she has eaten too much, and you want me to help her.'

Nicos came through the back door, closely followed by Vassos. The instant they recognised Big M, they gave her a good ear rubbing, the bent tail of Vassos lending a comic element to the scene.

'Ah, it is a friend of yours is it?' The old lady oozed hospitality, then made a gracious offer. 'Come on in then, my fat little friend, we will soon put you straight.'

The door closed behind them all; Big M had been saved. This house was turning into quite a little haven for cats, in fact a real cat sanctuary. I suspect that the old lady loved having a few cats to fuss over, so I gave the cat equivalent of a 'Phew' as we reached the road, my brilliant idea had turned out to be successful.

We celebrated Big M's adoption with a tour of the strip. Many humans who did not like their holiday to be too hot came to Cyprus at this time of year, and even though it was only pleasantly hot, the tendency of some humans to turn pink was much in evidence.

I remember Big Feet always used to say whenever he saw one of these pink humans. 'Oh look! There's a brand new TuT!' (Tourist under Training)

The recollection of Big Feet brought memories surging back. Brown Legs had not seen me for a long time now, and I know she longed to have me back. Many times I had been told of their search for me as other cats and other humans had seen them on the edge of Cat City, probably hoping to take me home.

Avoula, seeing my pensive mood nudged me, and brought me back to the present, 'You were far away then,' she smiled.

I felt I owed her an explanation, so I told her of my past life with Brown Legs and Big Feet. I told her stories of Tigger, TC, and Cleopatra; I told her the story of Maria, and the cannibal Cyclops. She gasped with horror at the story of the loss of Maria's kittens.

'I could go back to Brown Legs now,' I told her. 'The job I fell into here is now finished, all my kittens are self-sufficient, and I really could go back.'

Avoula's face took on a look of sadness.

'What's wrong?' I asked my dear companion.

'You have become dear to me, I do not want to lose you; you have become the daughter I never had,

'If I can find a way home will you come with me?'

Her eyes brightened, expectation lightening her sad expression. 'Could I?'

'Surely you can,' I replied convincingly. 'My mistress Brown Legs will like you very much.'

'How will I get there?' She asked eagerly, and then continued as an afterthought: 'I have not lived with humans for so many years now, I have almost forgotten the joy and the security of human companionship, your words have served to remind me of the feeling. OOOH!' She exclaimed with female exuberance, 'How lovely it would be to belong to a human again, just to share love and affection in perfect harmony.' She stopped as she noticed the look of surprise on my face. She had never let her thoughts slip out before; this had become something of a revelation.

'If you behave as you are now Brown Legs will fall over herself to make you welcome,' I assured her. 'She has a penchant for intelligent felines who answer her when she talks to them. A purr or a meow, or even a gurgle in reply always works wonders with her.'

'When shall we go?' Avoula asked abruptly, bringing me firmly back down to earth.

'I don't quite know the answer to that,' I replied truthfully. 'But I do know someone who will tell me.'

Avoula looked disappointed for a moment; I think she had expected us to be on our way immediately.

Surprisingly, few cats were around when we reached Cat City, all the Toms, both territorial and young hopefuls were enjoying the freedom of the hills on the other side of the path of death now that they all had the scope to exercise their individual needs for adventure. Doubtless, new territories were being formed at this very moment, and the young fighting Toms of yesterday would be spraying any unclaimed land, proudly displaying ownership.

Early next morning, those of us who had stayed in Cat City overnight were surprised to see the smaller beast with round legs called a pick-up truck roll into the city. Two humans started walking around as if looking for something. After a while they both seemed happy with what they could see, and each of them took an object out of the back of the pick-up truck. One of them took a long pole with human numbers written along its length, and stood a long way from the other man who stared back at him through a glass on top of three legs. All morning they went around cat city calling to each other from a distance. We cats were a bit timid at first, but when we realised that these humans meant us no harm natural feline curiosity took over.

Sometimes they knocked a peg in the ground, and sometimes built a small pile of stones, writing things in a book all the time. Finally, they put everything back in the pick-up truck, and disappeared as quickly as they had arrived, in the same direction.

We cats sometimes find it very hard to find a reason for human actions, so when the humans disappeared, some cats just glanced at each other in puzzlement, and receiving no return look that might suggest knowledge of what had just been witnessed, shrugged their shoulders and returned to whatever was their interest before the puzzling interruption by the humans.

Later that day, Avoula and I saw Nicos sitting with Vassos and Big M sunning themselves in the back yard of their human's house. According to mood, cats will either totally ignore each other, seek to be friendly with a quick ear rub, or fiercely confront any feline they meet. In our case we were rarely hungry, so any mood swings were reserved for those times when nature's insistence made us that way for reasons of reproduction, and then the essential protection of our young until they can fend for themselves. This territory belonged to old Nicos, and he was far too tolerant to create a scene, so consequently our meetings here were always on friendly terms.

'I see the surveyors have visited cat City,' he said, after we had greeted the three sun worshippers. He noticed our puzzled look. 'They are humans who measure the ground before the humans build anything on it' he enlightened us, then continued, 'I have heard my humans say that a new hotel is to be built there, so Cat City is going to be a very different place in a few years.'

'Where will all the cats live?' I asked, fearful of a lack of space for the new alliance to mature. We females were always wary of disturbing factors that included us.

'Oh, believe me, a big hotel creates nice little areas for cats,' Nicos said, smiling at the "not in my backyard" look on my face before he continued: 'As long as we don't try to enter the hotel, no-one will bother about a few cats in the gardens. They like us to make unobtrusive homes outside, just in case any vermin dare to creep into the area.' Nicos seemed so sure in his knowledge that the conversation proceeded no further.

The old humans watched us purring at each other, as Big M gave us a demonstration of how quickly she had made herself at home. She waddled out of the sun, and shaded herself under the legs of the master of the house. He leant over and tickled her ears; she reacted by tilting her head to one side the better to get full enjoyment out of the sensation. She was still a big fat lump, but now she was a happy big fat lump with a secure home.

Vassos lay stretched out at the feet of the old grandma, presenting a scene of total contentment, which only served to make me feel more homesick for Brown Legs again. We had nothing of pressing importance to be involved in, so I tested the air with a gently purred question: 'You said we would talk of Governors Beach at some convenient time, is that time now?'

Nicos did not react to my question immediately, which meant that the answer was going to be informative to some extent.

'Is it such a nice home that you have there? Do you yearn to leave us so soon after your triumph? You have achieved much that is very good here. From the time of your capture by the Trods, your subsequent breaking down of ancient barriers, and your selfless dedication to make unification a success has opened a vast area of our island to the shore-side cats. The mountain cats also have much to be grateful for, they now have access to the bounties of the tourist strip when times are bad in the mountains.'

His eyes remained looking into mine, as if ensuring he had my full attention; seemingly satisfied he continued, 'The cessation of hostilities has given all felines a new sense of purpose; and a new sense of identity, they are not now mountain cats, or shore-side cats, they are happily united Cypriot cats. This has been a most wonderful process to take part in, and it all came about because you were fearless in the face of adversity; stay with us here, and enjoy the fruits of your labours.'

He could not help but see the great disappointment that crossed my face. He realised that I was suffering an inner turmoil, and it all had to do with divided loyalties. He was not without an answer to the problem, just as would be expected from a far seeing old Tom. 'You know it is possible to live with your beloved Brown Legs, and still play a major part in the life of all Cypriot cats,' he explained. 'Once you have learnt the habits of humans, and become familiar with their comings and Goings, the major problem of distance and transportation disappear,' he grinned as he spoke, trying to allay my anxiety. 'I will tell you something now that will solve your problem of mobility, and hence provide you with the means to return to Governors beach. My humans have a pick-up truck, and every year at the end of the rainy season they go to their caravan at Governors Beach, it is a quiet place for them to spend some time away from the hustle and bustle of a tourist town. Now I have got used to their habits over the years, and I can tell when a thing is going to happen. For instance, I know that in four days they are going to take things to the caravan, and to clean the plot ready for the season.' He looked at me, almost teasingly now, and then grinned slyly, 'You and Avoula could be in the back of the pick-up truck when we leave. All I have to do is tell you how, and I will do that closer to the day they will be leaving.'

I could feel Avoula fidgeting beside me, this long speech that Nicos had subjected us to was leading to a poignant moment, she could feel the suspense in the air, and was just itching for Nicos to tell us when. He became aware of Avoula's impatience, and his grin broadened. The wise old Tom still retained an impish sense of humour. 'You call and see me in three days and I will tell you for sure when the journey is going to happen, and I will tell you how you can come with us, unseen, off you go now,' he added his grin broadening still further. 'And don't be late!'

As if we would!

He strolled over to his mistress and stretched himself across her feet; young Vassos shifted an inch without opening his eyes. Nicos glanced back at us again, and once more that impish grin flicked across his face.

To coin a human phrase: Avoula and I were on tenterhooks. Me knowing that I was very close to going home; and Avoula in suspense pondering over the joys of belonging to a new home. It had become very noticeable that Avoula had gained greatly in confidence. She had always shown reserve and polite attention in her conversations with me, but now she had added a bubbly brightness to her personality which I found quite appealing. She asked more questions, and then listened wide eyed while I answered them in great detail; I too was glad to ease the persistent eagerness in my heart, and pleasant chat was certainly a good safety valve. Far into the night we purred and gurgled at each other, and often a suppressed mew of delight would emit from our nest.

****

Mario still returned to cat City every night, and strolled around spraying and shaking his tail to emphasise his actions. Achilleas of late had rarely been seen, he now spent his time wandering freely among the hills to the north of the path of death establishing himself as a Tom of some importance amongst the many human villages tucked into the valleys, and perched on the surrounding hillsides.

Andreas, and his fellow territorial Toms, Yiorgos, Christos and Dimitri had developed little patches for themselves close to Zavosena, this ensured that should she ever need them, they were close at hand. Her old bodyguard had disappeared. Having been relieved of all responsibility they had melted into the countryside, probably returning to Zavoseanos and a situation that they could relate to. Their whole neutered life had been spent in the service of the King Cat so they knew no other way, completely institutionalised; they sought the safety and security of the only life they understood.

Zavosena now had a different role to play; self-imposed certainly, but that was the way she saw herself. The transition from savage determined leader to society lady had been quite simple for her, which suggests that the desire for such a lifestyle was predominant in her anyway. The members of her old encampment stared unbelieving at their ex princess preening self-confidently for admiring tourists. She was by no means beautiful in the way of some felines, but she was haughty, and imbued with a great sense of self importance, and that very fact made her a popular and most photographed female.

I made it my responsibility to inform her that Big M was firmly established in her new home, and that it was unlikely that she would ever get this far down the strip again.

'Oh good!' she answered Haughtily, and then went on somewhat spitefully, 'The big lump won't be barging into my pin-up pictures any longer, and I will not have to suffer the continuous and incessant rattle of an ice cream tub being frantically pushed around the table legs....cheery bye,' she added affectedly as another photo opportunity took priority.

Avoula stared unblinking at her, still unable to come to terms with this transformation. She walked away shaking her head in disbelief. I just sniggered under my breath, and took a position alongside her as we walked away.

The night before the third day, we were far too excited to sleep in cat City; we nestled under a well-kept row of bushes across from the home of Nicos and his humans. Such was the tension created by my thoughts of home that every little noise during the night, both familiar; and not so familiar jolted me out of my catnap.

Soon after dawn the old human grandfather came to the back door of the house in his pick-up truck. We vacated our bed for the night and watched the proceedings carefully. Nicos and Vassos noticed us from the back yard, and Nicos hobbled across the road to talk to us. 'In a few moments, you will see my old human put bags and cases in the back of the pick-up truck. When my mistress comes out she will be carrying Big M in a special crate in case she gets frightened. When you see all of us get into the front, and you hear the beast growl, you must run quickly and jump in the back, and hide amongst the bags. When we reach the caravan site you will recognise the area but do not jump out of the beast until my old human enters his caravan plot, you can then be out of the back and into the bushes in an instant.' Without another word he hobbled back to his house and watched proceedings attentively.

The old grandma walked out with a proper cat carrying basket gripped firmly in both hands, such was the weight of the cat inside stretched out sedately like a queen being carried on her litter. I reckon the clever old human had got Big M used to the basket over the last few days, realising that Big M may be terrified in the bowels of a beast with round legs for the first time.

The doors closed behind them as they all settled into their seats, and we were already running to the back when the pick-up truck started growling. With one simultaneous leap we were over the tailboard and amongst the bags and the cases. Avoula's eyes were wide and alert looking a bit frightened as she cowered down beside me; for an old cat I thought she had done very well.

My memory went back to my first time; look where my nosiness had got me, and I remember how frightened I had been. All this came flooding back to me as the beast jerked then ran forward in short bursts. Avoula cringed beside me dreadfully scared, but clenching her teeth determinedly.

After a while the beast found the path of death, and then, just like all the other beasts with round legs it ran very quickly in herds of two, four, and six. Sometimes the herd stretched far ahead and far behind, with the faster ones running past us. These beasts showed no fear at all, they were so fast on their round legs nothing could catch them.

They hurtled up the two paths that formed one side of the path of death zig zagging between the other beasts at speed, and disappeared into the distance in the blinking of an eye.

No wonder no side ever won when these beasts met in battle, they hurled themselves at each other with such ferocity one could only think that the humans who appeared to be in charge of them were very brave, or foolish beyond the point of stupidity.

We left the path of death, and within minutes I knew where I was. Caravans began to appear on either side of the road as we climbed the hill within the site. At the top of the hill the truck suddenly swung off the road and jarred to a halt. Instinctively I knew we had arrived, so with Avoula close on my heels we bounded over the tailboard, and before the beast stopped growling we were in the hedge. The road was clear so I swiftly led Avoula across, and we ran down the path on the other side.

'Hang on a minute,' puffed Avoula, 'I must catch my breath.'

Her call for a respite curbed my enthusiasm, we had arrived, and I was home. Two hundred metres down the path was the back entrance to my plot. 'Oh I do hope they are at home!' My thoughts were out loud again as I reacted to a moments consternation.

Avoula glanced at me, and the feeling transferred to her almost telepathically. 'Don't panic,' I reassured her, 'they are usually here still at this time of year.'

We cats are likely to show a bit of excited behaviour if something has hyped us up. For myself, the anticipation of coming back to Brown Legs had heightened my senses; the knowledge that we were only seconds away from our first encounter for many human months was almost unbearable as we neared the back entrance.

A suddenly remembered habit made me go past the back entrance and through the plot next door, and enter my plot by the front entrance.....I should have known it! There sprawled directly in the middle of the entrance was the tawny tabby prima donna form of my eldest daughter.

She jumped to her feet startled, she had not been aware of our approach. Her first reaction was a loud scowl accompanied by an aggressive stance.

'Don't worry Avoula,' I said gently. 'This is my eldest daughter, and she has probably grown to have airs and graces far above her station.'

We stretched out in the road together, and I stared directly at my daughter. She hesitated for a moment; my softly purred reassurance to Avoula had probably jogged her memory. At this moment the grey matter of my self-important daughter was probably churning through past memories, struggling to find the switch that would click on the area of brain associated with 'Mother.' I helped along by strolling up to her; our noses met as we stared eye to eye. Recall flashed through her mind, I noticed her body tense as the burgeoning realisation urged caution. Then, just as suddenly she rubbed me with an ear, I did not rub back so she repeated her welcome. This time I cocked my head and rubbed her determinedly, making her adjust her footing to resist the pressure. She then diverted her attention to Avoula, her curiosity giving her an excuse to back off. Avoula stood her ground as Tigger sniffed her backside, but laid her ears back as Tigger dabbed at her with a paw. Tigger did not back off at the signal of displeasure, so Avoula put her head close to the ground and her eyes narrowed as she emitted a low purring growl. Tigger backed off; Avoula's scent had told her nothing. She had never had contact with a spayed female before, so this puzzled her. She strolled back to me, having decided to ignore Avoula, who was not a competitive female in the true meaning of the term. She gave me another glancing rub with an ear and I replied by dabbing her lightly but firmly with a paw, whilst giving her a queenly scowl. The message got home, she rolled over, ears laid back in time honoured deference to the real boss around here; I took the action no further.

A sudden clatter of rocks and the sound of a human talking to herself turned my attention to the real priority of the moment. I strolled into my patch, and sat on my haunches looking up at the figure of Brown Legs still working at her favourite pastime of changing rocks from one place to another, having patted a much cared for piece of greenery affectionately but firmly into position. It crossed my mind that the pile of rocks was much bigger, and protected from cats seeking a soft patch for their toiletry habits by a covering of wire netting.

As if no separation had taken place, I walked between her legs, rubbing them with each ear. She looked down and said, 'Stop messing about Tigger, I am busy.' Her face suddenly took on a look of complete astonishment. She stood there mouth agape for seconds, the squeal of delight shattered the peace of the day. She bent down and hoisted me up in her arms, and cuddled me closely to her. She had just got the name 'Fluffy' out in the open when Big Feet came bursting out of the awning.

'What the hecks the matter!' His expression quickly turned to a dumbfounded gape as he saw me nestled in Brown Legs arms. 'How!...When!...How did she get here?' His stuttering voice was completely bemused, but it did not matter, Brown Legs had not heard him, she was too intent on chattering at me to be aware of anything he had to say.

Poor Avoula: completely confused by the loud squeal, and Brown Legs grab for me, she had run straight into the foliage of the bottom of the hedge. Brown Legs had caught the action, but was far too involved with me to think anything about a strange cat jumping out of sight, such things were an everyday occurrence for her.

The reunion calmed down after a while, so Avoula crept out of the hedge and looked up at my self-satisfied form, still cuddled in the arms of my beloved Brown Legs. Big Feet was fussing around me as well, which proved to Avoula I was a much loved cat.

Seeing Avoula creep from under the hedge; now only slightly apprehensive, brought me out of my luxuriating self-concern, and made me think of my duty towards my dear companion. I wriggled gently, and Brown Legs put me down saying a little peevishly, 'Oh, you've had enough already have you?'

I gave Avoula a couple friendly of licks to the head, and then sat on my haunches beside her looking up at the two bemused faces staring down at us.

'She's trying to tell us something,' Big Feet said.

'She seems very close to this other cat doesn't she,' Brown Legs said, bending over to give Avoula a closer inspection. Avoula did not flinch, her large round eyes looked straight into Brown Legs questioning gaze, her head cocked to one side in the manner of the attentive feline.

Brown Legs instantly warmed to the appealing stare. 'I do believe you are Fluffy's friend, and you have come back with her all this way,' she said, and then straightening up she said to big Feet, 'Fluffy's bowl is under the table, pass it out please, they must be ravenous after walking all this way.'

Within seconds we were both heads down into a large bowl of mackerel. As I ate, it occurred to me that there was no way I could explain our cleverly arranged journey. The thought disappeared and I concentrated on getting my share of the fish.

My humans were lost in conversation; they were swapping theories as to which direction we had taken to reach here in such good condition. Brown Legs came nearest to the truth when she said, 'Knowing the way she disappeared in the first place, and ended up in Limassol, I wouldn't put it past her to have found a similar method to return to us.'

Big Feet thought for a moment before replying, 'Yes, but that assumes she has the intelligence to know that her choice of vehicle was coming this way,' he argued, and then added as if to prove his point. 'The people she thumbed a lift to Limassol with are not here, so that means that if she came back in a vehicle, it has to be a different one. Honestly!' he exclaimed, 'How could even Fluffy know that, then choose the right moment to board the vehicle?'

Brown Legs was not convinced. 'She and her friend are far too clean and tidy and well fed, to have traveled all that way overland. You know how easily cats get diverted by surrounding events, it would have taken them weeks to do such a journey,' she pointed out our well-fed frames as she spoke. 'Look at the size of them; they have been well fed and cared for, look: the sheen on their coats tells us that.'

Big Feet caved in. Both had a convincing argument, but our well-fed bodies certainly seemed to deepen the mystery for them.

Avoula stretched out, making herself at home. 'Ah well,' Big Feet said with a broad grin, 'Looks as if you have gained another loved one; there is no way these two are going to be separated.'

That did not bother Brown Legs in the slightest, she knew full well that we felines self-regulated our numbers in our own patch, and we feral mothers always did our best to establish our young in other areas. My only problem had been that prima donna Tigger but, she knew her place so it was not a real problem.

Brown Legs continued to make friends with Avoula, who liked her new home very much. She showed Brown Legs just how much she enjoyed being with her by edging closer, and rubbing her ears against her in a show of total adoration and commitment.

Later that day Cleopatra strolled by with her brood of four, she gave me a glance of recognition, and continued on her way. Then something that amused me greatly happened. Big Feet had always assumed that a black and white kitten of mine, born in the same litter as Cleopatra, was a Tomcat; you can't blame him really, TC was a lumpy ball of fluff from birth, and appeared to have the size and head of a Tom. TC had presented her new humans who lived just up the road, with a litter of kittens, but only one survived, and somehow or other that solitary kitten had chosen my plot, and my humans as his favourite place.

Big Feet called his new friend Toopeas; at least that's how it sounded after Big Feet made absolutely sure of the gender of this absolute replica of his mother. Toopeas, just like his mother followed Big Feet everywhere. Toopeas had no siblings to wrestle and argue with, and every time he tried to get friendly with Cleopatra's brood she cuffed his ears and sent him on his way, she had enough to contend with, having four of her own. Big Feet became his substitute for playmates. It strengthened the little fellow up and gave him a certain robustness of character. Someday he would rise to be a fine figure of Tomhood; he already had the broad head and sturdy limbs of a future alpha Tom.

During the next few days, with Avoula constantly by my side, I met all my old acquaintances. Maria, who had suffered such a dreadful loss before my unplanned visit to Limassol, had her hands full Six little beauties of about a month old strolled serenely beside her, their little tails pointing skywards, proving just how happy and well cared for they were. We watched their wobbly progress for a few minutes and then stretched out to watch and grin widely from a short distance. Very soon the little imps got used to us, and included us in their favourite pastime of tail chasing. We obliged them by swishing our tails from side to side temptingly, this stopped young kittens getting bored if there was insufficient stimulus, while mum had a rest.

Avoula made friends with everyone, they sniffed at her enquiringly; some showed puzzlement because their eyes beheld a female, but their noses gave no verification of the fact. We enjoyed our short strolls together; it gave Avoula a chance to learn all the little places that were of importance in the area. It did however become very noticeable that she always hurried her pace a little when it became time to return to our patch, she always made a beeline to be around Brown Legs feet before me. She just could not wait to be a part of the natural affection that oozed from Brown Legs every time we came home.

She had just thrown some scraps over the hedge for the strangers, and Avoula, not quite familiar with all the routines yet, made a dive for them.

'No, No, No!' Brown Legs ran through the back gate scolding Avoula, and picked her up in her arms. 'You eat in here now with Fluffy,' she said, placing her on the ground next to me.

This did not upset Avoula; she soon became conversant with the rules of the house, and was very soon doing her toilets in the proper place like all of us well brought up felines.

On the fourth day back we decided to take a stroll to the top of the site and say hello to Nicos and company. They were all sitting outside under a sun shade enjoying breakfast as myself and Avoula nonchalantly stretched out at the entrance to the plot. Nicos, Vassos, and Big M jumped to their feet, and ran across to greet us. For a few moments a session of vigourous ear rubbing took place as we greeted each other. The old couple looked across at us, and laughed at our antics, but then the old boys face took on a puzzled look. 'Hey!' He said to his wife waving a finger at us. 'Isn't that the two cats who visit us at home?'

The old mistress put her glasses on, and looked closely at us from her seat. 'It surely is!' She answered, equally puzzled.

We wandered off and left them talking, and exchanging views on how it was possible for two cats to be here, when only five days earlier they had seen us at their home. Old Nicos gave us a sly wink, and grinned broadly as we got up to leave, he no doubt would get endless pleasure listening to his old humans discuss the mystery of how we could possibly be at their caravan plot.

For a couple of hours we thoroughly inspected the top of the caravan site. I pointed out all the little tunnels under the fence, and the Tavernas down by the beach, then, having sniffed at a few strangers hiding under caravans we strolled down the centre path of the site. The site cleaners were out keeping the site spick and span and doing the gardening. A group of felines had stopped by the bushes, always curious as to what humans were doing. For myself, I would not have bothered about the activity of the humans but a black form caught my eye sitting amongst the group of nosy cats. It was my mother, whom I had not seen for ages. You can imagine my absolute surprise as I drew closer to her, when I noticed old Nicos sitting on his haunches beside her. They both turned towards me, reacting to my gasp of astonishment.

'Oh hello again Fluffy,' old Nicos said.

My mother turned and frowned at him saying, 'How do you know my daughter?'

The question remained in her eyes as old Nicos answered her. 'Oh, Fluffy and I have had a great experience together over the last few human months.....'

Before he could continue, I butted in, 'How do you two know each other?'

My mother looked at me strangely as she opted to reply, 'I should know him very well my dear; after all, he is the grand old Tom who is your father!'

THE SEACAT

The pregnant pause created by my mother's statement seemed to go on for minutes. Both Nicos and I stared dumbly at the impassive face of my mother. She did not blink an eyelid; she just looked from one to the other of us with a smugness that only a cat's features can portray. I found my voice first, 'But I have heard my humans say that I am the living image of that Tom from the Tavernas, the one close to the beach.'

'That would be rather difficult my dear,' she retorted with a hint of scorn. 'He has never been my mate, in fact my only mate for two seasons was your father Nicos, and you are one of the offspring of the second season. Only a mother knows who the father of her children is, and I am in a far better position to know your parenthood than the humans who have become your friends.'

Old Nicos recovered from the initial shock of this revelation, and scraping his throat said in a slightly hoarse purr, 'Well, that answers a few questions that had occurred to me over the last few months....wisdom runs in the family,' he said pointedly at me. 'Only a wisecat could have worked so diligently at the job you have recently completed.'

I noticed my mother give Nicos an odd look. He in turn looked her in the eyes saying, 'My dear Sheba.' He stopped abruptly, noticing my loud gasp. He turned to me and explained. 'Do not be surprised my dear, Sheba has always been my name for your mother, you could never have been expected to know that.'

He turned back to my mother who had retained her querious look. 'It is a long story Sheba, our daughter and myself, through some quirk of fate, were thrown together to solve a long standing problem between two differing factions of the cat population of this Island. Thanks to her efforts, peace is now established between the cats from the mountains, and we shore-side cats. No cat need ever go hungry again, and all the young cats of the shore-side now have more space in which to develop their territorial traits.'

The cats in the vicinity, who, whilst appearing to be totally intrigued by the actions of the human cleaners had turned their heads towards my father as he spoke. They hung onto every word, news would very quickly travel all along the coast that all the lands were now open to all cats.

Hunger broke up the gathering and in the way cats do when confronted with a greater urge, we all broke up and went our different ways to the patches we shared with our tame humans.

Avoula, who had sat silently watching what had transpired, spoke up for the first time as we reached our patch. 'Well my dear friend,' she grinned broadly as she purred, 'Life with you is certainly a series of surprises; whatever is it to be next?'

I looked at her grinning widely. 'I have just had the most pleasant surprise ever. What could be nicer than suddenly discovering that the wisest old Tom around is actually your father.'

Avoula nodded in agreement saying, 'Your mother has a beautiful name; I don't recall ever hearing the name 'Sheba' before.'

I considered my answer for a moment. 'I think my father has lived with humans so long that he probably gives names to cats that do not otherwise have one, and, as you say, Sheba is a beautiful name to give the feline who is your mate.'

A fishy smell wafting through the hedgerow broke up our conversation. Avoula was first into the plot, and consequently the first to bury her head into our communal food bowl; she was not greedy though, she knew that one fish was for her and one for me. The milk bowl was full also, so we dined gracefully, and then settled back licking our chops clean, and then we nodded off for a while.

We awoke later to the sounds of Big Feet and Brown Legs chattering to Cleopatra. She was trying to shake off her cloying brood, and lose them somewhere else on the site. She had her own human friends now and the crafty little so and so was trying to show her brood what a nice person Brown Legs was. She had not thought out the whole equation though; there was me to consider, and the fact that my eldest daughter also had a claim to this patch thanks to my foolish forbearance.

Avoula and I were watching Cleopatra, with her youngsters unsuccessfully trying to suckle. Out of the corner of my eye I could see Tigger watching the show with narrowed eyes. It was obvious that her territorial feelings were about to snap, and if she did let go all hell would break loose, and the youngsters would stay clear of the territory she shared with me forever.

Just as I thought, Tigger's patience snapped, and she hurled herself at the three teenagers. The ferocity of her attack was such that the three youngsters were sent reeling, bowled over by the speed of her attack. They recovered from their surprise, and let out the most ear piercing yowls. These screams, mixed with the adult screeching of Tigger created a scene from hell. All other cats close by-except those close to Brown Legs-scurried for cover, they did not want to be on the end of the uncontrolled anger of a cat jealously ensuring that no unwanted cats would interfere with her livelihood.

Tigger did not just chase them off the plot; she harried them down the road, ramming the message home with feline determination. Cleopatra jumped up on Brown Legs lap, and pretended to ignore the whole scene; the job that she should have completed probably a week ago had been done for her. I looked up at her, comfortably curled up on Brown Legs lap with eyes half closed. 'Yes madam,' I growled to myself, 'You thank your lucky stars that my humans are here, and they protect you, otherwise that would have been you off down the road, with your offspring also.'

No doubt she would find her brood waiting for her when she went home, but Tigger had ensured that they were not dispersed around our patch, much as Brown Legs would have liked it.

Tigger stalked back into our patch on stiff legs, the hackles on her shoulders still raised, but that did not stop her tail from rising in the air triumphantly as she paced towards Brown Legs and stretched out across her feet.

Big Feet always had a good word for Tigger, and he voiced his opinion about Tigger's ferocious action. 'If it wasn't for her we'd be overrun with cats you know, at least she shares them around.' He leant over and stroked the prima donna; she reacted by jumping to her feet and doing figure of eights between his legs, giving him a possessive ear rubbing at the same time.

'Ah, but she is not here all the time,' Brown Legs said defensively. 'They all end up round the back if they are starving, have a quick snack and disappear again.'

Big Feet grinned, and replied jokily: 'I'll bet, if I left my arbeitzimmer open you would have that full of cats in next to no time.'

'Don't leave the keys loafing,' she grinned back.

Big feet raised his head and gave a quick laugh. 'Come on Tigger, you can keep guard for me,' he said, getting up and going to his work room.

Tigger followed him faithfully and draped herself across the doorstep. 'You see,' he shouted pointedly, laughing like a jackass.

Later on in the afternoon, everybody; that is, cats and humans were enjoying an afternoon snooze in the gentle sunlight. The humans were stretched out on their sun lounger seats, and all us cats were stretched out heads on front paws.

To all intents and purposes we gave the impression that we did not have a care in the world. Suddenly this air of contentment was disturbed by a weird sensation surging through my mind; this was a new feeling never experienced before. A sudden premonition of danger followed the odd sensation, and I gazed around uneasily. I was not alone in whatever it was that was disturbing me. Tigger; TC, Cleopatra, and Avoula were all standing heads high seemingly bewildered. Little Toopeas was on straight stilted legs, his nose testing the air.

The sensation did not go away, it increased. Suddenly we were all on our feet, backs arched, hackles raised; real fear was in the air now, and we all had sensed it. Brown Legs and Big Feet remained dozing. Whatever it was that initiated this fear worsened, all of us cats rushed into the road, most of us meowing uncontrollably. We were not alone; every cat on the site appeared to be seeking an open space. The noise stirred my humans; they arose from their loungers, concern etched across their faces.

Aloud bang that shook the earth came from miles out at sea. We could not see it, but the sound wave rippled across the water as it passed over deafeningly. The bang galvanized all us cats into action, as one body we all made a beeline for the perimeter fence. None of us went through the little cat tunnels that went under the wire, we all hit the fence at the run and were over it and into the open land on the other side in seconds.

Big Feet and Brown Legs looked on open mouthed; a second later it was their turn to be forced into action. The ground heaved suddenly, and trembled ferociously, then seemed to wobble backwards and forwards interminably. My humans clutched at anything to hang on to, but stumbled onto their knees. Just as suddenly as it had started shaking, the earth became still again.

All the cats were now stretched flat out as if clutching the ground. Some got up instantly and started rushing around aimlessly, first in circles and then in little short straight bursts. This was interspersed by short pauses with head held high, and eyes darting this way and that way fearfully. The madness seemed to go on for ages, and I suddenly became aware of Brown Legs looking over the fence at me, calling my name. Big Feet had Toopeas clutched in his arms, the little fellow had not made it over the fence, but now appeared calm nestled safely in the arms of his pal.

Not one cat made a move to go back into the site. The ones who had felt inclined to rush around madly slowly settled down, but still remained out in the open. Many were taking advantage of the stillness of the earth to move downhill, further out into the open. I had no desire to move further downhill towards the sea, perhaps because it would take me further from Brown Legs; however, I still made no effort to react to her calls.

Glancing seaward I became aware of Avoula crouching behind a bush. Her body was tensed as if pulling away from something. I watched for a moment; noticing her tugging actions getting even more frantic. Whatever it was that held her, appeared to have her by the front leg. Still very uneasy I looked back at Brown Legs again, she was calling me more determinedly now, anxious to protect me from whatever pending danger confronted us all.

I looked back to Avoula, who really was getting more scared by the second. I could see that she could not free herself from something, and like any trapped animal was doing damage to her leg as she frantically tried to get loose.

In an impulsive moment my mind was made up, I raced down towards her only to find her whole leg was tangled in a discarded fishing net that had just been dumped in the bushes. She was gnawing savagely at the manmade fibre, and her leg, but all to no avail. Her eyes searched mine as I reached her, the horror of her predicament reflected in them, but I had no quick answer, other than to join her frantically chewing at the nylon net.

Big Feet saw us, and instantly knew we were in trouble. He rushed to the bulky carob tree that the fence ran under, and clambered up into the lower branches. He then lowered himself on our side of the perimeter fence. In the minutes it had taken him to do this; a loud rushing of surf had gone unnoticed. As he reached the ground he looked upwards and turned to face the shoreline. For a long moment he stood transfixed, his mouth gaped as he stared at the sea. One of nature's most dangerous creations was bearing down on us at tremendous speed. 'Good Lord!' Big feet gasped, 'a Tsunami.'

Without a moment's hesitation he was over the fence again urging Brown Legs to get a move on and run further up the site. He had judged the wave to be about ten feet high, but growing bigger as it drove up the shallow seabed.

'Get in here!' He shouted at Brown Legs, pushing her through the door to the ladies toilet. 'It does not look high enough to reach here,' he shouted. 'But if it does, it will be a spent force; the steep ground up to the fence will deaden it.' He offered up a silent prayer that his estimation was correct.

The cats became aware of the wall of water racing towards them, and with huge bounds retraced their headlong flight over the fence. Brown Legs and Big Feet heard their screeches of fear as they scrambled past the toilets in an attempt to put as much distance as possible between the small tidal wave and themselves. 'O please let one of them be Fluffy,' Brown Legs offered up a silent prayer.

The wave, now fifteen feet high, powered up the beach collecting chairs, tables, sun beds, parasols, and all sorts of children's beach toys, as it forced its way relentlessly inland. It flattened the outside areas of the Tavernas, where minutes earlier fearful tourists had scrambled for their cars and raced away uphill from the beach areas.

The Tsunami raced on uphill getting noticeably shorter by the second, it bowled people over who had not quite reached the total safety of the steepness of the hill, but they were seen to stumble to their feet, only to be swept of them again as the wave started its return.

I had been forced upwards by the savage rush of water. Now I felt myself tumbling backwards as the water rushed back to its source. My head cleared water a couple of times and instinctively I sucked in life sustaining air. Seconds later I was part of the debris left floating two hundred metres out at sea, as the turbulent water ceased its foaming rush back to sea level.

The surface of the sea was absolutely littered with every form of beach paraphernalia. I clambered out of the water onto a sailboard, my first instinct being to shake of the sea water clogging my fur. My next reaction was to counter the motion of this lively sanctuary.

I hadn't noticed at this stage that a slight current created by the retreating waters was carrying me away from shore somewhat faster than the surrounding flotsam, which was not quite so aqua dynamic as my sailboard.

Assisted by a light offshore breeze, the sailboard, with me, it's still dazed rider, was soon a kilometre from the beach. I watched hopefully as a fleet of small boats that had been hurriedly overturned and emptied of seawater started to come out to the line of floating beach furniture. The occupants started loading the rescued furniture, but not one of them bothered to come and see if anything had floated a bit further out to sea, so I was left adrift and at the mercy of the elements.

The waves lapping over the edge of my sailboard quickly made me realise that my position was not at all secure. The board dipped and rose, and was continually awash, several times I found myself slipping to one side or the other. Only my claws acting as a brake prevented me from going over the edge. It was then I noticed a projection jutting out of the smooth surface of the sailboard.

I chose my moment and scrambled towards it. I clutched the projection firmly with my front paws, and immediately felt more secure, I was not now at the mercy of the rocking and rolling motion of this very shiny platform. My feet and lower body were constantly wet, but the sea was not so rough as to drench me totally.

I quickly learnt to turn away from the direction of the spray, so my only view of the sea was as it reappeared having passed under the board.

The sun began to sink below the level of the sea. The apprehension that grew in my inner being, and culminated in the frightened darting movements of my eyes, turned to total fear as darkness began to descend. If total blackout occurred I would be totally blind. My eyes were very efficient at making the most of any glimmer of light, but total darkness meant total blindness. Of my other senses, I could smell the sea and I could hear it, I could feel the motion of the sailboard, but these were secondary senses compared to the ability to be able to see danger and make any allowance necessary to avoid it, or meet it head on.

Fortunately total blackness did not occur; the stars shone brightly, and later on a thin crescent moon appeared. Sleep was out of the question, I had to stay constantly alert to retain my grip on this very welcome projection on the surface of my lifesaver.

I don't know how I survived the night. I kept drifting off into a catnap, and then wake up startled as my body relaxed its hold on the projection. It was with great relief that the first glimmer of dawn appeared to the east. I was barely aware of it, but my fight to retain total awareness had sapped my conscious strength. My eyelids were like lead weights, I believe at that moment I was losing the fight to remain awake.

I was vaguely aware of the motion of my sailboard, at least aware enough to realise that it had stopped moving awkwardly to the motion of the waves. Through a sleepy haze could see that the surface of the sea was flat and totally calm. I slipped away into a catnap, the pleasure of approaching oblivion lost to me; such was my need for sleep.

How long my catnap lasted I do not know, but I was brought back to consciousness by a sudden lurch of the sailboard. Every muscle in my body tensed, taut as a bowstring as I scrambled to grab a hold of the projection.

The board lurched again; and then the part behind me seemed to dip backwards, and the part I clung to rose out of the water. I swung around on my foothold to face the back of the board and froze in horror at the sight that met my eyes.

The head of a huge sea monster was pointed straight at me, the grey mass with its round black eyes and long beak like face with open mouth showing small teeth, gaped directly at me making a chattering squeaky noise in some unintelligible language. For a moment I thought the sea creature was laughing at me as its beak like mouth opened and closed rapidly. It seemed to nod its head at me, almost tossing me off my precarious perch. I clung tightly to the projection determined now to fight to the death to avoid being thrown from my raft by this laughing monster that appeared determined to eat me.

Then, a surprising thing happened. The monster slid slowly off the sailboard, and gripped the back gently between his teeth. I prepared for my doom by crouching lower onto my life saving projection.

Suddenly I was being propelled through the water at great speed; I was now in danger of being washed off my raft by the occasional torrent of spray that was sent up by the front of the sailboard. Quickly, I turned to face the monster again; his grinning face showed he was highly amused by my discomfort and the sight of my fear filled eyes.

The thought flashed through my mind that its grinning face made it look quite a jolly creature, but the movement of the sailboard quickly brought me back to reality. I dispensed with my hasty opinion as my aching muscles reminded me that I was clinging on ever so tightly to prevent myself from falling into the jaws of this grinning beast from the deep.

Suddenly my craft came to a jarring stop and seemed to climb upwards. The force of the sudden stop in forward motion broke my grip and I was sent sliding up the shiny slope created by the upward angle of the front of the sailboard.

My tormentor had let go, and was wagging his head up and down laughing at me. I suddenly realised I was on dry land again; my sailboard was firmly aground on a pile of huge rocks forming a breakwater.

I stared unbelievingly at the monster, instantly realising that this most intelligent looking face with its friendly eyes and laughing mouth had actually saved me from a watery grave.

The agile swimmer dipped below the surface, and seconds later burst through the surface in a great high leap out of the water. His head turned towards me with that fixed smile; I'll swear he was saying goodbye to me because after entering the water again he turned away and disappeared into the distance in a series of short leaps that gave the impression of a farewell display.

I sat staring in the direction my lifesaver had swum away for ages; my new circumstances caused me to see this intelligent animal in a completely different light. We had never seen each other before, we were not even aware of each other's existence, yet this beautiful creature had deemed it necessary to save my life, it must have sensed that I was a land animal, but we had something in common: we both breathed surface air.

The reason why this jolly looking creature should save me was way beyond my comprehension, had it have eaten me; yes I would understand that because that is the more usual way of life for a wild animal. I pushed it from my mind and got on with a feral cats natural obsession: survival.

Looking around me I still appeared to be all at sea, the sliver of land I was upon disappeared into the distance, and then seemed to join a bigger piece of land. This was a place where humans kept their boats, not a big harbour or port where huge ocean going vessels berthed and unloaded and loaded, this was a smaller harbour for fishing boats and smaller craft, called a Marina.

The sea was deeper here; it did not have such a steeply rising continental shelf so the effect of the earthquake at sea making a huge pressure wave which developed into a tidal wave had not battered this small port as badly as the beach areas. The breakwater had taken a lot of the force from the lower part of the wave, but a deluge had descended into the Marina from the crest of the wave.

The breakwater was made up of huge rocks of all shapes and sizes interlocked together in what appeared to be a hap hazard manner, but in fact many of the rocks were strategically placed.

To something as small as a domestic breed of cat the breakwater presented the human equivalent of a climb through rocky country; after much leaping and jumping I finally found myself on the mainland once more. People were rushing hither and thither like ants, working singly and in groups. No one paid any attention to me, but just in case they did, I darted from cover to cover, belly low to the ground and eyes alert.

A pile of knotted fishing nets all jumbled together in one great disorganized heap provided a good vantage point to survey my surroundings. Some damage had been caused inside the Marina, mainly swamped boats, mooring lines separated, and some boats had been swept into contact with other vessels causing minor hull damage.

The old port of Limassol had been battered, but human endeavor would quickly bring things back to normal.

Now that I was safe, and had time to think, I suddenly realised just how hungry I was. A smell wafting on the breeze had brought on this sudden need; someone was cooking a fish for lunch, and quite naturally my taste buds had reacted to the delightful smell. I tested the air with my nose pointed upwards; the enticing aroma was coming from a big fishing boat tied to the jetty almost opposite my hiding place.

A ramp ran from the jetty up to the deck of the boat, although there was no sign of the crew. Humans were hurrying up and down the jetty carrying ropes and all forms of rigging so I took my chance when a break came in the human chain. I ran across the intervening space and ran up the ramp onto the deck of the big fishing boat.

All the new ropes had been piled in a heap on the deck, and they provided a decent hiding place for the time being whilst I surveyed my new position. The smell of cooking fish was coming from a door that was open just a little way from where I watched. I crept from beneath the nets and cordage, and edged my way towards the open door.

I paused, and then tentatively put my head forward slightly the better to peer inside, but ready to run if any danger lurked within. A short, but very strongly built old man was cooking over a stove his thick brown arm waving a frying pan over a flame whilst the other arm jiggled a cooking tool inside the pan.

The aroma of the cooking fish was mind boggling, in fact the aroma was so enticing I became careless and allowed my whole body to come into view. The old man caught the movement out of the corner of his eye; his head swung round, and his grey moustachios seemed to bristle, but I could not help but notice the sudden light that danced in his friendly eyes.

I had ducked down below the doorstep as his eyes caught me, a natural reaction under the circumstances. The old man raised the pan off the flames and tipped the contents onto a plate, scraping the pan clean with the cooking utensil. I turned swiftly, slightly startled as a fish head and tail attached by a long backbone landed beside me. 'Here!' The old man chortled. 'Is this what you have come for?'

I dived at the fish head, and the old man stepped over me as he took the meal he had cooked through another door further to the front of the big boat. Soon, the loud talk of jolly men interspersed with an occasional burst of laughter came through the door. I became less ill at ease, I had lived with humans long enough to know when I am welcome.

The fish was a big one, with plenty of flesh around the head bone. I chewed away contentedly until I reached its eyeballs; I crunched them up savouring this delicacy before proceeding to devour the remainder of the head followed by the juicy and generous lump of tail flesh that had been left on the bone.

Having eaten my fill, I lay down on the deck below the door sill. My mind did not dwell on the events that had brought me to this position, we cats had enough to worry about concerning the present and the near future; the past was gone, any lessons to be learnt from it were locked away, and would only be brought into use if the occasion demanded it.

My reverie was disturbed by the sound of loud voices coming from the door further forrard. Suddenly three men seemed to burst through the open door all full of jollity. 'There she is Stavros,' said the old man who had fed me.

Stavros bent down and looked me in the eyes, saying, 'We need a cat to catch a rat.'

His two companions roared with laughter, which I suspect was enhanced by a liberal portion of wobbly water with lunch.

Stavros grinned even more broadly in response to the mirth shown by his shipmates. He bent down again and tickled me under the chin, 'My ship is plagued by a master thief,' he said with the pretence of being serious, then continued in the same vein.

'I have a clever rat aboard my ship who has evaded all attempts at capture, and certain death; the food we put in rat traps he steals with great skill, having tripped the latch by some clever means.'

He stroked my head, and I reacted in a friendly manner by cocking my head first to one side, and then to the other, the better to enjoy the sensation.

'You catch Mr Rat,' he went on, 'and your payment will be one fish per day for life.'

My belly was full so his promises meant very little to me at that moment, but the sport of rat catching; ah now, that was a different kettle of fish!

The old man picked me up in his thick brown arms, and stroking me soothingly carried me through the door into a room with a wooden wheel in the middle surrounded by all sorts of dials, clocks, and screens. The whole room had windows that went all the way around in such a manner that if you stood in a certain spot, you could see all around you.

He took me through a hatch in the deck and down a short ladder into a communal cabin, this was obviously the place where they all ate and slept.

He opened a door at the back of the cabin, and the smell that hit me indicated that this was a store room. It was not a big room to a human, but to a cat it was quite a large room.

A few rings of shelves went around the room, each shelf holding different types of stores. The old man left the storeroom door open, and put me down facing the entrance. 'Now I shall leave that door open so that you can have a good sniff around without being locked in there, I don't think you would like that,' he added kindly.

He climbed back up the ladder, closing the hatch behind him. As the latch lowered I heard the voice of Stavros saying to the old man: 'Glafcos stand by to let go forrard!'

The hatch closed, and I heard no more.

Looking around the cabin, I began to feel at home. I sniffed in all the corners, and began to realise that in human terms this was a man's world. All the paraphernalia that hung on the bulkheads; the smell of stale tobacco smoke, and other manly odours designated it as male territory; although the human male did not appear to spray his territory in the same manner as the territorial Tom Cat, but the end result was the same.

The store room was much more interesting. I was becoming absorbed with a scent that was definitely that of Mr Rat, when a sudden roar like a beast with round legs startled and distracted me, causing me to jump back on the shelf I was investigating, and disturbing a spiky metal plate.

I calmed down as the engine reduced to a low purr, and then after a series of higher and lower rumbles seemed to settle down to a steady purr.

The boat began rocking and pitching gently, reacting to the surface of the sea it was ploughing through. The motion was not unpleasant, much nicer than the jerky movements of the two beasts with round legs I had ridden in to date.

Soon my legs got used to counteracting the light rolling motion. In human terms, I was finding my sea legs. I looked at the contraption I had bumped into. How odd, I thought, as I gave it a thorough examination. Several pieces of metal fitted on to a plate with a spike in the middle with a large chunk of cheese skewered onto it. I became very wary of this unfamiliar thing, the smell of rat was everywhere around it.

Deciding to give the contraption a wide berth, I continued my investigation. It soon became very obvious that Mr Rat did not live in the storeroom, so that meant that he had access to the stores from some outside source: but where was it? I sniffed out all the corners of every shelf, and then gave the deck a most particular investigation. There was not a single crack or gap in the wooden planking that made up the deck of the storeroom, yet the smell of rat pervaded the ambient air of the room.

Looking upwards, my eyes scanned the deck head. Apart from a length of rope going from port to starboard, and a slatted air vent directly above the length of line, the remainder of the deck head was clear space. I squatted down on my haunches behind a sack on one of the shelves, and settled in for a long wait. Mr Rat would get hungry sooner or later, and then he would show me how he gained access to this well stocked pantry.

Dozing off onto a catnap with my ears pivoting in all directions to catch all the sounds around me I began to realise that boats were never silent. The throbbing of the engine, creaking boards, the constant swish of water passing along the hull, the hum of a fan pumping air below decks, the sounds of humans working on deck. Surprisingly, even though the noises were all jumbled up together, each of them could be picked out individually. I decided it was not an unpleasant situation to live in; there was something reassuring about ship board noises.

Very soon, the creaking of the winch told me that the big fishing net was being streamed out. This was a night fishing trip so that fish could be fresh on the fishmongers slab next morning in the Limassol fish market.

After the noise of the net going out, the winch stopped, a few moments later I heard feet descending the ladder and old Glafcos poked his head through the storeroom door. 'Ah there you are,' he said, as his sweeping stare settling on me behind the sack. 'Have you seen Mr Rat yet?'

He hunched his back slightly so that we looked into each other's eyes. The red glow of the night lights gave him a devilish contour with his shining eyes and huge drooping moustachios.

'I see you are hiding where he cannot see you, you must be alert, he is a very clever Mr Rat,' he chuckled as he ducked out of the doorway, and ascended the ladder once again.

Sometime later I became aware of a scratching sound. It was a new sound, but easily discernable amongst all the other noises I had become accustomed to. Glancing into the crew's cabin I could see that it was empty. The scratching sound occurred again. This time I caught the direction of the sound, and looked upwards just in time to see the rats head squeeze between two of the slats of wood that formed the vent that allowed a circulation of air in the storeroom. The clever fellow had chosen the middle of the slats where they were more bendable, and could be pushed apart a little. Having squeezed his head and his front paws through the gap, he proceeded to pull the rest of his lithe frame through; then amazingly, he hung on the bottom slat with his front paws whilst his back legs searched for the length of line somewhere beneath him. His legs waved about for a moment then contacted the line. He let go with his front paws and scurried along the line to the safety of the sack just below the line of the shelf with all the practiced flair of a circus acrobat.

I watched in silent wonderment as this master thief chewed an onion free from a string that was hanging on the end of the line. Carrying the onion by its string he staggered along the sacks until he looked down on the piece of cheese skewered to the metal spike on the contraption below him. He appeared to be lining the onion up on something. When satisfied, he released the onion and the round vegetable descended onto the front of the contraption. A loud metallic clap filled the storeroom as the onion hit the trap, and it appeared to jump in the air.

In an instant Mr Rat was down on the trap; he grabbed the cheese, and clawed his way back to the top of the sack again. His nose tested the air as he reached the top of the sack again, he was uneasy and with good cause; the unusual smell that disturbed him was me, and my feline mind was already devising a plan of attack. There were plenty of hiding places for him in the store, but due to the stacking arrangements they were all easily accessible to me.

He nibbled at his cheesy prize holding it delicately between his front paws, his little eyes flicking this way and that as they penetrated the reddish gloom.

I judged the distance between the shelf I watched from, and the shelf three metres away on the other side. Could I reach it in one mighty leap? My muscles tensed like coiled springs, the potential energy stored within about to be released in one huge explosive burst of feline power. Making an instant decision I launched myself into space. My eyes caught the rat's first startled movement as he dropped the cheese and scrambled for the line. At almost the same instant my front legs were clawing for the shelf I had launched myself at. I gained a hold and quickly hauled myself up onto the shelf, and then leapt for the top of the sack. Mr Rat had already got his head and front legs through the slats of the air vent as I hurled myself at him. My teeth clamped on the on the base of his tail where it joined the rump, at the same time as my front claws found purchase on the air vent. He began squealing loudly, he was a strong little devil and clung on the slats he was between with great tenacity. His front armpits were lodged over the slat, and I was clinging onto that slat with my claws, the only way I could pull him through was to release my hold on the slat and thereby allow my suspended weight to pull him through. I had just started that move when a loud thwack from above silenced Mr Rat and he suddenly went limp.

I crashed to the deck with the now dead rat in my jaws. Almost immediately I heard the pounding of feet descending the ladder, seconds later the head of old Glafcos appeared through the storeroom door. I had just changed my grip on my victim to ensure that the kill was efficient, my teeth severed the vertebrae, and any glimmer of life that may have remained was snuffed out.

Glafcos held a hefty piece of wood in his right hand; he had been attracted by Mr Rat's loud squeals, and belted him on his exposed head to prevent his escape. He looked at me standing over our kill with that self-satisfied smug feline look that all we cats have on our faces when the hunt turns out to be successful. Stooping down he grabbed hold of the corpse by its tail and ran up the ladder with it.

'Look here!' He shouted at his skipper Stavros. 'No more Mr Rat, she got him!'

I followed him up the ladder, jumping from rung to rung. I stood on my hind legs sniffing at our kill now swinging in the hand of an excited Glafcos.

'Okay, okay!' He shouted laughing loudly at my possessive stance. 'I know it's yours, and you shall have it in a moment.'

Stavros grabbed a camera that he kept on the chart table, then Glafcos picked me up in his other hand, and nestled me in the crook of his elbow. A blinding flash emitted from the camera and instantly Zavosena sprang into my mind because I associated bright lights with her.

Glafcos put me down and gave me the rat; I snatched it up and ran out onto the upper deck with it clutched firmly between my jaws, its long tail dragging on the deck. I found a quiet corner, and devoured most of the rat closely watched by other members of the crew who appeared fascinated by my tugging and chewing as I disemboweled the rat.

One of them fastidiously swept the remains overboard, and with a bucket on a length of rope collected some seawater and scrubbed the spot clean. I crept back into the wheelhouse, and curling up in a corner, fell soundly asleep.

I was rudely awakened by the roaring of the engine some time later. I rushed out onto the deck to find that we were alongside the wall in the Marina. The nights catch was being unloaded to begin its short journey to the fish market.

My body suddenly told me that I had not been to the toilet for a very long time. I gazed about me; there was nowhere in sight suitable for a cat to do its toilets. I ran down the gang plank, and started searching for somewhere to dig a hole.

Finding a suitable spot I hid behind a large stone and completed the job at hand, following it up with a good grooming. With a belly still full of rat; fur shining nicely, and wrapped in a sense of well-being, I found a comfortable spot and dozed off again in the warmth of the morning sun.

My rest did not last long. Shortly after settling down I was rudely awakened by shrill human voices close to me. The laughter and the loud squeals of delight were coming from a large group of young humans prancing along the jetty in great good humour. Whatever it was that delighted them so much was not immediately obvious, so, ever inquisitive, I jumped from the rock and followed this group of jolly and scantily dressed young humans.

No-one noticed me as I trotted along directly behind them along the jetty to a much bigger boat than the fishing boat I had recently served on.

The all smiling, and very handsome members of the pleasure boat crew helped all the giggling young females on board, and one who was dressed like a skipper was saying, 'Welcome to the Love Boat' as he took their hands gently, inviting them aboard.

I scurried up the gang plank, and unnoticed by the crew mingled with the feet of the happy young passengers out for a day trip. With no fuss at all, the smiling crew hauled the berthing ropes on board, and in minutes the pleasure boat had cleared the harbour, and was rising and falling to the gentle swell of the Mediterranean Sea.

The Skipper sailed south for about half a kilometer, and then turned east to leave the beach areas of this popular part of the south coast on the port side.

The happy passengers were wasting no time, and before they had even ordered a drink of wobbly water, they were wriggling and writhing their bodies to the loud music. Even I, a cat, whose only rhythm was the cycle of feline life, could sense how cleverly the humans contorted their bodies to the loud beat of the music.

One human male who appeared to be older, sat alone at the end of the bar his head hidden in a cloud of his own making. He had just come along to enjoy the trip in his own way, and take advantage of the cheap wobbly water.

Everybody seemed to be doing their own thing. Some danced on their own, some danced in two's, whilst others stood at the ships guard rails and chatted, the movements of their bodies suggesting that they were just enjoying the sound of the music.

A few humans sat at tables enjoying a drink in the gently warm breeze created by the ships motion. I noticed a young couple with their lips glued together, it did not appear painful; they seemed to be enjoying the sensation very much.

A short time later, the Skipper turned the boat towards the shore, and a loud clattering sound signified that he had dropped the anchor. The crew lowered a ramp to the water, and the small boat that had been towed astern was tied to the platform of the ramp. The ships engines had stopped and all was safe. Some humans were then allowed to dive in the water to swim from the platform.

I cast my eyes along the shoreline, and had a sudden feeling of awareness. Looking further inland from the beach line I could see caravans scattered amongst the trees at the top of the hill. Somewhat surprised, I suddenly realised I was staring at my home. I looked around me desperately; I had no fear of water, but that distance was too far for me to paddle.

My eyes lighted on a group of humans climbing into the boat tied alongside the platform. Without hesitation, and not really knowing why, something made me rush down and jump into the boat amongst the giggling humans. They were not bothered at all; it was almost as if they had not noticed me.

The boat swung away from the platform, and raced towards the shore. Some happy individuals did not wait for the boat to reach the shore; they jumped into the sea laughing loudly, and swam to the beach. I waited, poised at the bottom of the boat. I felt it run up the sand, and was up and over the bow into the water in an instant.

'Hey look! a swimming cat!' I heard a human shout.

His friends looked my way, 'Go on cat, you can do it,' they all shouted; cheering me on.

I reached the sandy beach and immediately burst into a gallop, heading for the scrubland around the caravan site. I did not stop running until I reached the fence surrounding the site.

The big wave had washed all the loose debris from the scrubland right up to the fence, and had deposited all sorts of rubbish that seem to litter open ground these days.

I took all this in without a break in my stride; taking the fence at a gallop, and dropping down the other side exhausted. I paused for breath then strolled through the plot alongside the fence. I checked the road out of force of habit; then sauntered across to my own patch overcome by a sense of relief.

Somehow, I had never expected to see my home again, having fallen victim to the awesome power of the sea when disturbed by another great force. I had survived by some good fortune, and the aid of a stranger from another element. The memory of this sea creature was still in my mind; I wonder how long it would stay there.

The recollection was already fading as I sat down staring at Brown Legs and Big Feet enjoying a cup of tea.

Big Feet was shuffling a sheaf of papers, chattering lightly to Brown Legs who was half absorbed in an embroidery project. She caught sight of me out of the corner of an eye and paused in her work. She turned to me and her gaze met mine, and held it for a number of seconds; then her mouth sagged open, but not a sound came out.

The embroidery dropped to the floor as she slid forward out of the chair her arms outstretched towards me. As if in slow motion she sank onto the tiles beneath her knees and took me into her arms. Not a word was said as she cradled me between her head and her shoulder. In that moment words were not necessary to convey deep feelings. Poor Brown Legs had thought I was lost, and this moment proved without doubt that humans are capable of great loyalty towards animals that they have built up a rapport with; but it was not until this precise moment that I realised that I belonged to them, just as much as they belonged to me, and they felt totally responsible for me whenever I was with them.

Big Feet had noticed her sinking to the floor, and a worried expression flicked across his face. It was then that he noticed me. He gazed on us for seconds seemingly devoid of speech, and then he found his voice,

'Where did you spring from madam?'

His astonished question leant an edge to his voice, but then he continued in a softer much more possessive tone.

'We thought you were lost little lady.' His hand came across and tickled me under the chin in one of his rare acts of overt affection. Brown Legs still had her cheek against my head, her eyes were moist with the tears she was trying her hardest to contain; she finally found her voice.

'Never mind, you are back with us again, and that is all that matters,' she said soothingly.

Big Feet helped her up, and still cradled in my arms we all walked into the awning. At last she put me down and opened the door to the cold white box. She took out a can of fish, opened it, and poured the contents into my bowl. I dived into it gratefully while they stood back gazing at me fondly while I devoured the whole contents of the tin. They had kept my water bowl full of fresh water, so having washed this nice meal down, I settled onto my cushion and proceeded to groom myself extra thoroughly, then without a care in the world I curled up and went to sleep in my own favourite corner.

'It never ceases to amaze me,' Big Feet said as his eyes followed me into the corner. 'Where does she get to, and what does she do? Did you notice her fur was soaking as if she had been fully immersed in water?' His face broke into a grin as a thought flashed through his mind. 'Perhaps she had to swim back from this adventure.' His grin broadened as he added, 'I wouldn't put that past her either.'

Brown Legs, watching me curled up on the cushion, answered his incredulity, but her view was more circumspect. 'She always comes back here, and she looks well when she does come back, so no matter what she gets up to she has discovered an art of survival far beyond her natural feline instincts. I think that is because of us; we have taught her that humans can be kind and loving; this means that she can manipulate suitable humans to her own advantage. That has got to mean that she is a wise little pussy cat.' She looked at Big Feet; he smiled back saying simply: 'Great to see her curled up there again, isn't it?'

Later that day all my daughters paid due homage to their mother. All of them gave me a cautious rub with their heads; then sat at a safe distance away from me.

Safely back with my humans, one would have thought that my mind would be totally at ease; but it wasn't. Something was bothering me; there was something, or someone missing. So far nothing had happened to encourage an association that would jog my recall system.

Later on that day as evening approached Brown Legs threw the scraps out at the back, and then fed us residents with a lump of liver each. She put my bowl down, and I dived into it greedily.

That feeling of something missing came over me again. I continued puzzling over it as I chewed away at the liver. Suddenly it came to me, Avoula; that is what had been nagging at me ever since I came back.

We had become accustomed to eating together, and she had always run to be first with her head in the bowl.

A momentary sadness flashed through my mind, all my other familiars were here, and judging by the scowls and growls coming from the other side of the hedge, so were all the other cats who congregated here at this time of day.

So where was Avoula? She had not ended up in the seas as I had done, and it was unlikely that she was under the wave long enough to drown.

I continued mulling that fact over in my brain while finishing off my meal. The only way to solve this one was to retrace my steps, and then my water assisted tumble down to the sea.

Big Feet noticed me leaving my empty bowl and then stroll to the road. 'Hey! Where do you think you are off to?' The sound of his voice made me pause and turn my head around to look at him. 'Yes you,' he grinned as he spoke. 'What big adventure are you cooking up now?' He started to walk towards me. I turned and hurried across the road; eyes swing right and left instinctively. I passed through the plot on the other side, and crawled under the fence. Big Feet was close on my heels, apparently anxious to watch my every move. He watched me walk down to the bushes and sniff around, but he did not go as far as to climb over the fence.

I found the spot where Avoula had got tangled up in the discarded fishing net- it was no longer there. I went further downhill sniffing around every bush I came to it, it was then that I came across a most awful and unexpected sight. There tangled up in the fishing net which was firmly entangled in the top branches of the bush was the inert body of Avoula, her fluffy light grey body completely entwined in that terrible net. Her gaping mouth, and her widely staring eyes told me she had not drowned, she had been choked to death by this man made ligature that was binding deeply into her neck fur.

For several minutes I sat there staring up at her body; perhaps inwardly hoping to see a twitch or some other indication that life had not left her body. The silence was broken by a shout from Big Feet. He could see me and the bush from his position on the other side of the fence. His shout encouraged me to turn away from the horrible sight of my poor friend, and look upwards towards him. He could not understand my look, but he knew I was not transfixed to this spot for no reason at all.

'What is it Fluffy? What have you found?

I remained rooted to the spot, and turned my head back to the body of my dear companion who had surely suffered an agonizing death, wrapped in a terrible shroud of carelessly discarded fishing net.

I became aware of Big Feet clumping down the hill towards me. He stopped beside me, his eyes following the direction of my fixed stare.

'Aw my God!'

The compassion in his quietly spoken exclamation made his voice sound husky. He untangled Avoula's body from the top of the bush, and walked up the hill with her laid in his hands. Reaching the fence, he called for Brown Legs.

'Look at this,' he said quietly holding the body of Avoula up. The look on his face had turned to sheer anger now as he looked into Brown Legs white face. She in turn gazed at Avoula's body the horror that she was feeling reflected in her eyes. But just like Big Feet her horror turned to an expression of disgust as she stared at the reason for this unnecessary extinction of life. This once vibrant and companionable old feline had fallen victim to one of the scourges of our modern age: careless and thoughtless disposal of none biodegradable material.

'She did not drown,' Big Feet said, containing the anger that burnt in his eyes. 'I suspect that the swirling of the waters wrapped the net tightly round her neck; the poor thing had the life choked out of her by that fiendish garrote.'

His anger faded away into exasperation, 'Fetch me the shovel dear,' he asked, his head shaking from side to side as he spoke through pursed lips.

We watched as he laid Avoula in a shallow grave, and then, after putting stones over her body, filled the hole in.

'The dogs won't get her now,' he said, the compassion returning to his voice. He climbed over the fence, and we all went silently back to the plot.

****

When I felt like it, I stayed in the awning with them. For this reason Brown Legs always kept an old cushion wrapped in an old towel in the corner. It was quiet in the awning tonight, a complete contrast to the usual badinage that interspersed with whatever was on the radio. The death of Avoula had saddened them greatly; they would both be recalling it long after I had pushed it from my mind.

Early next morning, a low feline growl was heard from the plot alongside ours. I pricked my ears up and crawled under the canvas. My daughter Tigger was standing on stiff legs her head and neck straining forward as she peered into the hedge. I stood beside her, also straining to see, or catch a scent that I could recognise. A strong purr from a young Tom came through the hedge. 'It's me, Vassos, I must see you.'

I dived through the hedge, and came out quickly on the other side prepared instinctively to fight or run. Vassos backed off visibly at the speed of my appearance.

'Nicos wishes to see you,' he purred softly, regaining his composure.

We hurried up the path through the middle of the site together, the speed of our advance making other felines crouch down on their bellies at the sight of us. All of them were familiar with me, and the speed of our feline trot indicated trouble to their alert minds; they did however relax as soon as they realised that they were not about to be the victim of a territorial good hiding.

Minutes later we trotted through the entrance of the patch belonging to the humans who had cared for old Nicos all of his life.

The wise old Tom was stretched out on a rug specially put out for him. I noticed immediately that something was not quite right about him. He was stretched out lying on his right side; his left side had a look of limpness about it.

'Hello my daughter,' he greeted me. His purr lacked the old strength that I had become used to, it was also noticeable that he purred out of the right side of his mouth; the left side of his lips seemed to be floppy.

'Hello Nic...' Habit made me use his name; I stopped myself. 'Hello father,' I greeted him fondly.

His right eye seemed to hesitate as it joined the remainder of the right side of his face in a grateful smile. Looking at his reaction, I realised that he had never been called 'father' before.

It is good of you to come so quickly,' he purred in a husky whisper. 'As you can see, I am not my old self today; the ravages of old age have caught up with me, the shock of the earthquake was too much for my old body.'

I could hardly hear his soft purr so I moved closer to him on the rug and lay beside him where I could place my ear close to his mouth.

'Thank you my dear,' he purred softly, then continued with some difficulty: 'When the quake shook the ground, I jumped up to run with all the other cats, but something seized in my brain and I collapsed unable to move the left side of my body, thank God for humans. My old mistress saw me collapse, and instantly picked me up. I think it was the warmth of her body that saved me, because the shock of the quake had left me feeling very cold. I knew I was fading away, but her cuddles warmed me, and gave my system the will to fight.' A tear seemed to mist his right eye. 'Sadly, the old lady has to pick me up to feed me now, but she has learnt to roll me on my belly so that my head is over the saucer, that way I can feed myself, but very slowly. I am very lucky you know many humans would consider it an act of mercy to have taken me to the human who puts animals away forever. My old humans can still see the twinkle in my eye, and they can see that I am helpless and not in any real pain, so they show their love for me by helping me do everything.'

If I had been capable of human emotion at that moment, I am sure I would have shown my deep regards for this old Tom in a much more overt manner, but somehow all I could bring myself to purr was, 'If there is anything I can do to help you father, I will stay with you.'

At that moment we were disturbed by the old grandma bustling out of her awning carrying a bowl of bread soaked in milk. Close on her heels wobbled a still very large Big M. Her gross body broke into a trot as she saw me. Our heads met a few times in greeting as we rubbed each other and licked ears. 'Oh Fluffy,' she purred. 'It is so good to see you again, where have you been? We all expected regular visits from you,' she chided me good naturedly.

'Believe me,' I replied. 'It is a long story and now is not the right time to relate it.'

'Oh yes of course,' she replied, slightly chastened herself now.

Nicos smiled on the good side of his face as his old mistress laid him flat on his belly with a paw either side of his bowl, and his head in a strategic position, the better to allow him to help himself the best he could. 'There you are my old boy,' she said, patting him affectionately. She watched him for a few moments to make sure he could manage properly.

She had noticed me of course, and now she spoke. 'Ah, it's you again pretty one, you do have a habit of turning up at poignant moments, are you sure you're not psychic?'

Old Nicos spluttered in his bowl, and coughed gently as he heard her statement. He turned his good eye to me and winked as if to say, 'If only she knew the truth of it all.'

His mistress eased her old frame into a plastic armchair and Big M draped an ample body over her feet possessively.

My father struggled to finish his bowl of food and finally succeeded. He smacked his lips gratefully, and actually managed to groom his left shoulder and leg; the old boy had some life left in him yet.

'My mind is unharmed,' he explained simply, noticing my concerned gaze. 'But I shall never again be able to react to the call of my brethren when they seek my guidance.' He looked wistful for a moment. 'One thing I shall be eternally grateful for is that I have lived to see a peaceful outcome of the differences that developed between the cat communities on either side of the path of death. You played no small part in that peaceful outcome my dear, and all those that carry that knowledge forward to future generations will forever sing your praises. No doubt they will always refer to you as Fluffy, daughter of old Nicos; and that will make me very proud. To have given Tomkind an advisor and mediator, and certainly a wise feline leader for the future has made my life complete, my existence on this beautiful Island has been justified. How wonderful it is to have reached the last stages of my life, and be able to look back on events with great satisfaction.'

He looked at me pointedly, his eyes aglow with pride. 'I have instructed Vassos to inform the whole of Cat City that you, my daughter, will now assume the exalted position of "Wisecat" in my place. May you be blessed with the same good fortune that has been the hallmark of my life.'

QUEEN OF CAT CITY

My father continued to visit the site with his humans until the autumn of that year. My dear friend Big M began to look less of a monster as the year drew to a close, and Vassos had become an assertive Tom: both on the site, and in the society of the tourist area of Limassol.

The rainy season hit us very late, and the shortage of water due to years of low rainfall caused the need for control of the use of this precious element. All the humans were talking constantly of having to build desalination plants at selected places close to the shore. We wisecats became very aware that not all the humans who shared this island agreed upon which were the best places to build these industrial plants that extracted the salt from the sea water, leaving it fit for human consumption.

Desperation point had not yet been reached, but the shallow water in all the major dams served as a reminder to all at government level that action must be put in place now, to prevent a major shortage in the not too distant future.

The people of Cyprus had other thoughts on their minds as the end of the year drew closer. A great event was about to happen in the human calendar, the millennium year of 2000 was upon us, and all those people in the world who regulate their lives by the Gregorian calendar were organizing huge celebrations. Many people of the world who regulated their lives by other calendars were also caught up in the great excitement that had gripped the world, mainly because there was only one chance every thousand years, and that is a long time between big parties.

The people of Cyprus who worked long hours on the land, and looking after tourists, always looked forward to any date that called for a party, so when they threw parties they did it with huge enthusiasm. Unlike many of the richer nations however, they did not make it a terribly expensive event. The prices for all those people who came to Cyprus, and all those humans who lived in Cyprus were kept at a very sensible level so that everybody; rich and poor alike, could afford to celebrate this great occasion in a true community manner.

Three months later, the rainy season was coming to an end, and I had weaned and dutifully dispersed a litter of kittens. I was looking forward to a bit of rest and social intercourse with Brown Legs; but that was not to be it seems.

Early one morning, I was eyeing up a Stone Chat who had made a tree in my hedgerow, her perch for greeting the new day with her constant prating.

A low growling purr came through the hedge from the plot next door. I sprang into action immediately because that sound came from a Tom. My youngsters were weaned and gone, but the instinct to defend and protect was still strong in me. I rushed through the hedge ready to fight whoever it was.

Poor Vassos leapt back, assuming a defensive stance as I burst into view, but then relaxed as he saw instant recognition put the brakes on my attack impulse.

'That's the second time now you've surprised the life out of me, why don't you come round the front where I can see you,' I blurted at him, and then grinned as I saw his scared face relax.

He could tell that I had only recently weaned a brood, so his first words posed a question: 'Do you have young with you?'

'No, they can all hunt and beg for themselves now, I was hoping to enjoy my rest period until you appeared on the scene,' I answered, letting the grin stay on my face.

'Oh good!'

The sound of his reply, and the look of relief that dashed across his face, brought a look of puzzlement to my face, quickly wiping the grin away.

'You are needed back at the tourist area a problem has occurred that needs the attention of a wise female before it grows into a major problem. Can you come up to our site now, I have much to tell you, and I don't want to be interrupted by some over-zealous territorial Tom.'

The look on his face, and the almost imploring tone of his voice made me react immediately. Silently we started our journey to the top of the site. We didn't run because that would bring attention to ourselves. We loped along side by side in total silence for the first part of the uphill climb.

After we passed the halfway point Vassos tried to make light purring conversation, but I could not help noticing some tenseness in his attitude; he had something further on his mind.

Just before we reached the plot of his humans he stopped and blurted it out in the only way he knew how, 'Your father will not be there to greet you,' he said hurriedly, looking at me in a way that preceded bad news. I stared back at him silently, my eyes indicating that he should complete his statement.

'I am afraid he died a week ago.' His eyes did not leave mine as he spoke, and I was aware of his personal sadness also. I remained silent. The news tugged at my feline sensitivities, but not in a sentimental manner, more a sudden sense of loss which increased momentarily as recent memories of that wise old Tom paraded through my recall system.

One iota of memory remained vividly constant; the moment of revelation when I discovered he was my father. It was a comforting thought that this wise old Toms genes were alive in me, and the many offspring that I had nurtured and weaned.

We had reached the top plot by this time, but did not cross the road. Vassos dropped onto his haunches in the bushes alongside the road; somewhat surprised, I followed suit.

Without hesitation he continued his news, 'The great Zavoseanos has also died.'

Zavoseanos meant very little to me, his passing, whilst of concern to those close to him, raised no sense of loss in me.

Vassos, aware of my lack of reaction continued, 'His death has caused a problem. Zavosena, the most forceful of his offspring is insisting that she must now be instated as Queen of the Trods. She believes that she is the only one of his heirs who has proved herself fit to lead all the diverse breeds of felines who form the nation of the Trods. This has brought her into direct confrontation with Mario and Achilleas, who insist that rule, can only be right if it is by mutual consent of the majority of the cats on both sides of the path of death now that we are all united. They believe that unelected hereditary rule is wrong, they insist that all Tomkind on this Island should be free to pick their own leader, and if that leader turns out to be no good then there should be a system in place to deselect that leader and elect someone else.'

He paused in his long speech to collect his thoughts. I looked at him sitting there on his haunches with his bent tail stretched out in a buckled arch. It flashed into my mind that this was a far more experienced Vassos sitting before me that the eager youthful Vassos who came to public notice during my time as a peacemaker. He interrupted my thoughts by continuing his explanation:

'Before he died old Nicos told us that our humans invented a way of life called 'democracy'. He explained that the great masses of humans who have adopted democratic ways are not ruled directly by one person who has gained a position of power from his or her forefathers. Democracy is not hereditary, it is not achieved through class distinction or privileges, it is government chosen by the majority of the people, they elect the leaders to act in their name, and to ensure that their leaders do not let power go to their heads and then abuse it, every four years or so they have new elections which can put someone else in power if the people are not satisfied with the way they are running a country.'

He paused again, and this time noticed that I was staring at him wide eyed and incredulous. 'I hope all that is clear,' he said.

'My father told you all that?'

My continued incredulity turned the statement into a question.

'Oh yes, he did!

Your father had such a way of explaining things that you just had to pay full attention to what he was saying, I just could not help understanding what he passed on to me.'

I knew what he meant; he had purred away so lucidly that his repeated version of my father's lecture was ingrained within me. I suddenly knew why I was what I was. The wish to live in a democratic manner must be strong in all species. Even amongst so called dumb animals, all will follow the member of the species who by natural talent has gained the leadership because nature has imbued that individual with the ability to reach the top. I now know why I reacted so strongly to those who would dictate to me, and those who would try to curb my natural air of freedom of thought and speech.

My father learnt all this because he was susceptible to the way of life of all free thinking humans, his understanding of them and their ways had made him a wise old Tom. The sudden recollection of him made me feel sad, Tomkind had lost a very good and wise old Tom, and now I had been chosen to carry on where he had left off.

I snapped out of my reverie as I realised that Vassos had been watching me intently.

'So once again I must have a confrontation with Zavosena?' I asked matter-of-factly.

He thought for a moment before answering, 'Mario and Achilleas feel that you are the only female who has the natural strength of will to combat her sense of superiority, they doubt if she would even listen to any other feline in the community. Anyway, now that your father has passed on, all the females consider you to be there natural spokescat; they refuse to even consider anyone else. Mario and Achilleas are of course strong enough to stand up to her, but this is a talking matter and must not develop into a fighting matter; otherwise we slide back into the bad old days of confrontation.'

I still hadn't quite caught up with the realisation that this young Tom, who gave so fully of himself as a fighting Tom, had now assumed the mantle of diplomacy. I had to realise that I was purring to an intellectual equal, and that was not easy considering that he was a young Tom, and I was a far superior feline mother. I pushed aside my feelings, and tried a pertinent question.

'What about Christos, and Yiorgos, and the other territorial Toms whom Zavosena had appointed as my escort group? What about the brave Trod Females who formed the initial discussion group? They are her own people by birth and long association, cannot they convince Zavosena that her self-serving inclination is not acceptable now that we are all democratically joined as one nation.'

Vassos frowned deeply, his forehead creased as he considered the words I had put to him.

'They are all firmly with Mario and the leadership group, but it is very difficult for them to face the cat that was their princess, and had the power to make their lives unbearable. You know that Zavosena would not accept them on equal terms. The council of Cat City has spent hours discussing what can be done; everything that I say to you is as a result of these meetings.' He stopped purring abruptly, searching my face for acceptance of his well-expressed words.

I did not answer immediately. During these last few months with Brown Legs I had grown used to the regular routines that humans live by; routines that come naturally, and are not instigated by a chemical impulse. We talked to each other, I could always tell by her stance, and other actions, what would happen next. When she looked at me and said: 'Oh look, it's time for lunch!' I would look up at her and answer with an expectant meow. 'Are you thirsty?' She might ask, and I would answer affirmatively with a meow. In the evening I would watch her closely until she said, 'Time for walkies!'

I would follow her with my tail high in the air. Inevitably all of my offspring cottoned on to this ability to talk to humans, and to react to their habitual ways. The evening walks became an entourage of Brown Legs with me directly alongside her, and then the remainder. Tigger; Cleopatra, TC, and her son the ever bigger lump called Toopeas. All four of them had got into the habit of being outside my plot at exactly the right time, and their tails shot into the air as Brown Legs and me walked out onto the road.

Quite honestly, I was reluctant to leave this homely situation; hence an inner battle was raging between what I loved, and the onerous duty that had been placed on my shoulders.

Brown Legs and Big Feet were used to my frequent disappearances, they reasoned that I was a feral cat, and quite rightly exercised my right of natural freedom whenever the feeling moved me. They were not aware of the major dramas that occurred during my absences.

Vassos could see the indecision in my eyes, so did not force the issue for the moment, a sure sign of his acceptance of human wisdom.

'I will run and tell you when I see my humans loading the pick-up truck ready to leave,' he said diplomatically, and then without another word ran across the road to his humans.

Big M sniffed at his fur, then her tail shot high in the air, and she stared alertly towards the bushes I was hidden in. She had caught my scent and instinctively knew that I must be quite close. I could not help but notice that Big M was a lean normal feline again, her silvery tabby coat glowed with health; a sure sign that the old couple who had adopted her had succeeded in training her to respect regular meal times.

Seeing her new slimline body made it hard to believe that she had gone through a bad period due to her addiction to Danish ice cream. I suddenly remembered how I and my dear departed friend Avoula had been unable to contain our mirth at the sight of a bulbous Big M. The recollection of my dear friend forced my mind into a fit of nostalgia as my mind brought forth the memory of my time in the tourist area.

The memory of old faces sprang back into my mind, individually, and in groups. The joy of seeing the confidence of the female discussion group grow: as their bodies reacted to regular feeding.

The sleek black coat of my mate Mario lodged firmly in the memory circuit blotting everything else out. For an instant I felt selfish at having delayed my acquiescence at the end of Vassos's well delivered explanation. I hurried across the road to make up for my tardiness in making a reply to him.

Big M saw me break cover. She dived carelessly into the middle of the road to greet me with a frantic full on head bashing.

I retaliated with equal force, and then scolded her for not checking the road properly. We strolled into her humans plot, tails erect and bodies close together.

Vassos jumped up from where he was stretched out across the comfortable slippers of his old mistress, and looked at us with Tomlike expectancy. His mistress glanced at me and Big M and her old eyes brightened visibly.

'Ah it's you again my pretty one,' she said, and then her eyes clouded as she went on, 'You look so much like my old Nicos, I think you must be one of his daughters, you are too much like him not to be.'

She leant forward and hoisted Vassos onto her lap. 'This is my new Nicos,' she said happily. 'He is a lovely boy too.'

Vassos had gained another name. It would not bother him in the least. When an amply filled plate of goodies is placed under ones nose: who cares what the benevolent one calls you.

Vassos jumped off her lap; like all felines he liked to choose his cuddly moments, not have them forced upon him, anyway, he preferred to be draped across her slippers, they were comfortable; reassuring; fluffy, and smelled of himself.

'Come and fetch me the instant your humans prepare to return to the tourist area,' I purred.

The statement made him stare into my eyes, and after a few seconds he acknowledged my determined statement with a grin, and then draped himself back across those beloved slippers. His mistress had returned her attention to the elaborate lacework pattern she was working on. Like many of her fellow senior citizens she was so thoroughly adept at lacework that her fingers seemed to move under their own volition, without any mental effort.

Big M followed me across the road to the bushes. 'Are you returning to the tourist area with us again?' She asked, her eyes taking on a sly glint as she added, 'Missing Mario are you?'

I paused before answering; her question indicated that she had no idea of what was going on outside of her own home.

'Do you know that Zavoseanos the King of the Trods is dead, and that his daughter Zavosena is trying to set herself up as queen of the alliance?

Her jaw dropped, and it took her a moment to reply. 'I um, er I um, I have not been to Cat City since you left,' she stammered with a hint of guilt. 'I have grown so comfortably attached to my humans, I rarely leave their company for more than a few moments.'

Her demeanour, as she explained awkwardly, indicated that something else was the cause of her feeling of guilt.

'What are you frightened of?'

My question sounded stern, yet I was trying to get a point across as gently as I could. I was genuinely concerned; it was most unusual for a cat not to be nosey. She must be worried about something, and perhaps even fearful of something.

'What is it M? Come on, you can tell me, I am your best friend.'

'I love them so much,' she blurted out, and then a stream of sentences came forth which fully explained the inner fears that plagued her sensitive pedigree soul:

'I am Frightened they won't be there when I get back. I am frightened they may not want me. If I have kittens, will they be angry? When Vassos sniffs me, I cringe in case they see it and throw me out.'

'Stop, Stop! M, don't upset yourself like this,' I cried soothingly. This poor friend of mine was lost in a field of broken glass, her imagined fears preventing her from taking a step in any direction. I had seen other females on this site suffering the same feelings of insecurity that Big M was going through. They had been rescued by cat loving humans on the site, and remained on the site during their human's absence.

They stood on the roofs of the caravans waiting, and searching the road for their companions to return. They slept under the caravan, and only left the plot for toilets, and to hunt and scavenge. Their only true release from feral insecurities was when their humans returned.

One could almost feel the sense of relief emanating from these females when they looked up at their returning humans purring obsequiously, 'Look, I have kept our plot free of mice, and snakes, and lizards,' then pounce gratefully on the bag of scraps tipped out for them to gorge on greedily.

'Your humans would never consider losing you now that they have seen how beautiful you have become,' I consoled her gently. 'They love you, they have made you a part of their life, come on silly!' I rubbed my head against her. 'Forget all these worries and lead a normal feline life.' I paused for a second as a thought flashed through my mind. 'I tell you what; you can help me when I talk some sense into that self-centered Zavosena. She knows you very well, and the sight of the new you, cured of your addiction will give her something to think about.'

I gave her a friendly nudge to emphasise my regard for her. She reacted by licking my ears and the top of my head. What she had been lacking was sisterly assurance, she had isolated herself from the general population of cats, and the price was the fear of loneliness, another brood of kittens would do her the world of good, there is nothing like motherhood to cure self-worry and self-orientation.

****

The pleasantly warm sun that attracted so many visitors from colder climes had exchanged duties with a bright, and in human terms: romantic moon, twice before I had the visit from Vassos that I had been expecting.

This time his visit was noticed by Big Feet and Brown Legs. With typical human male one track mind, Big Feet glanced at us walking across to the path, and said: 'Flipping heck Fluffy! You've only just got shut of the last lot; surely it isn't that time again so soon.'

Brown Legs, hearing the tone of his voice looked up from the row of Marigolds she was tending. I gave her a long stare, and felt momentarily undecided. It took a second or two to shake off the feeling; as much as I loved her, I had made what amounted to a promise, and must stay true to my word. I dragged my eyes away from her worried expression; she made no move to intervene, but I could tell by her stance, and the concern on her face, that she was forcing herself not to interfere in my personal feral life.

I could feel both sets of eyes watching us as we strolled up the path. Just in case Big Feet did follow us and discover our destination, I encouraged Vassos to slink into the bushes with me, and make the rest of the journey up the site under cover.

Before we were out of earshot, I heard Big Feet's voice saying, 'I wonder when we shall see her again?' A lump came into my throat, his voice held a note of sadness.

By the time we arrived at the old Cypriot couples plot, they had placed all the items that made for a comfortable weekend in the back of the pick-up truck; and were making sure the awning was secure, and properly zipped up. 'Jump in the back now,' Vassos ordered.

I obeyed instantly, and hid between two bags that propped each other up. Minutes later the pick-up roared into life, and once more I was setting off on another adventure.

****

This was my third ride in a beast with round legs, but I still had that feeling of apprehension as the pick-up truck growled; sometimes loudly, and for long periods of time, yet at other times just stood purring gently as if it had stopped for a short rest. After some time it stopped completely and no sound came from it at all. I now knew that this was my cue to jump from the truck and hide.

From my vantage point under a bush I saw Vassos leap from inside the beast, and then his old mistress struggled out on stiff limbs, but still clutching Big M to her bosom.

Big M made no attempt to jump free, and even tried to cling on as she was lowered to the ground.

Vassos immediately started scenting his territory, and I had to dive back quickly as he squirted the bush I hid beneath. His actions did not bother me at all, because I too scented my territory on the caravan site. I had in fact been scolded by Big Feet and Brown Legs a few times, until I learnt that they did not like their awning squirted at. The sight of Big Feet rushing to get a bucket of water startled me on a couple of occasions. I suppose the combination of the scolding, and their reactionary jump, told me in no uncertain terms that humans do not consider peeing anywhere at will a terribly polite thing to do.

Big M dived straight indoors as the master of the house unlocked the door. Her eagerness to be securely at home with the people she had grown to love was patently obvious. She truly had become a fully domesticated cat.

Vassos saw me spring back under the bush, and when he had finished squirting everywhere joined me in slinking up the road and under a beast with round legs that was half on, and half off the pavement. We waited until the old couple had emptied the back of the pick-up truck, and closed the door behind them. We were now free from caring eyes so we strolled up the road towards Cat City. It was nice to see that the Russian waitress was still cheerfully at work in the corner café.

'Chu, Chu, Chu,' she said to us, bending over and patting her right leg in an invitation to join her. The visit was worthwhile, when we had let her stroke us we were rewarded with a few titbits of sausage and bacon pieces, very palatable as a mid-morning snack. Other people, noticing the lovely Russian girl feed us, threw portions of their breakfast meal at us. By the time we continued our short journey to Cat City it was as if every human was glad to see me back scavenging around the cafés.

Crossing the road to get out of the sun, we searched for somewhere to sleep off our early lunch. We settled down under some bushes, and for the next two hours completely forgot about my purpose for being here. In typical feline manner nothing had greater importance that the desire of the moment, any other priorities would have to wait, and take their turn, after this immediate desire was sated.

Two hours later I stirred; yawned widely, and arched my back giving all my muscles a good stretch. I jumped back startled as I became aware of a big ginger Tom staring at me absently, whilst perched on his haunches. My startled jump aroused Vassos, who also leapt to his feet, instantly ready for action.

With a wide grin across his broad features Achilleas looked straight into my eyes saying: 'Well-well-well, you've come back!' and then added slyly, 'Mario will be pleased.' He glanced at Vassos, and his ears went flat against his head as he growled, 'Steady boy!'

This was in reaction to the defensive pose that Vassos had assumed. His back was arched; with his ears laid back, and his broken tail curved to one side. It would take him minutes to settle down.

Territorial Toms were always inclined to be offensive when another Tom was too close, which of course made them useless negotiators. It was up to the females to keep order in our own areas, and encourage some discipline.

'Let's go then,' I purred, breaking the air of hostility that surrounded us. I did not take the lead for long though, Achilleas jumped to the front with a few decisive bounds, this was his patch, and no female, or young stripling was going to be allowed to lead him.

Big black beautiful Mario came bounding across as he noticed that I was in the group he had suddenly become aware of. I curbed his natural enthusiasm with a hiss and a spit, and a tap on the nose with claws retracted. That had the effect of steadying him down, whilst putting him in his place, so I immediately changed tack and gave him a rub with my head, followed by a lick of his ears.

Chastened now, he laid flat down on all four paws, and showed his interest in a more diplomatic pose with his eyes closed to mere slits.

'It is good that you have come so quickly,' he purred. 'None of us can do anything with Zavosena. Now that her father is dead, she insists that she should be Queen of all the Trods. That in itself does not worry us; she is quite welcome to be Queen of the mountain cats. What we find offensive is the fact that she believes because we all co-exist peacefully now, and that all cats have access to all parts of the Island from the mountains to the shoreline, she should be Queen of all the cat population. We cannot allow this, so we need someone to talk some sense into her, and break this stalemate before it causes division and brings back the old troubles. Some of the shore cats are already saying that she should be escorted to the other side of the path of death before too many cats fall under her spell, and begin to back up her claims. That could be very dangerous.'

He had presented his worries simply, and it was easy to understand why all of them were so worried. I nodded my head understandingly as he finished. 'Vassos explained the problem to me quite clearly,' I purred, and then after a moment's thought I continued, 'I am not going to rush down to here right at this moment, I must have time to mingle with my old friends, and listen to their views. Are the females who helped me break down the barriers that divided us still with us?'

'They certainly are, they are firmly settled in Cat City, and are a popular part of the community, as are Christos and Yiorgos, who are now part of the ruling council of territorial Toms.'

'Good,' I purred happily. 'Then you will not mind if I involve all of them and my friend Big M.

'It's about time she had babies,' he scowled at the mention of Big M's nickname. 'She is far too interested in her own comforts, she should get to work and have kittens, that is what female cats are supposed to do.'

I purposefully ignored the tone of his purring criticism. 'Perhaps being with me, doing something useful for the whole community will help her to get over the insecurities that have made her this way,' I said gently.

'Don't rely on her too much,' he growled back, his attitude leading me to believe that his male ego had been offended by a rebuff from Big M during one of her natural fertility cycles.

Achilleas joined the conversation, 'Not a natural female that one, she has all the scents of a receptive female, but runs and hides; even young Vassos who shares the same human house is warned off.'

I could have explained Big M's difficulties to them, but I did not bother to try. Nature had imbued Toms with two basic instincts in life: one, to gain a territory, and the second to pass their genes on to as many receptive females as they could service by any means fair or foul. How could I explain such a sensitive issue such as Big M's problem to creatures who were not endowed with the necessary grey matter required to form an understanding of such delicate feelings.

Seeing a lack of response to their male posturing brought the discussion to an end; suddenly grooming took on an air of importance, and for some minutes we were all contorting our bodies into seemingly impossible positions to give ourselves a thorough cleaning.

Vassos finished grooming first, and as if ordered by some inner mechanism, padded silently away out of Cat City in the direction of his home. That inner clock had just reminded him that it was that time of day when his humans put out a meal for him. If he was not there when it was put down on the floor for him, it would be placed outside the back door.

Time had taught him that other cats were always watching and ready to pounce on that plate should he not be there in time. This act by his caring humans had taught him that an orderly life with orderly habits and a natural instinct for punctuality had its own rewards.

Being a cat, albeit a Tomcat, he learnt good habits very quickly; particularly when they were to his own advantage.

Mario and Achilleas both strolled off together towards the tourist area, and I was left to my own devices; but not for long. It appears that I had become a very famous pussy cat. I was being hailed by young felines I had never seen before, felines I knew vaguely, and then most pleasant of all I bumped into the four Trod mothers who had joined me to negotiate the peace. We banged heads together; licked, and purred greetings to each other. The one called Lala finally purred, 'We all knew that the ruling council had sent for you, so we were looking forward to seeing you very much.' The other three echoed her sentiments, and a great deal of affection was shown to me, which I enjoyed very much.

During the remainder of the day, we all dispersed around the tourist area, making sure that only one or two of us were at any café at any one time.

I bumped into Yiorgos, who greeted me with typical Tom like interest until I cuffed him round the head, hissing nastily. Having been thus disciplined he joined me for a meal. When we had eaten, and drank our fill at the watering point, we sat down and had a chat.

'You have come to talk to Zavosena?' His voice was a gentle purr; as we lay down to digest our meal. Before I could answer, he continued.

'You will not find her easy to talk to now. The humans in her area have grown to love her, and care for her when she lets them. The tourists always run to take pictures of her preening and posing. She thinks she is absolutely wonderful, and terribly superior to all us other cats, she really does consider herself to be the cat's whiskers, and a most deserving candidate for the self-imposed title of Queen.'

I let his gently purred information sink in for a moment before I asked, 'Does she ever come to Cat City?'

He looked away, not wishing eye contact, but answered assuredly, 'She has never set foot in cat City since the day she was shown to the territory by the Danish ice cream parlour. Every human in that building has accepted her as the local feline, so her and her cronies have undisputed access to the whole area, all the way up to the path of death. None of the other territorial Toms argue with her, so she is virtually Queen of the whole area. As you know, she does not give off receptive scents, so no Toms go near her anyway. She does however have a following of felines, all of them entranced by her haughtiness and total self-love. It is they who feed her ego and encourage her Queenly intentions, simply because her popularity rubs off on them.'

'So she has never been to Cat City proclaiming her Queenly intentions?'

'Not once,' he confirmed, shaking his head from side to side emphatically before continuing, 'It is her statement that she is Queen of all the cats, and the autocratic manner in which she proclaims herself as Queen since the death of her father that worries the rest of the cat population, who prefer a more democratic form of selectivity. Not one of us mountain cats who have remained here permanently with the shore cats, agree with her intentions, we have learnt to enjoy our democratic freedoms.'

His strong words gave me food for thought, in fact, I got lost in my thoughts, and did not notice Yiorgos rise; stretch, and pad softly away. He had obviously thought that my glazed eyes meant I had heard enough.

The knowledge that Zavosena had never been back to Cat City planted the seed of an idea in my mind. All I had to do was translate the idea into something that Zavosena would accept. The idea would also have to be acceptable to Mario and the other Territorial Toms who formed what was loosely considered a council. I am sure my father, old Nicos, would have approved of the diplomatic approach I had in mind. Why go into this Tom headed, if a gentler approach could work.

Later that night I approached Mario, who was stretched out below his tree on all fours, majestically surveying his territory, somewhat reduced now by the construction of another building. I purred to him pleasantly as I stretched out on all fours before him. He reacted with a superior yawn; this was a natural cat reaction so it did not bother me in the slightest.

My first question however, gave him cause for thought: 'How many territories are there in our tourist area?'

'Er, um er.' He growled, and then thought for a while. 'I don't know,' he purred back at me finally, and then began to explain what he did know.

'All the territorial Toms use Cat City as a base, and many of them sit around at the council when we are all together in one place. Many territories are controlled by a strong female such as Zavosena, but we never see any of them because they are further up the tourist strip, or further down the strip, and generally go along with whatever is decided in Cat city.'

'Okay then,' I purred back, but continued to press my point. 'How many do you know of that use Cat City as a base, beside yourself?'

'Well er, there is me, Cat City is my territory.'

'Yes I know that,' I purred, a little impatient at him for stating the obvious.

He carried on, totally oblivious to my impatience. 'Then there is Achilleas. His territory is from Cat City to the tourist strip. Vassos has taken over old Nicos' territory, which are all the human houses and hotels. Yiorgos has the territory surrounding McDonalds. Christos has the water park. Zavosena holds the territory around the area of the

Danish ice cream parlour. That leaves all the young Toms to fight it out for the hotels and apartments along the seashore.'

'That's a lot of territories,' I said. 'Do they all congregate at Cat City from time to time?'

'Yes frequently,' he purred, and then added gratuitously, 'Cat city has more felines than anywhere else, so they all pop in from time to time to help out. All except Zavosena that is, she seems too proud to mix with us common cats.'

He paused thoughtfully and I waited in case he had anything to add.

After a few moments I broke the silence, and asked my next most important question. 'What names are all the other territorial leaders known by?'

'You know all their names,' he said frowning, you know I am Mario.

'Yes -yes! But what other names have you popularly been given by the other felines?'

He looked at me strangely for a moment before the penny dropped, then beginning to grin broadly he said, 'I am the Black Knight.' He looked at my face waiting for a reaction but I could see he was poised to go further.

'Old Nicos was very wise in the ways of the humans,' he continued, 'and because he could understand their speech and their habits he gave us all names that relate to human leaders. He called Achilleas, Alexander the Great, and his young friend and pupil Achilles. His explanation for the name Achilles was that Vassos walked with a limp, caused by the same moment of danger that gave him a bent tail.'

I stopped him before he could go on. I had obviously touched on a subject that he found very amusing, and perhaps he was showing off a bit. He didn't realise it, but he was actually adding credence to the plan I had in mind, so I asked another leading question. 'And all the felines in all the territories enjoy calling you by these names?'

'Oh yes!' His reply came across with enthusiasm, and he continued in the same tone, 'Few of the felines who know me well ever call me Mario in private. They say that the 'Black Knight' is a much more respectable name for their leader, and you should see Achilleas strut and preen when his females boast that the father of their kittens is 'Alexander the Great'.'

I had a sudden feeling that I had broached a good idea. Mario's enthusiasm for these historical names, and the apparent preference by the main population to call their leaders by these names was quite encouraging, so I decide to introduce the main theme of my thoughts to him.

'You and the council gave Zavosena her territory, and I remember that we all agreed that it was right that she should have a territory of her own due to her standing in the minds of her own people. Surely, what she calls herself in her own territory, and what her followers call her matters very little to all the felines in surrounding territories. If I can convince her that her self-appointed title is quite alright in her own backyard, and that all the other leaders are called by chosen names in their own territories, but it is the council as a whole that make all the important decisions by which we all live, do you think that will satisfy all the felines she has upset with her grandiose ideas.'

He fully understood what I was getting at now, and his facial expression showed approval 'you go ahead Fluffy,' he said supportively. 'It you can diffuse this problem, with this simple ruse, you may save the unity that was won such a short time ago. You surely have been blessed with the wisdom of your father,' he added approvingly.

'I may as well start tomorrow then, but please do not discuss what we have just decided with anyone else, I don't want Zavosena getting wind of my idea. You know, and I know, that one hint of subterfuge and she will be unmanageable.'

The conversation ended, and with typical cat like disdain we parted and went our own ways. I had intended to make a nest for the night in the bushes around the home of Big M's humans, but a sudden screech from Lala halted me in mid stride.

'There's plenty of room here, stay with us Fluffy,' she purred with loud invitation. I accepted gratefully, noticing that all four of the Trod females had set up home in my old area. I bore them no grudge; I had not been using it of late.

I felt no urge to rush into the job next morning. We all breakfasted, spread along the tourist strip, and then congregated at the water pedestal trough and drank our fill. I briefed my ladies on the job at hand, but purposely left out the politics of my plot. I instructed them that their main task was to take Zavosena's immediate followers to one side and engage them in friendly discussion, leaving me to rebuild my association with their self-orientated leader.

I encouraged them to be patient and thoughtful to the local felines, and even sympathetic if the occasion asked for it. I did however insist that they should be made to feel that their standing in the shore community was not subordinate to any other group, whoever's territory it happened to be. I insisted that everything we had achieved in the past was accepted in such good faith, because we had all worked for totally democratic classless integration.

Up to this moment it appeared we had succeeded, so we could not allow Zavosena's wish to create a class structure, just to satisfy her innate lust for aristocratic recognition.

I fully appreciated that my four friends had lived under Zavosena's viciously autocratic rule; they had witnessed the absolute power of this preening feline at her worst. I looked at them to see if any of the fear still remained, but if any of them had any doubts or fears, it did not show in their demeanor as we started to stroll along the strip in an easterly direction.

Calling at the home of Big M's humans, I was met by a gasp of surprise from her mistress. 'How do you get here?'

Her gasp of surprise was followed by the shout, 'Come here!' Her husband hobbled to the doorway, and his jaw dropped as his eyes fell on me. For a moment he was dumbstruck, and then his face began to crack into a grin. He wagged a finger at me as if to emphasize his statement.

'Someday pretty lady, we will find out your secret. You really are as clever as old Nicos.' The smile dropped from his face the instant he mentioned his old friends name, but his wife broke the nostalgic moment as she said, 'Look at her sitting there. We have often said that she is the image of old Nicos, I am convinced that she is his daughter.'

The old boy nodded as he answered, 'She looks just as intelligent as well, doesn't she?'

I gave Big M a knowing glance, and she rose off her hind quarters and stood beside me. We were stepping out onto the pavement together, to join the other four females, when the surprised voice of the old grandma made us turn and stare at her.

'Oh! You have decided to go out at last have you?'

Her voice rose noticeably as she hobbled to the hedge, just in time to see us join up with our four friends. 'Don't you be late for supper; and be careful on that road!'

Big M looked back at her old mistress, and noticed the look of worry ease a little as their eyes met in mutual understanding. Big M broke away and joined us as we disappeared from the view of her humans.

Nobody hurried, I was in the lead with Big M at my shoulder as we passed McDonald's with the other four stretched out behind. We ambled past the water park listening to all the human kids having a great time hurtling down water chutes, and flopping around in paddling pools, closely watched by park attendants.

The Danish ice cream parlour came into view, as we moved from the pavement onto some rougher ground cleared for future development.

Suddenly, with a loud screech, a young male sprang from behind a pile of rubble, his back arched, and tail bent sideways. His ears were laid back, and his eyes were mere slits of glowering savagery. He stood on stiff legs trying to present as formidable a figure as his feline instincts would allow. His wiry youthfulness and lithe outline combined with the natural attack and defence mechanisms made him a dangerous adversary. If he had have attacked immediately, he would have had the full advantage of surprise, and we would have had to retreat hastily to avoid a full frontal attack. His youthful savagery had not been put to the test before, and that became instantly obvious to us older females. I shrank to the floor, every sinew tensed ready for the attacking pounce.

My body was just being projected forwards and upwards, when a screeching bundle of silver tabby hurtled past me and met the young Tom head on. I immediately controlled my headlong leap, and dropped just short of the screaming, screeching, writhing, and slashing bundle of fur in front of me.

Anyone seeing Big M at this moment would have undoubtedly realised that no matter how much a feline becomes domesticated, they can transpose in the blink of an eye. Big M was instinctively using all her weaponry to the best advantage, and it was not until the youthful Tom realised that he was losing the initiative and turned tail; that I noticed that he too had silver mixed in with his grey/black tabby markings.

Big M did not chase after the retreating young Tom, and he, realising this stopped in his headlong flight and faced us all brazenly spitting out a tirade of feline abuse, and then shrieked, 'What do you want here? This is the territory of Queen Zavosena, and nobody enters here unless she allows it. Who are you, and why are you here?'

I walked towards him purposefully. He poised as if to run, a quite natural reaction, having just suffered a sound beating.

'Don't go!' I purred loudly, but gently. 'I am here to see Zavosena, I am her old friend Fluffy, and she will be pleased to see me.'

His ears pricked up at the sound of my name. 'Fluffy the peacemaker?' he asked, his attitude visibly changing, his ears erect.

'Yes, that is I, you can take us to Zavosena; she will not berate you in front of me.'

He led us across the open ground towards the Danish ice cream parlour. He strutted proudly now as he led us, indicating to every cat that we met that he was escorting important felines.

Big M came up alongside me. 'You remember we both had a litter of kittens at the time we were working towards a peaceful settlement,' she said conversationally.

'Yes.'

'Well,' she started, a hint of amusement in her purr, 'That silver furred little devil is one of my own, so perhaps it is natural justice that his mother is the first one to give him a damned good hiding.'

I grinned widely, by way of reply, greatly appreciating the irony of the moment.

The young Tom led us around the back of the buildings, and there, perched on a large concrete flower pot was Zavosena. The beautiful colour of the flowers in the huge pot provided a regal backdrop to her throne.

Stretched out all around her, in various feline poses lay those of her subjects who were in favour at this moment in time. I have no doubt that the carpet of cats at her beck and call changed regularly according to the whim of the moment.

She looked up as we approached unable to hide her initial surprise, but she quickly gathered her wits and posed the obvious question, 'Fluffy' she said loudly, her composure intact in the moment it took her to utter my name. 'Whatever brings you here after all this time?'

She paused, and then went on primly, 'So much has happened since we were last together.'

'I have come to engage you in discussion,' I answered bluntly, and then added, 'We have much to talk about.'

Her eyes narrowed, but never left mine. 'Does it take six of you?' she asked tersely, nodding towards my companions.

'They will be visiting with me, but they will not be involved in what I have to say to you.'

'You make it sound as if your words will be of earth shattering importance.'

The cold manner of her retort reminded me of the old Zavosena I had known before the peace talks. She was steeling herself for an icy beginning. I decided to ease off a bit, in case the stubborn streak in her overcame her natural respect for me. It would serve no purpose to alienate her at this stage. With an ego as well developed as hers, it would not be beyond the bounds of possibility for her to deny us entry to her self-ordained Queendom.

I regulated my tone to a friendly purr as I reminded her, 'The four females are the very ones you yourself gave the powers of a discussion group to. They are the ones who negotiated the peace we now share. Big M you will recall, is my firm friend, and constant companion of that time.'

My words had sunk in, her features softened for a moment, but then a puzzled look crossed her face; with knitted eyebrows she asked, 'Where is Avoula? Where is the old female I directed to be your constant companion?'

My face dropped visibly. Her keen eyes caught the brief look of pain that clouded my eyes. I paused before answering giving my mind time to formulate a reasoned reply. 'Dear Avoula was killed as a result of the earthquake,' I told her with sadness, and then before she could pursue me about the unpleasant realities of her death, I said: 'Perhaps I could explain the details at a more appropriate time.'

There must have been the hint of a plea in my statement, her puzzled expression quickly turned to one of sorrow, and then understanding. 'Yes!' She almost whispered. 'Let us leave such sad talk to a more appropriate time; will you join me when we all go out to eat shortly. I have a favourite old English lady who looks forward to my company of an evening; she will be delighted to meet you.'

Having made the invitation, she jumped from her throne, and walked regally through her subjects, who had jumped respectfully to their feet; their fawning attitude of obeisance appeared pathetic, but I ignored it.

Initially surprised at her sudden movement, I quickly collected my wits and followed her. Big M and the four Trod females gave me a 'what do we do now look'.

Zavosena, noticing their unsure glance, spoke up immediately. 'You other ladies,' she said haughtily, 'Can join my subjects for a meal, our tourists are particularly generous, and the taverna owners like to see a cat around, especially when sniffing for vermin, so you can be assured of a welcome.'

By now we were walking up a quiet road that ran towards the path of death, but did not join up with it. Small but tastefully built villa's lined the road, and before we had walked far, an old human female voice shouted, 'Yoo-hoo-Queenie, here I am.'

I caught sight of the old woman leaning over her front wall and waving at us. I looked sideways at Zavosena: 'Do you understand what she has just called you?' My eyes must have betrayed my surprise at the old ladies call.

'Of course I do! My old friend has always called me Queenie; I understand English as well as Greek you know.'

By this time we had reached the old ladies villa, and Zavosena led us through the gate that the old lady held open, with our tails high in the air.

'Hello my beauties,' the old lady coo-ed, obviously delighted to have another guest. Wait here, both of you while I get the milk.'

She hopped up the back steps into her kitchen quite nimbly, she may have looked old, but she was agile for her age.

'Here you are ladies,' she said pleasantly, placing two saucers on the ground and filling them with milk. Zavosena and I dived into the saucers and lapped the milk up greedily.

'My word you are thirsty, aren't you?' She leaned over and filled the saucers again, and this time took a closer look at me. 'You are a pretty pussy cat,' she murmured, stroking my back gently. Brown Legs instantly leapt into my mind, and I had to force the recollection away, because I always missed her terribly.

'Your fur is beautifully groomed,' she continued softly. 'Just like my precious Queenie. That means that you are both well brought up pussy cats. So someone must care for you as well,' she went on with a possessive tone to her voice.

After we had finished the saucer of milk, she placed a small red scaled fish on each of our saucers. They were fresh and uncooked, just how we cats like them. She watched us gnawing at the fish with our side teeth, chattering away cheerfully, oblivious to the fact that we were not human. She called Zavosena Queenie all the time, and of course she loved it. This old dear had inadvertently provided Zavosena with all the assurance that she needed for her Queenly ambitions,

Very soon, the energy required by our systems to digest the hearty meal left us feeling drowsy, so we both stretched out at the old dear's feet and drifted off into a good cat nap. This pleased the kind hearted old lady greatly, and before long her muted snores mingled with the slight fluttering that emanated from the lips of us two lucky 'pussy cats'.

Darkness had descended by the time we roused from our nap. The kind old lady's chair was empty. 'Looks like dear old Gladys has gone to bed,' Zavosena said, using her old friends name for the first time.

My mind flicked back for an instant to the other two English ladies I had met when I first came to the tourist area; Ethel and Maude, and now I had met Gladys. What strange names these English ladies had been given, not a bit like the names of our Cypriot ladies.

Zavosena and I strolled down the road together; we would be out until the early hours of the morning now, meeting old friends, and old enemies. All would be intent upon asserting their authority, or superiority, and those in the mood would be courting. Those with new families would be aggressively protective, and those weaning a litter would be keeping an eye on the playful antics of their offspring. Mature mothers would be lying on one side twitching their tails encouraging their young ones to pounce. The cat world during the early part of the night was a world full of action of one sort or another. All ages joined in the bickering and squabbling that is ever prevalent in cat communities.

As for myself, I had a job to do, so as Zavosena and I strolled down the road, I opened the conversation with a quietly posed question, 'Has your friend Gladys always called you Queenie?'

She turned to me, 'Yes!' The word came out in such a manner as to indicate she had taken umbrage at the question, and then she uttered firmly, 'The moment she met me, she clapped her hands together and said: 'Oh what a Queenly cat; so elegant, and so proud in bearing.'

'Does Gladys know you have been deprived of the ability to have kittens?' I posed the question as nicely as I could.

'No she does not!' The retort was emphatic, and stayed the same as she added: 'How could she know? Anyway, what has that got to do with the fact that she can see I am a Queen, she realises that I am of royal birth.'

I walked alongside her deep in thought for a while. What I had to get over to her needed to be put forward with diplomacy, not easy for a cat, our instincts make us react quickly, and violently if necessary.

'Who was King of the Trods before your father?'
She turned and glared at me, realising that I had changed tack.

'No-one!' The answer was very blunt, but she did elaborate: 'My father was left behind when a rich European family sold their house in Platres. He had to fight for survival amongst the local feral cats, and gradually he beat all the competition and set up the Kingdom of the Trods. Slowly but surely his powers increased, and soon all the Troodos Mountains were his domain, but he had many problems.

When the winter snows came to the upper reaches of the mountains, there was little food to be had. The cold, and the wet, and the snow, caused great hardship until the snow was deep enough, and crisp enough for the humans to come and play in it. Food became more plentiful then. During the bad times his followers became wandering bands of hunters and scavengers; they had to, to survive, and that is when the first confrontations began with the shore cats.'

I listened to her politely, taking in every word she said. It was also very noticeable that her voice became less strident the further she got into the explanation of her father's difficulties. Every word she said sank in, but I still had to pursue the purpose of my being here, after all, I am the wisecat of the whole area, so I pressed on.

'Zavosena,' I said, politeness oozing out of me. 'I am going to explain a few things to you which I learnt from listening to my humans. I hope it will make you understand why you cannot call yourself Queen of all the shore cats.'

'Why not!?'

The ire had returned to her voice, angered by my straight forward denial of her self-imposed ambition.

'My father was a King; and my lovely friend Gladys says I look like a Queen.'

'Because direct monarchic rule is out of date nowadays,' I began to explain. 'Nearly all the countries of the world are ruled by a democratically elected parliament or a senate, and the people are guided by those whom they themselves have elected to office as a Prime Minister or a President, or sometimes a President and a Prime Minister. Some nations, like that of my humans, have a long line of royalty, but it is not an imposed royalty. They are there because the majority of British people wish it so, and they are generally well loved because of their stoicism, and the good example they set in the field of duty. I must also explain to you why Gladys calls you Queenie. Many people breed pedigree cats to pass on to other cat loving humans. The cat that gives birth to these kittens is called a Queen, but she is only the mother of a superior line of felines, she is not a leader of cats. So when your friend Gladys refers to you as Queenie, she is praising you for your beauty and your haughty bearing. She can also see that you have grown to love being pampered.'

'Do you think so? Do you honestly think I am beautiful and have a lovely coat?'

She preened with pleasure at the somewhat lavish nature of my praise for her elegance. Those few well-chosen words had changed her from a scowling self-possessed feline, into a malleable personality whom I hoped to manipulate with some verbal dexterity.

'Look, why not come to Cat City with me now, we are walking that way already. Come and show all those Toms just how breathtakingly beautiful you have become, now that you have a civilised area to live in; join in their council and thrall them with your superior intelligence.'

Her beaming countenance darkened momentarily. 'They won't welcome me. I have never been back there because they are all so loud, so common, and so bombastic. They will chase me away because they don't like me. They think I am odd, because I don't give off the scents of a normal female.'

'No they will not! You come with me,' I encouraged her. 'You will soon see that they want you to join the council with them. You are the most important female with a territory at this moment, and the council is not complete without you in it.'

'You stay with me all the time then,' she pleaded.

I continued building up her confidence until we reached the edge of Cat City.

A sudden stir under a newly erected street light caught our attention as we gazed towards the group of Toms staring at us from beneath the street light, their outlines a little ghostly bathed in the incandescent glow of a sodium lamp.

'It's Zavosena, one of them gasped as a buzz of purrs and growls issued forth. They fell silent as we strode up to confront them. I purposefully tested their reactions by saying firmly, 'This is Queenie, leader of the Zavosena territory,'

My introduction was met by a barrage of hisses and growls by all the council except Mario. He just sat there on his haunches watching developments.

'We don't want a Queen here,' Achilleas spat out. 'We have a council leader, Mario. We have elected him, and that is enough.

'Queenie is her name,' I threw back. 'Queenie is what the English tourists call her, because she has the appearance of a feline Queen.'

'That may be so,' hissed Vassos, looking perhaps a little ridiculous with his already broken tail bent aggressively to one side. 'She cannot be Queen of the shore cats; we do not recognise such a title. Mario is our leader,' he echoed Achilleas.

I took a chance on my judgment of Zavosena's mood, and her acceptance of my lecturing. I turned to her and said determinedly: 'You don't want to be Queen of this rag tag bunch of thick headed Toms, do you Zavosena?'

She surprised me, and the group of glaring Toms. Even Mario who until now had kept his peace, gave in to a catty grin, as she replied confidently, 'What female in her right mind would want to lead such an ill-educated; ill mannered; single minded bunch of morons such as these. The IQ's of all five of them together would barely reach double figures. No, what this lot need is a fierce female in amongst them to beat some much needed sense into their posturing egos. If Tomkind on this island is going to be led by a duly elected council, then that council will have to be a balanced group of cats, and I can assure you that it cannot be a balanced council if there are no females amongst all you Toms. Females must be included to promote common sense. I am a good candidate for inclusion into this group because I do not give off the scents of the females who become mothers. I have no diversions; my whole being can be given to the services of our felines. Other females must be brought into the council; mothers with children, and old females who have the wisdom of age. This council must equally represent all Tomkind; young and old, male and female, fit and poor, all must be of equal importance.'

She stopped speaking abruptly, and as if to add emphasis to her short determined speech she pushed through the small group of Toms, and stretched out beside Mario. The rest of the Toms gazed on in awe; they glanced at each other not wanting to be the first one to say anything. It took Mario to break the spell; he jumped to his feet and gave Zavosena such a head licking that her head moved from side to side under the determined force of his tongue. The ice was broken, and so was the silence, as all of the council meowed their approval of her speech. She may not have achieved her ambition to become Queen of all cats, but for sure, every cat edict from this council would bear her stamp of approval. In her own way, she had surely won the day.

Mario peered over the heads of his yowling council and looked me in the eyes for a moment, his eyes closed in a cat like wink, and his mouth moved into a wry grin which meant to say: 'Well, you won again Fluffy, but look what I'm lumbered with now!'

THE GREAT DIVIDE.

Once again natures wonderful process of procreation kept me in Cat City long past the time needed to mediate in the affairs of Zavosena, and her acceptance into the Cat City council of territorial felines. True to her initial haranguing of the council members, she had proceeded to cajole suitable females to join her, to achieve a fair balance of gender. One female; not unexpectedly to me, had strongly resisted her approaches.

Big M, as ever, unsure of herself; had opted for the comfortable life of a much loved feline who had now lost all her feral attributes, thanks to the affection shown by her old humans. They, like all sensible cat lovers who intended to keep their feline friend, had taken her to a human animal doctor to have her spayed. Big M now had no desires to be anything more than a cuddly companion to her favourite humans.

Vassos, of course, was her companion cat in the human household, so I suspect that his presence had been the deciding factor in Big M's operation.

When Zavosena was made aware of Big M's new status in life, she became very forceful with my best friend, explaining to her in no uncertain terms that her operation made her the ideal candidate for council membership. Big M however, remained adamant, but did make one very small concession.

'I shall always be here if Fluffy ever needs me though.'

Zavosena scowled, and bitterly accepted defeat.

****

Four months later I had weaned my brood and was enjoying a break from nature's duties. My reverie was occasionally broken by one of my youngsters sneakily testing my resolve by edging towards me and craftily trying to suckle. The good hidings I now dished out were more purposeful, and added meaning to the loud throaty growls that emphasised my determination.

During one of these intense scolding moments, I became aware of Vassos approaching me. He sat patiently on his haunches at a respectable distance, until he considered my temper had eased. 'I would speak with you Fluffy,' he purred finally.

My look remained non-committal, so he edged over to me. Settling down on his belly, his proud head raised in a sphinx like pose, he flicked his broken tail and purred: 'The picture box that stands in the corner of a room in my human's house, is giving out images that cause my humans great happiness. Apparently our Island is to join with many other countries that form a great alliance that is democratic, just like our council. Your father often said that our feline troubles were as nothing compared with the problems of separation suffered by the two races of humans on this Island?'

'I certainly remember an occasion when he said that,' I interrupted his speech, my interest aroused, as an image of my dear father flicked through my mind.

'Well,' he went on. 'A new government on what the humans call the Turkish mainland has said some words that have given our Greek Cypriot humans cause to feel that very soon this Island will be just called "Cyprus", and the people will just be known as Cypriots, not Greek Cypriots, or Turkish Cypriots.'

I caught on instantly. 'So this means that all the cats from the northern part of the island, and all the cats from the southern part of the island will be able to cross into each-others territories, and give all cats absolute freedom of all the island?'

'That is what my humans believe,' he replied, and then elaborated a little more. 'According to the images on the picture box, this will be a very great moment for all the humans of this island when it happens.'

I sat considering my friends statement, and then asked, 'Do you think I could come into your home and watch these images with you?'

My request took him aback momentarily. I grinned cattishly at the perplexed look that covered his features. 'I could come and visit my friend Big M, and perhaps get myself invited that way,' I said helpfully, my grin broadening as the frown left his Tommish forehead.

Without another purr we both got up from our prone position, and began a slow stroll towards the built up area of human homes where the old couple lived. My kittens made as if to follow me, but a sharp hiss from me made them run off and seek other diversions.

Big M was sunning herself outside in the back yard when we arrived. The instant she saw me she jumped to her feet and gave me a very affectionate ear rubbing. I retaliated with the same fervour, and then all three of us lay side by side and enjoyed the warmth together, and even enjoyed a short cat nap.

We were aroused some time later by the pick-up truck stopping at the back gate. They both hobbled in carrying bags of food which they placed at the back door of their home. When they had taken the food inside, they both settled into their sun chairs in the yard, puffing slightly from their exertions. It was then that the old ladies eyes dropped on me. 'Ah, you have come to visit us again pretty one,' she said loudly.

I was used to the look of surprise that always spread across her face whenever she saw me, and the slight tone of astonishment my presence always seemed to inspire.

After the old couple had caught their breath, the old grandma went inside, and we could hear her clattering about in her kitchen.

Vassos and Big M were gazing up at the door expectantly, and after a few minutes their expectant looks were rewarded with a bowl of brown food each. 'Here you are pretty one, some for you as well,' the old lady chortled as she put a bowl down for me.

She watched me as I wolfed the lovely food down, and then showed my appreciation by rubbing my ears against her old stockings. 'You did enjoy that, didn't you pretty one,' she said, reaching down and tickling my ears as she spoke. I reacted by moving my head under her hand in order to luxuriate in the pleasant fondling of my ears.

A good sleep followed the nice meal, and we only woke up when the scraping of the humans chairs told us that the old couple were going inside. Big M and Vassos were already at the heels of their humans when I joined them. They rushed inside as the door opened, and the old lady was just closing the door behind them when she noticed me staring up at her. 'Oh,' she said gently, with a kindly smile.

'You want to join us too, do you? Come along then, we have room for another pretty one.'

I had not expected it to be quite this easy, but then a further statement made me realise why the old lady had been so accommodating. 'You are the image of old Nicos; it is almost as if he is still here alive when I see you.'

How I wish I could have told her that her beloved Nicos was also my father.

The door closed soundlessly behind us all. The old lady disappeared into her kitchen, and all three of us cats settled down on the carpet beside the old man's chair. The picture box in the corner was lit up and images of humans appeared and disappeared as if by magic.

Sometimes one person was sitting in the picture box talking to us, and sometimes many people were talking together, but at the same time talking to us. At one time we cats thought it was hunting time early, because men in the same uniform were standing in lines, or running around in the wild areas.

We all ducked suddenly, and dived under the old man's chair as those long sticks that go bang were being let off everywhere. We all settled down quickly though when we realised that the bangs were not meant for us.

Then, as if a huge bird was flying over the land with us in its talons, we were taken for a long flight over a long line following a huge fence. The ride came to an end on a street with a great barrier across it where hundreds of people were jostling around on both sides; laughing and shouting joyously. Between the people on both sides, men dressed in hunters clothes stood impassively on both sides of the barrier, seemingly to stop the people on either side reaching out to touch each other.

I began to understand. The barrier shown on the image was similar to our tunnel under the path of death. We had overcome our feline differences, but the humans had not fully succeeded in overcoming their difficulties. 'I wonder if felines are allowed through that barrier,' I thought.

That thought stayed in my mind, and I began to drift away from the images on the picture box as my inner thoughts stayed on the human barrier. I had not seen one cat in those images, were there no cats there at all? If not, what had happened to all the cats that must have been there?

That serious part of my inner being started to take over, there must be cats there but no-one is interested in their well-being. My mind suddenly told me that I must go there and find out what is happening to the feline population of this great divide. If humans are reaching out for each other, then so must the feline world.

The old lady suddenly bustled in with two trays, disturbing my thoughts. She thrust one tray at the old man, and sat down with the other, and proceeded to eat. The images on the picture box had changed; several humans were jigging about on a platform, their bodies moving to that horrendous din that seems to pass for music these days. I stretched my body, looking upwards as I enjoyed the stretching motion.

I froze as my eyes lighted on a glass box hanging on the wall. My back arched, and my fur stood on end. There, in the glass box, his head turned towards me, was the figure of my father. His glazed eyes stared at me but, his face almost held the pure smile of wisdom we had all loved so much. I screeched, as only a female feline can screech when confronted with the totally unusual.

The old couple nearly dropped their trays in surprise, and their eyes swung round to me simultaneously. The old boy followed my gaze and immediately realised what had disturbed me.

'Come on pretty one,' he said quietly. 'It is only our old Nicos. He could see that his words had not registered so added, 'If you don't like it, I will let you out.' So saying, he opened the door, and I raced past his legs as if all the ghosts of dead cats were on my heels. I ran towards Cat City until I was exhausted.

Slowly the terror began to subside, so stopping under a street lamp; I proceeded to adjust my fur. It was all over the place, partly due to my fear, and partly due to my mad rush in my haste to run away from what appeared to be the reincarnation of my father.

Vassos appeared in my peripheral vision, up went my hackles again, but they quickly subsided as I recognised who it was.

'Why the sudden rush to get out Fluffy?' Vassos asked his face creased with as much concern as a Tom was capable of showing.

'My father is dead, yet there he is as large as life in that glass box, I do not understand this.'

He continued staring at me, but now his face was split by a grin that stretched from ear to ear.

'When our humans brought the glass box into the house with Nicos standing in it as large as life, both myself and Big M wondered how it could be, and showed our fear in exactly the same way as you did. Slowly we got used to the idea, even when our humans speak to him now; we try not to pay any attention, because he is dead and cannot answer them. When you look at him closely you can see that the eyes are not real, you can also see that he is rooted to the spot somehow.

We think that they loved him so much that they put him in a box so that he will always be with them. How this comes about I do not know, but it makes them happy, so we do not bother about it now. You must also get used to it, now you have seen it.'

'It is very strange,' I replied, happier now that I had some idea of how this thing had come to be. 'Is that why you followed me out?' I asked him conversationally.

'No, I do not stay in the house at night; there is nothing to do once they get ready for sleep. I don't think cats are meant to stay useless at night; it's the best part of the day. But there is another reason I ran after you. You probably did not realise that when they were talking, they were saying that they would have to visit Nicosia and join in with the celebrations, and show how happy they are at this possible chance of re-unification. They will take us with them when they go, because they may be away a day and a night; do you want to come with us? I thought that was why you wanted to watch the images on the picture box.'

'Yes, I will come.' I jumped at the chance to see what the cats on the other side would be like. 'When will they go?' I asked eagerly.

'You will have to be ready to go at any time early in the morning. Big M and I always know when we are going somewhere, because they put our metal carrying cages in the pick-up truck. If they are just going shopping they don't bother to take us.'

'I shall stay close to your house then,' I replied determinedly.

For three days I stayed close to the old couple's house. I ate regularly with the pretty Russian waitress, and socialised with Achilleas and the other cats who he allowed to congregate in his territory. When all the night activities came to an end, I curled up under a bush in sight of the old couples back gate.

On the morning of the third day, I had just returned from foraging at the back of the restaurants, and was sat on my haunches watching the back of the house. Vassos was lying atop the gate waiting for the back door to open so that he could join Big M for breakfast. The lucky devil did not have to forage anymore now that he had been adopted.

It seemed we both waited patiently for hours, looking for some sign of activity to bring our vigil to an end. Suddenly the back door opened, and Big M squeezed past the old grandma's legs. Vassos leapt off the gate, and they both dived into the separate feeding bowls without so much as a glance at each other.

The old lady tutted at her two pets for their indecent haste, and returned indoors, closing the door behind her.

I strolled out into the road and walked down to the back gate. I leapt over it just as my two friends were finishing breakfast. I looked on, amused as they pushed their bowls around the yard trying to extract the final hint of flavour attached to the bottom.

I now knew that much of their food came out of a tin, because I had shared with them the other day.

Big M rushed across to greet me. Vassos cast his eyes my way and then stretched out to digest his meal.

Later, the old man emerged from the house, crossed the road, and brought his pick-up truck to the back gate. We watched as he began to put things into the back, and then finally he appeared carrying two cat cages which he placed on the back seat. I could not help but notice that each cage had a nice piece of fish in it.

I was amazed at the speed with which my two friends leapt into the cages, and sank their teeth into the fish. It did not bother them at all when the old man closed one end of the cages.

The old lady came bustling out, locking the back door after her. She wriggled into the front seat, and closed the door.

The old man glanced down at me and gave me a soothing stroke on the head. 'We shall be away with your friends for a little while, but I shall bring them back safely,' he cooed, in that gentle way he seemed to reserve for us felines.

I waited until he had settled down inside the beast with round legs, and then, as it roared loudly I jumped into the back unnoticed.

The truck moved forward and carried out movements left and right which I was familiar with. After several minutes the winding motion stopped and the beast began to roar more loudly as it joined other beasts that were also racing in the same direction.

The journey this time was much longer; in fact I began to wonder if we would ever stop. I would have loved to look over the top of the back of the beast, but they might have seen me, and that could have ruined my self-imposed mission.

Finally, just as my patience was becoming very difficult to sustain, I became aware of towering buildings either side of my hiding place. The pick-up truck began to weave left and right. It stopped several times then surged forward again. At each stop I prepared to jump out of the back, but no door opened so I stayed put. Very soon we came to a stop and the beast stopped growling. The doors clicked open so I leapt over the back, and hid behind a round leg.

From my position I could see two cages being lifted out with my two friends looking up at the old man totally unconcerned with the procedure. The old lady knocked on the door we had stopped beside. The door opened and amidst joyous sounds of greeting, the two old couples embraced each other. They all went inside, and the door closed behind them.

I did not move from where I lay hunched up beside the round leg. I was aware of people walking both ways, but I could not see a cat anywhere. One thing was uppermost in my mind; I knew I could not find the great barrier without human help, I therefore decided to stay in this position until the old couple came out of the house again.

So deeply was I concentrating on the door of the house that I failed to remain aware of what was going on around me; a gruff, 'Who are you,' startled me greatly, and caused me to jump up hackles raised, and back arched.

'Whoa-whoa!'

The gruff voiced old Tom stepped back and added hastily, 'I can see you are a stranger, and I thought maybe I can help you. I am certainly too old to be of any danger to you.'

I did not answer him immediately, but my readiness to defend myself gradually eased. 'You surprised me,' I told him bluntly, settling into my normal hunched up position again.

'Where are you from?'

'I am from Limassol,' I answered a little tersely.

'Ah Limassol, I used to have an old friend from Limassol. He always came here with his humans to visit that house,' he indicated with a nod towards the door I had been concentrating on.

'What was his name?' I turned my head towards him, my interest aroused.

'He was called old Nicos, the wisecat. His life with humans had given him a knowledge and insight rarely shown in felines.'

'I know, he was my father,' I stated matter-of-factly; but now the last sight of him in that glass cage sprang into mind before my usual recollection of him.

'How is he these days?' His tone had not changed; he was not in the least amazed by my admission and continued, 'He was an old Tom when I began to show my age, he must be very old by now. Is that why I see the new Tom with the broken tail in the carrying cage?'

'He is dead now, but lives on in our minds. His humans will always remember him fondly' I said, thinking of the glass cage.

'That is sad,' the old Tom muttered wistfully. 'It comes to us all, but I shall miss him, he was a special friend. We used to spend hours purring together on that doorstep.' He stopped, and a puzzled look replaced the nostalgic glaze in his eyes. 'Why are you not in the house with the others then?'

I could not answer that question in one sentence, so I told him briefly of what had come about in the cat population of the Troodos Mountains, and the shore-side cats of Limassol. I then ventured to tell him of my reason for coming to the divided city of Lefcosia (Nicosia).

'There are hundreds of cats here by the great barrier,' he replied. 'But very few from either side venture through the checkpoint on Ledra Street. Those of us that do cross from side to side, go further away where there are not so many humans congregating.'

'So cats from either side do meet each other then?'

'Oh yes, all the time, in fact all the feral cats along the line regularly mix with each other, to us there is no divide. It is only the cats who belong to humans who do not mix, because they live in human households and take on human beliefs, and human rules. The law on the Turkish side does not really like the people of either side meeting each other, so domestic cats do what their humans do.'

I hunched down deep in thought for a while, In fact I thought so deeply, my eyes closed in concentration. My new friend hunched down also, waiting for me to show interest again.

'What is your name?'

His eyes shot wide open, surprised at my sudden question, and he spluttered, 'Leonidas, my name is Leonidas. Somebody long ago named me after a great Spartan King; I used to be the toughest Tomcat in Lefcosia.' His face took on a knowing grin as he added. 'The lovely females could never escape the advances of the handsome Leonidas.'

I ignored his boastful statement, and brought the conversation back to my level.

'Can you take me to a place where I can see the other side of the Great Divide?'

'Sure I can, you follow me, and I will take you to where many of us feral cats live along the barrier on this side. There are many passing holes in the barrier where feral cats from both sides live closely together.

Without another purr, he rose stiffly on straight legs, had a good stretch, and a wide mouthed yawn before stepping from underneath the pick-up truck.

I followed him closely, adjusting my pace to the old Toms slow stroll. It was not a long way, but we seemed to zig-zag along many narrow streets before reaching a wider street.

He turned his head to me and said, 'This is Ledra Street; the place in the barrier where the humans are let through is just ahead of us. There are not many here now, but tonight when they have finished work many humans come to this place to air their grievances, and hold big boards with words on, and carry images of humans that they love, and do not know where they are, or what has happened to them.'

He did not take me to the crossing point, we went left, and after a short while we were in a space where the ground had been heaped up into a long mound with sharp metal passing along the top of it.

'This is where most of the feral population live, whenever we want to we climb up this mound and go under the wire, so you see, we feral cats are not stopped by this barrier at all.'

I looked around me, taking in my surroundings. A movement on top of the mound attracted my attention. It was a human dressed like a hunter standing in a tower looking all around him. I noticed the stick that goes bang in his hands, and was stricken by a short moment of fear.

The old Tom caught my sharp intake of breath and followed my eyes. 'Oh don't worry about him,' he reassured me. 'A cat has never been shot along this barrier: but humans have.'

We stayed by the barrier for some time while he showed me a nice spot where I could make a little den for myself. Cat City jumped into my mind, there was not a great deal of difference. The mound along which the path of death passed was vaguely similar to this great mound, when looked at from the side. It suddenly dawned on me that I would not get back to Limassol with the old couple if I stayed here. I quickly settled down realising that one night here could not hurt, because they were staying with their relatives for at least two days. 'Anyway,' I muttered to myself. 'You have a mission to carry out.'

'Are you ready to eat now,' he asked.

'Yes, yes,' I repeated, as his words brought me back to the present

'There's a well-used Taverna just over there,' he indicated with his head, 'It is my territory, so you are most welcome.'

I was amazed at the number of humans eating in the Taverna. Not a cat was in sight, and that meant that the generosity of the patrons was heaped upon me and my new friend, tasty little titbits seemed to appear from all directions.

'This is where you will eat while you are with us,' the old Tom said. 'No-one will ever bother you, I may be old, but my reputation has not reduced in strength as my body has.'

I nodded my thanks, not wishing to be too demonstrative.

We strolled back to the barrier. He went to his favourite spot, and I tried out my new home. After a short while scraping together some grass and old bracken, I had a very comfortable, temporary little home. Without any hesitation, I curled up and was soon dreaming full bellied dreams of all the nice things in a cat's life.

Hours later, I sprang up, totally alert. A gravelly voiced purr had brought me out of my slumber.

'Fluffy,' the hoarse purr called again.

I crawled from my shelter, and looked at the old Tom.

'Something is going on, on the other side of the barrier,' he stated urgently. 'I thought you might like to go over for the first time now, whilst something is happening.'

I followed him up the mound and under the fence. Suddenly I was in another state, part of my own Island home, yet another state. It felt no different than my own side of the barrier, even the other cats we met along the way spoke exactly the same cat language that I did. We began to walk around a place where many humans had gathered; in fact more humans than I had ever seen in one place before. I understood what they were shouting about because many of them were shouting in one of the human languages that I understood.

Some of the humans, however, were shouting in a language that I did not understand. One thing became very certain though, no matter what tongue they spoke in, they were all shouting for the same thing. They all wanted to be with my side of the Island of Cyprus when it joined with all the people of Europe. No-one was fighting, or making a disturbance, every one of them was shouting for what they wanted in a peaceful manner.

I had been a negotiator and a peacemaker, and my group of females had succeeded in joining two bitter enemies together. These people would surely achieve what we felines had achieved before them.

I suddenly made my mind up to stay here until this great event happened. I would go out and meet the cats who had human homes and tell them of a united Cat City on my side of the Island. I would tell them that every territorial feline had got a territory of their own, and a home where hunger would not strike at any time of the year; a place where democracy reigned, in its truest form.

I became so involved in this vast meeting of humans of Northern Cyprus that I lost my friend Leonidas. 'No bother,' I muttered to myself, 'I do not feel a stranger here.'

For hours I wandered around the fringes of this vast crowd. When I was hungry I ate; such was the abundance of food available from these thousands of humans.   Other felines I bumped into took absolutely no notice of me. They too were so amazed at the number of humans in this place, that nothing else seemed important. I suddenly felt in need of a wash, so in typical feline manner I succumbed to the mood of the moment.

With my back resting against a house wall, I proceeded to giving myself a thorough licking, all over. I finished, and ran my tongue along my lips, feeling much refreshed and thoroughly contented.

Suddenly my hackles rose, as I sensed a Tom near me. I sprang to my feet back arched, ready to run or fight, whichever was the more prudent. My eyes focused on a large Tomlike shadow surrounded by the glow from the street lights. His outline seemed slightly unusual, thick around the shoulders, and rising to the head. He sat there on his haunches staring at me with an air of total confidence.

He purred something at me, but I could not understand him. He rose to all fours and approached me. I reared up against the wall and lashed out with both forepaws. He drew back hastily, having recognised my defensive shriek of warning.

'Ah! You are from the other side,' he purred. 'Don't be frightened, we too are civilised you know.'

'You frightened me,' I hissed at him, still prepared to run or fight.

'My name is Kemal,' he introduced himself. 'I live in that Villa there, to the left of you.'

I did not follow the nod of his head; I kept my eyes firmly on his form, ready for any sudden attack.

He, realising that my female defences were on the alert, drew back a little and sat on his haunches looking at me attentively.

'Why have you come over to this side? He purred.

He now spoke in the other language which I had learnt, by listening to my humans. He asked pleasantly so I decided to tell him my name.

'I am Fluffy, and I have come here to see your part of the Island for myself.'

'Why on earth should you do that?'

'I have been elected to be the wisecat of the united cats of Limassol, and I want to get to know the cats of this separate state.'

'Ah, I understand. The humans are all trying to get together again, and you want the cats to do the same?'

'Yes I do. My side of the Island is going to join with all the people of Europe. I think we cats should all join together and be just simply Cypriots, and then maybe your state will come together with ours again. Surely that is what all the humans are shouting for out there.'

'You are nearly correct,' he answered a little haughtily. 'Actually they are calling for our president to resign, so that the barriers that divide us can be pushed to one side and be forgotten about in time, and then we can join you and all the other countries of Europe in one great brotherhood of nations.'

'Yes, I understand all that. I have listened, and watched the picture box in the corner of a human's house and seen many images on it. That is the real reason for my being here, and you have now told me that only one human stands in the way of this happening. That seems very strange to me, how can one human stop all the people from doing what they feel is best, that does not sound very democratic to me. What are your feelings about this situation?'

He stood thoughtfully for a moment before he answered. 'The history of our two peoples on this Island has not always been on the friendliest terms. From my great grandfather's time when we won independence from Great Britain, Greeks and Turks fought each other. Then a group of people tried to assassinate a holy man who was president of the whole Island, and this caused the greatest split of all. The Turkish mainland invaded with thousands of soldiers, and separated this one third of the Island from the rest. Then all the countries of the world sent there soldiers to stop us fighting each other, and they are still here to this day, keeping the peace.

If we can join this great community of Europe, it could mean that this Island would be one state again. So my feelings,' he looked at me meaningfully, 'are that we must not miss this wonderful opportunity.

For sure, there will never again be hostility between the two peoples of this Island, because a government of equal opportunity will be set up that must satisfy all of the peoples, regardless of ethnic origin, and that's how it should be.'

He looked at me for a reaction, but I remained none committal while I mulled over the facts. I had agreed with the final part of his statement instantly, because whatever affects the humans of this island certainly works its way down to us cats. If the humans are not happy and prosperous, then our lives are that much harder.

We are their pets when we are domesticated, some of us are kept by humans purely for the purpose of keeping natures balance by not allowing vermin to become a nuisance, so there is a natural symbiosis between us and humans, this fact had been proven to me by my two humans.

Then there is the old couple who love their cats Big M, and Vassos, and who have made a shrine of their most beloved Nicos-my father.

This was all proof of the affinity between cats and humans, so I definitely agreed with this beautiful stranger that peaceful co-existence is far superior to a hostile environment.

'You talk the talk of the wisecat,' I complimented him. 'My father too, was a wisecat before he died, and he has told us all about the difficulties between the two ethnic races of this island, but I have never heard it voiced with quite so much detail by a feline.'

'My humans are employed by the government of Northern Cyprus,' he replied. 'They are what are called 'civil servants' in the other language of our island. Do you understand English when you hear it spoken?'

'My humans are English,' I confirmed, then told him of how I adopted Brown Legs and Big Feet when I was a youngster. 'But I still stay absolutely free to be a feral cat,' I added.

'Sounds Ideal,' he purred in English. 'But how on earth did you get from Governors beach to Limassol, and then from Limassol to here? Come to think of it, how on earth are you going to get back?'

I explained my travel arrangements, and how they came about from the first time my father had showed me how to use humans and their beasts with round legs.

'My word you are a wisecat, aren't you?' A nice smile played around the edge of his whiskers as he acknowledged my simple way of getting from place to place. The smile remained as he asked, 'What's your name, by the way. You do have a name don't you?'

I returned his smile with a grin. 'My name is Fluffy,' I stated simply.

He paused for a moment looking slightly quizzical, and then his look brightened. 'Ah!' he replied quickly: 'Your humans are English of course, hence the unusual name.'

We both grinned at each other, in unison this time, before he caught himself and continued with what he was originally going to say before my name made him pause.

'Look,' he said. 'My villa is only there, next door, we have a huge garden with numerous little hidey holes in which to make a bed for the night, why don't you join me for a bit of the feline night life around here, then you can choose a bed for the night---if you wish, of course,' he added politely.

He took my return smile to mean that I had accepted his kind offer; and his invitation to join him on a night out on this side of the barrier. I must admit to being impressed, but this polite Tom was only one of many, so I reserved my judgment for the time being.

This time I did not follow the lead of my guide, I strolled through the night alongside him, quite comfortable to be in his presence. The huge crowds were dispersing now; they had voiced their opinion forcefully and peacefully, but were now going to enjoy the remainder of the evening socializing.

The police of Northern Cyprus stood around chatting to each other as they watched the host gradually dispersing, and then walked away to carry out traffic duties as the cars of the protesters began to fill the streets of Northern Nicosia.

Many of the locals filled the cafes and bars, all of them celebrating what to them, had been a successful and pleasant day of demonstration. Loud music began to echo along the streets, and it was noticeable that groups of humans were dancing in the style of their own ethnic upbringing, not the wriggling and writhing I had become accustomed to on the tourist strip of Limassol.

As we passed a café, a scrap of food landed in front of me. I stopped immediately and wolfed it down. Other scraps of food began to appear, and I made the most of it, grabbing them up as quickly as I could. I noticed my companion did not make a move for the food, most unusual for a cat. He sat there patiently waiting, while I took advantage of this opportunity to fill myself up.

It was some time later, when completely sated, I fell in behind him licking my chops, and we continued our night prowl. For a few moments I concentrated on cleaning the edges of my mouth with my tongue, and then I looked up in the direction we were going.

A short gasp of admiration left my lips as I noticed his tail for the first time, in all its glory. Never had I seen such a pure white, hugely bushy tail before. He was aware of my gasp, and turned his head wondering what had caused it. My eyes were fixed on this delightful indicator of a cat's mood.

'You like my tail?' He asked pleasantly.

I looked up, and for the first time saw him in all his glory, as a bright street light highlighted his beautiful head and totally extraordinary neck. For a moment he stared back at me, probably confused by the awe that still reflected from my gaping mouth.

'Haven't you seen a Turkish Angora before?

I gathered myself together, although a female shiver did run through me as I looked up into those attractive eyes that gazed at me steadily.

'No,' I admitted. 'I have never ever seen such a beautifully coated Tom.'

He was obviously flattered by my astonishment at the beauty of his gorgeous pelt, and with his head turned round at me we started walking again. 'Come on Fluffy,' he urged, let's go and see what games the ferals are up to.'

I shook myself, and tagged along beside him, still unsure of the feelings this lovely Tom had aroused. He was obviously top Tom in this area, all the felines we encountered – both male and female stared at him hopefully as we passed. He was out of his home territory, but not a cat protested at his presence.

We rounded a corner, and it became clear that we were approaching a human building site.

As we drew near, a gang of immature Toms were visible as we passed a small alleyway. They had not noticed Kemal pass the entrance, but the awareness that someone else was around, caused them to turn their heads towards the entrance to the alleyway just as I strolled past.

'Wowee baby,' one of them called loudly. 'Down here, this is where it's all happening.'

I ignored them completely, my nose rising in the air to show my disdain. That did not appeal to their immature egos, and they all rushed to the entrance in one yowling mob. They ran round the corner; and straight into the glaring eyes and raised hackles of Kemal. They came to an abrupt halt. 'Hey, we meant no bother,' one of them hurriedly purred. 'We just saw the chick, and thought she was alone and needed some company.'

I watched Kemal stand his ground in complete silence. The immature bunch backed away around the corner; and were gone in the twinkling of an eye.

He looked at me for confirmation that I was untroubled by the event.

'Immature Toms are the same wherever they come from,' I assured him. 'But thanks anyway, you saved me from teaching at least one of them a lesson he would not forget quickly.'

His smile assured me that he understood that I was quite capable of handling a situation such as had just occurred.

I know them all very well,' he said. 'In a year's time they will be a little harder to discourage, but that is how it should be in our feline world.'

We reached the building site, and I was soon fraternizing with all sorts and colours of cats. The cross breeding between several types of domestic feral cats had produced varied tortoiseshell mixtures over the years. I did however notice that not a single Turkish Angora was amongst them. I was slightly puzzled at that because Kemal was certainly an Alpha Tom around these parts.

I shrugged free of these thoughts quickly as I met an oldish female who was the image of my old friend Avoula. She gazed at me disinterestedly as I hunched down close to her. She remained in her resting position, head bending slightly forward, eyes closed to mere slits, but the swiveling ears said that she was alert to everything going on around her.

'Hello,' I said in my friendliest purr. 'My name is Fluffy: what is your name?'

Her eyes opened and she glanced my way. 'Only cats that have been with humans have names,' she replied tersely; and then turning away, closed her eyes once more.

She had answered in my language. It was true then, just as Leonidas had said. All the cats along the "great divide" acted as if it was not there, probably, because they were born to it. They didn't even question why it was there, they treated it just like they would any other feature of the landscape; I tested my theory, 'How do you feel about the barrier that has been raised between you, and we cats on the other side, being torn down?'

She opened her eyes again and turned to me with puzzlement etched across her eyes and forehead. 'What are you talking about?'

The question came across very bluntly, her eyes holding mine this time. 'What barrier? What cats? What other side?'

The fact that I was staggered by her ignorance of the facts: and more so her lack of interest in her surroundings must have shown in my face.

'What are you talking about?' She repeated her initial question, glaring in my eyes as she awaited an answer.

'Don't you know, the humans of this Island have been separated since the time of our grandfathers, and that big mound with human guards, and sticks that go bang is meant to keep them separate?'

'Oh that!'

Her reply, whilst looking at me as if I did not belong to the real world, showed me that not all of my species lived amongst humans who showed great concern about the physical division of our island, and her second statement proved it.

'What is so unusual about humans fighting, and then separating from each other; just get on with your life and ignore them. While they squabble amongst themselves, they are no bother to us.'

I looked at her dumbfounded. She had not made her statement callously. To her, everything that humans did was perfectly natural to their species, so she just carried on with her life as if nothing was out of the ordinary.

Having no answer to her inbred tolerance of human traits, I arose from my hunched position, and in typical feline fashion wandered off to seek other things of more interest to me.

As the night wore on, I learned that every female I chatted to was as dismissive of the problems humans created for themselves as my first encounter. All of them purred the language I knew, and none of them cared one iota about what the humans got up to as long as they remained generous to the needs of felines. In fact the major topic of conversation in any of the gatherings on the building site was what their last meal had consisted of, and boasts of extraordinary acts of generosity they had encountered in their feral lives.

'I wonder if some humans, just like these single minded cats, are so casually dismissive of the sufferings of others, just as long as it does not confront them, and disturb their comfortable lives.' My natural thoughts disturbed me a little, I was not at all happy with the indifference I had encountered this night. One lesson I had learnt though, and that was: it is impossible to defeat a community's ignorance of dominant facts, without a system of imparting knowledge to all members of that community, in such a way that draws their attention to the politics of life surrounding them.

Later, while I sat contemplating, and listening to all the purrs, and the odd screech of dissent going on around me, I realised I had come here fully expecting a situation similar to the long standing differences between the shore cats of Limassol, and the wild cats of the mountains called the Trods. But here I was now, seeing for myself at first hand, that none of these cats were in the least bit worried about anything that was going on around them. They had become so inured to life as it was for them.

Kemal's gentle purr aroused me from my thoughts. 'It's time I was returning to my garden,' he purred quietly, 'My mistress gets cross with me if I wander the streets.'

I fell in obediently behind him, and in a very short while we had reached the iron front gates of his human's villa. I hopped through the iron bars behind him, and he pointed out a wooden lean- to with a few garden tools jutting out.

'You will find it very comfortable in there, and if you wish to stay with us for a while, that can be your home.'

I thanked him, and just as it appeared that he might stay a while, a demanding human female voice echoed around the garden.

'Where have you been Kemal? You know I forbid you to go out gallivanting with all the street cats around here. They are not good company for a pedigree such as you, God knows what you will be bringing home with you, veterinary fees are not cheap you know.'

I watched poor Kemal being harangued by this very strict mistress from behind some flower stalks. I saw him rush towards the closed door, and then disappear as if by magic. His mistress opened the door, and then slammed it loudly behind her. I would later learn that he had disappeared through his own little door cut into the lower part of the main door.

Before dropping off to sleep I thought out a simple plan for getting back to Governors Beach sometime in the near future when I was satisfied with what I had learnt here. I would dearly love to be here when this 'great divide' is torn down, and I could share in the pure joy such an act would bring to the humans who no longer see any need for this barrier that separates them.

Early next morning I took steps to see if my plan was feasible. I hurried over the mound, and sought out Leonidas in his den.

'Whosat!' He growled defensively.

'It's me Fluffy,' I purred quietly, having no wish to aggravate his old Tommish sensitivities this early in the morning.

His head appeared at the entrance to his little hole in the bushes.

'What do you want so early in the morning?' He grumbled, licking a paw, and then rubbed the sleep out of his eyes.

Without hesitation I laid my plan out to him, explaining everything in detail.

'You see all, and hear all around these parts,' I said persuasively, knowing that my words would appeal to his old male ego.

'So my plan cannot be successful without diligence on your part, you are the key to my plans successful outcome.'

'This Vassos and Big M you talk of, are you sure they will act on a strangers advice when the time comes?'

He continued his morning ablutions with great concentration, whilst appearing to listen to me casually.

'Oh certainly, they are my greatest friends. Once I tell them, and show you to them, they will always look out of their cages eagerly to see if you are there, whenever their humans visit this place.'

'Come on then,' he urged. 'Let's have an early breakfast before we go and sit under your friend's pick-up truck.'

One hour later, we both hunched up under the old couples pick-up truck, not knowing at this stage whether they would return to Limassol today, or whether they would stay with their relatives for a bit longer. This part of the plan was trial and error, there was no other way to play it, just hang about until it happened.

I offered a silent prayer to cat heaven as we settled down to wait, and one human hour later, as if my prayers had been answered, the door opened. The old boy came out with the two cages, I held my breath whilst hoping he would put them down where one or both of my friends could see me under the pick-up. He placed the cages on the floor, and reached up to open the door. 'Psst Vassos,' I hissed loudly.   'Psst, look this way.'

Big M saw me first. 'Fluffy,' she purred, her delight showing in the tone of her purr.

'Hush a moment M and listen to me,' I hissed back sharply. 'This is Leonidas; he will watch for your next visit, and then come and tell me you are here. I must stay a little longer, very important things are about to happen. As a wisecat it is my duty to stay and learn how it will all come about.'

Both my friends opened their mouths to speak as both cages left the ground. I could just discern Big M's: 'Take care Fluffy,' before her voice became muffled.

Old Leonidas and I quickly scooted from under the car while the four humans were saying their goodbyes. I could just make out the final words of the old couple as they climbed into their pick up, 'See you in six weeks,' the old boy shouted as he pulled away from the pavement.

'Six human weeks,' I said breathlessly to Leonidas, as we disappeared around a corner. 'Did you hear what the old boy said as they drove away?'

'No, I could not make out his words for the noise of the beast,' he admitted.

'Can you judge six human weeks,' I asked.

'I don't have to,' he replied nonchalantly. 'I spend every morning on that street, being patted and fed by all the old ladies who have known me for years.'

'I shall come and see you often then Leonidas, then all you will have to tell my friends is whether I am ready to go back or not.'

'Are you staying on this side then?'

'No! But if you need to tell me anything quickly, just get in touch with Kemal...you do know him, I trust?'

He looked at me, and I noticed a slightly scornful curl come to his lips.

'Oh you've met that toffee nosed git have you? Typical Turkish nobility, and boy, does he know it. But I will do as you wish if it is that important. Just you don't forget who your real friends are while you are on the other side,' he continued icily, then turned and made his way back up the street with as much composure as his old body would allow him.

I stared after him; I suppose I should have realised that even at his age, he still had the heart of a territorial Tom, even if time had robbed him of his competitive edge. I did however feel absolutely confidant in his reliability.

****

For four human weeks I mixed with the feral cats along the 'great divide'. They were all mainly clustered like one great clan along that part of the barrier that passed through the historically important city of Nicosia.

I co-habited with all sorts along that line, realising more every day that when the great moment arrived; when Cyprus became totally united again, it would not mean a thing to these cats. They would just continue their daily routine of survival, absolutely oblivious to the social enormity of the occasion.

All of the domestic cats I met could not talk of anything else but the historic importance of the great day when it arrived. Even Kemal, who was pure bred Turkish from the tip of his beautiful ears to the pads of his huge paws, could only talk of what it would be like to belong to a united island for the first time in his life.

It was bound to happen of course. Like all female felines, my fertility period crept up on me, and suddenly I forgot my mission, and could only think of Tom Cats. One Tom Cat to be totally truthful, and so it came about that before the next few days were up, I was well and truly pregnant again. I suppose it was natural that Kemal was the father of my future brood; we had formed a bond during my weeks of chatting with all the local felines.

He became very protective when the scents I exuded told him I was a receptive female. He ignored the shrill scolding of his mistress and stayed with me for the whole of my fertility period, hence all my kittens would have his genes alone.

Suddenly everything came back to normal again, the hormones that caused this disturbance in the name of procreation, switched off, leaving me with the results of their period of activity.

A couple of mornings later, my time clock, that had developed due to my association with humans, told me that the time had come for the old couple to visit their relatives again. Later on that day, as if by some telepathic message Leonidas appeared at the building site.

'Ah, there you are,' he said hoarsely. 'That saves me having to meet your personal guide, a great relief, I must say.'

I grinned at his casual dislike of pedigree Toms, but said nothing.

'Human conversation on the street has it that your friends will be visiting today, they could be arriving at any time,' he went on informatively.

We agreed that we should breakfast at his Taverna first, as there was no hurry, but first I had a little job to do.

'Can you hang on here for a few moments while I go and say goodbye to someone?'

His eyes took on that scornful look, and with a curled lip affecting his hoarseness, he said acidly: 'If you must go, I suppose I shall have to wait; wont I?'

I made no comment at the bitter edge to his voice, I merely assured him, 'I won't be long,' and disappeared before he could change his mind.

I found Kemal sniffing at the entrance to the lean-to, and purring my name. He turned and looked at me as he became aware of my presence approaching from behind.

'Ah there you are, up and about early eh?'

I rubbed his head and gave it a couple of licks; he retaliated affectionately, and then asked where I had been.

'I knew it was about time my friends visited again, so I was on my way to see if there was any news, when I met Leonidas at the building site.'

He sat back on his haunches staring at me'

'So the time has come for us to part then has it Fluffy?'

'I must go Kemal,' I purred quietly. 'I have duties as a wise cat, the cats of our City will want to know what I have discovered, and my humans will be worrying about me as they always do.' I looked affectionately into his staring eyes, he did not want me to leave, but knew that I had to.

'You know the humans will take ages to arrange the reunification of our island. I had expected it to be completed by now. I had failed to realise that everything of great importance that involves humans does not happen automatically, just because it is the right thing to do. Oh no! They must discuss it for ages until every ordinary humans patience is about to break with the slowness of officialdom.

Not until the last stone is turned, and the last piece of bureaucratic paper is stamped and counter stamped, signed and countersigned, and then reaches the hands of the two leaders will the people suddenly realise, it was not a dream after all. I cannot wait here at their convenience, I am a wise cat, and I have important things to do.'

We rubbed heads and said goodbye, I promised to come and see him again when the time was right, and then turned and walked away. I was aware of his eyes following me as I hopped through the iron bars of the gate, then as I strolled down the road I turned to see his beautiful head stuck through the iron bars looking after me longingly. I paused in my stride, and looked back at him with promise in my eyes, but did not wait to see his reaction.

Leonidas greeted me cheerfully; time is a great healer, particularly when it concerns jealous old Toms. We breakfasted together and chatted about my encounters with all the ferals and domestics on the other side, some of whom he had never encountered, because he had not journeyed to the end of the barrier in the city and back again. He was well aware of the apathy I had encountered amongst those whose minds only stretched to the end of that day, but like me he did not blame them for their ignorance.

He did have something else to add though, and his statement raised his knowledge above that expected of a doddering old Tom Cat: 'I blame the greater powers for the division of the island,' he stated determinedly. 'The humans of this island have been like a pawn manipulated by those who should realise that war divides people for a very long time, and it seems ridiculous that intelligent people cannot get their heads together and thrash out their differences, without descending into the pit of violence and death, it is the ordinary people who are still mourning their loved ones, and it is the ordinary people who suffer the most in the long run, their whole lives have been blighted by their losses.'

He fell silent, having released his deeply felt feelings, but his words had rung truer than even the words of old Nicos my father.

We finished our meal in silence, and having groomed ourselves, strolled off to where the old couple's pick-up truck would park when they arrived.

We did not have to wait long, I knew this pick-up very well by now, and I heard it coming as soon as it turned into the street. I urged Leonidas to get under a car in front of where the pick-up would stop. No sooner had the old human stopped the beast from growling than I was underneath it.

'How long are you staying?' I hissed at a very surprised Vassos as his cage settled on the ground.

'We are going straight to Governors Beach when he has unloaded something out of the back, but I think we will stop and eat here first.'

The cage suddenly left the ground, cutting him off.　　Leonidas and I hunched up on all fours underneath the pick-up, listening to the scraping sounds of something being removed from above us. The two old humans staggered to the front door of the house carrying a polished piece of furniture between them. The door closed behind them, and we were left to wait it out once more.

We were both drowsing fitfully when the door opened again. We witnessed the goodbye hugs again, and just as the beast began to growl I hopped over the back end, and squeezed myself between the weekend baggage. It all happened so quickly that Leonidas looked at me a bit stupefied, and only just managed to miaowl, 'Goodbye Fluffy,' as my tail disappeared over the back.

I meowed a quick response, but I have no idea whether he heard me or not because the pick-up started to move the instant I had embarked.

I was used to all this by now, so I just settled down and thought over everything that had happened over the last few weeks, whilst the pick-up ate up the miles. My mind settled on the image of Kemal, and a certain glow filled my physical being. It suddenly occurred to me that I was about two human weeks pregnant, and that means that in another fifty human days or thereabouts, I shall become the mother of a new generation that will be able to boast. 'We belong to both sides of the island of Cyprus; therefore we are the first offspring of a new Cyprus.'

END.

www.ingramcontent.com/pod-product-compliance
Lightning Source LLC
Chambersburg PA
CBHW070351290526
45790CB00004B/1439